THE

HARM IN

HATE

SPEECH

THE
HARM IN
HATE
SPEECH

Jeremy Waldron

HARVARD UNIVERSITY PRESS

Cambridge, Massachusetts

London, England

First Harvard University Press paperback edition, 2014

Publication of this book has been supported through the generous provisions of
the S. M. Bessie Fund.

Library of Congress Cataloging-in-Publication Data

Waldron, Jeremy.
  The harm in hate speech / Jeremy Waldron.
  p.   cm.—(The Oliver Wendell Holmes Lectures, 2009.)
  Includes bibliographical references and index.
  ISBN 978-0-674-06589-5 (cloth : alk. paper)
  ISBN 978-0-674-41686-4 (pbk.)
  1. Hate speech—United States.   2. Freedom of speech—Philosophy.   I. Title.
  KF9345.W34 2012
  345.73'0256—dc23   2011046700

Acknowledgments

I have incurred many debts in writing these chapters. Some of the most substantial debts are owed to those who disagree strongly with me on the issue of hate speech: Robert Silvers of the *New York Review of Books*, who invited me to review Anthony Lewis's book *Freedom for the Thought That We Hate;* Lewis himself, who generously attended the Holmes Lectures; Ronald Dworkin, who has been a constant critical presence in the development of these ideas; and the late C. Edwin Baker. I am grateful also to former dean Elena Kagan, to the current dean, Martha Minow, and to the faculty of Harvard Law School for the invitation to deliver the Holmes Lectures and for their hospitality in October 2009; to the editors and staff of the *Harvard Law Review;* to Elizabeth Knoll at Harvard University Press for her patience and her outstanding suggestions; and to the Filomen D'Agostino and Max E. Greenberg Research Fund, which provided a summer research grant at NYU for the development of the Holmes Lectures in 2009 and the completion of this book in 2011. I am grateful also to Amnesty International for permission to use the text of Chapter 8, which was originally delivered as an Amnesty Lecture at Oxford in May 2010.

Thanks, finally—for comments, criticisms, suggestions, encouragement, and practical help—to Amy Adler, Anita Allen, Timothy Garton Ash, Lavinia Barbu, Eric Barendt, Teresa Bejan, Rebecca Brown, Wendy Brown, Winfried Brugger, Norman Dorsen, David Dyzenhaus, Richard Fallon, Noah Feldman, James Fleming, Charles Fried, Dieter Grimm, Amy Gutmann, Moshe Halbertal, Ivan Hare, Bob Hargrave, Stephen Holmes, Sam Issacharoff, Sanford Kadish, Frances Kamm, George Kateb, Henning Koch, Christine Korsgaard, David Kretzmer, Mattias Kumm, Rae Langton, Charles Lawrence, Liora Lazarus, Catharine MacKinnon, John Manning, Jane Mansbridge, Larry May, Leighton McDonald, Frank Michelman, Martha Minow, Peter Molnar, Richard Moon, Glyn Morgan, Liam Murphy, Thomas Nagel, Jerome Neu, Gerald Neuman, Rick Pildes, Ricky Revesz, Robert Post, Michael Rosen, Nancy Rosenblum, Alan Ryan, Michael Sandel, T. M. Scanlon, Sir Stephen Sedley, Joseph Singer, Geoff Stone, Adam Swift, Scott Thomas, Mark Tushnet, Roberto Unger, Joseph Weiler, James Weinstein, Ajume Wingo, and, as always (and with love), Carol Sanger.

Contents

THE
HARM IN
HATE
SPEECH

I   Approaching Hate Speech

I want to begin by explaining the position I am going to defend in this book, and I want to say something, too, about what has led me into this controversy. Let me start with the position and the concerns that underlie it.

Dignity and Assurance

A man out walking with his seven-year-old son and his ten-year-old daughter turns a corner on a city street in New Jersey and is confronted with a sign. It says: "Muslims and 9/11! Don't serve them, don't speak to them, and don't let them in." The daughter says, "What does it mean, papa?" Her father, who is a Muslim— the whole family is Muslim—doesn't know what to say. He hurries the children on, hoping they will not come across any more of the signs. Other days he has seen them on the streets: a large photograph of Muslim children with the slogan "They are all called Osama," and a poster on the outside wall of his mosque which reads "Jihad Central."

What is the point of these signs? We may describe them

loosely as "hate speech," putting them in the same category as racist graffiti, burning crosses, and earlier generations of signage that sought to drive Jews out of fashionable areas in Florida with postings like "Jews and Dogs Prohibited." Calling these signs hate speech makes it sound as though their primary function is expressive—a way in which one or another racist or Islamophobic element "lets off steam," as it were, venting the hatred that is boiling up inside. But it is more than that. The signs send a number of messages. They send a message to the members of the minority denounced in the posters and pamphlets:

> Don't be fooled into thinking you are welcome here. The society around you may seem hospitable and nondiscriminatory, but the truth is that you are not wanted, and you and your families will be shunned, excluded, beaten, and driven out, whenever we can get away with it. We may have to keep a low profile right now. But don't get too comfortable. Remember what has happened to you and your kind in the past. Be afraid.

And they send a message to others in the community, who are not members of the minority under attack:

> We know some of you agree that these people are not wanted here. We know that some of you feel that they are dirty (or dangerous or criminal or terrorist). Know now that you are not alone. Whatever the government says, there are enough of us around to make sure these people are not welcome. There are enough of us around to draw attention

to what these people are really like. Talk to your neighbors, talk to your customers. And above all, don't let any more of them in.

That's the point of these signs—that's the point of hate speech—to send these messages, to make these messages part of the permanent visible fabric of society so that, for the father walking with his children in our example, there will be no knowing when they will be confronted by one of these signs, and the children will ask him, "Papa, what does it mean?"

Many of my colleagues who are not Muslim say that they detest these signs and others like them (the racist slogans, the anti-Semitic signage). But they say that people like us, who detest hate speech, should learn to live with it. Less often, and only under pressure, they will say that the father in our example (who is not a First Amendment scholar) and his children and others like them should also learn to live with these signs. But they say that uneasily. They are more often confident in their own liberal bravado, calling attention to their ability to bear the pain of this vicious invective: "I hate what you say but I will defend to the death your right to say it."

That is the most important thing, in their opinion. The signs that we have been talking about, the bigoted invective that defiles our public environment, should be no concern of the law, they say. People are perfectly within their rights, publishing stuff like this. There is nothing to be regulated here, nothing for the law to concern itself with, nothing that a good society should use its legislative apparatus to suppress or disown. The people who are targeted should just learn to live with it. That is, they should learn to live their lives, conduct their business, and raise their children in the atmosphere that this sort of speech gives rise to.

I disagree. I think there is something socially and legally significant at stake. We can describe what is at stake in two ways. First, there is a sort of public good of inclusiveness that our society sponsors and that it is committed to. We are diverse in our ethnicity, our race, our appearance, and our religions. And we are embarked on a grand experiment of living and working together despite these sorts of differences. Each group must accept that the society is not *just* for them; but it *is* for them too, along with all of the others. And each person, each member of each group, should be able to go about his or her business, with the assurance that there will be no need to face hostility, violence, discrimination, or exclusion by others. When this assurance is conveyed effectively, it is hardly noticeable; it is something on which everyone can rely, like the cleanness of the air they breathe or the quality of the water they drink from a fountain. This sense of security in the space we all inhabit is a public good, and in a good society it is something that we all contribute to and help sustain in an instinctive and almost unnoticeable way.

Hate speech undermines this public good, or it makes the task of sustaining it much more difficult than it would otherwise be. It does this not only by intimating discrimination and violence, but by reawakening living nightmares of what this society was like—or what other societies have been like—in the past. In doing so, it creates something like an environmental threat to social peace, a sort of slow-acting poison, accumulating here and there, word by word, so that eventually it becomes harder and less natural for even the good-hearted members of the society to play their part in maintaining this public good.

The second way of describing what's at stake looks at it from the point of view of those who are meant to benefit from the assurance that is thrown in question by the hate speech. In a sense we are all supposed to benefit. But for the members of vulnerable minorities, minorities who in the recent past have been hated or despised by others within the society, the assurance offers a confirmation of their membership: they, too, are members of society in good standing; they have what it takes to interact on a straightforward basis with others around here, in public, on the streets, in the shops, in business, and to be treated—along with everyone else—as proper objects of society's protection and concern. This basic social standing, I call their *dignity*. A person's dignity is not just some Kantian aura. It is their social standing, the fundamentals of basic reputation that entitle them to be treated as equals in the ordinary operations of society. Their dignity is something they can rely on—in the best case implicitly and without fuss, as they live their lives, go about their business, and raise their families.

The publication of hate speech is calculated to undermine this. Its aim is to compromise the dignity of those at whom it is targeted, both in their own eyes and in the eyes of other members of society. And it sets out to make the establishment and upholding of their dignity—in the sense that I have described—much more difficult. It aims to besmirch the basics of their reputation, by associating ascriptive characteristics like ethnicity, or race, or religion with conduct or attributes that should disqualify someone from being treated as a member of society in good standing.

As the book goes on, we will look at a number of examples of this, of the way in which hate speech is both a calculated affront to the dignity of vulnerable members of society and a calculated assault on the public good of inclusiveness. I offer a characterization of these concerns at this early stage in order to give readers a sense of what I think is at stake in the discussion of hate speech, a sense of what legislation limiting it or regulating it might be trying to safeguard. The case will be made in detail as the book goes on, and various objections confronted and answered.

The argument is not easy, and many readers will be inclined to dismiss it at the outset, because they just "know" that these sorts of publications must be protected as free speech and that we must defend to the death their authors' right to publish them. Most people in the United States assume that that's where the argument must end up, and they are puzzled (not to say disappointed) that I am starting off down this road. I think it is a road worth exploring, even if no one's mind is changed. It's always good to get clear about the best case that can be made for a position one opposes. However, for those who are puzzled about my involvement, let me begin with a little bit of intellectual biography.

A Tale of Two Book Reviews

In 2008, I published a short piece in the *New York Review of Books*, reviewing a book by Anthony Lewis on the topic of free speech.[1] Lewis is a distinguished author and journalist who has written a number of books on constitutional issues, including *Gideon's Trumpet* (1964), which was made into a TV movie starring Henry Fonda, and *Make No Law: The Sullivan Case and the First Amendment* (Random House, 1991).[2] Lewis's 2007 book, *Freedom for the Thought That We Hate*, is a fine essay on the history and future of First Amendment protections in the United

States. *The New York Review of Books* does not seem to mind if a person reviews something in which the reviewer has been criticized. In *Freedom for the Thought That We Hate,* Lewis said that "[o]ne of the arguments for allowing hateful speech is that it makes the rest of us aware of terrible beliefs"—the depth and intensity of racist beliefs, for example—"and strengthens our resolve to combat them."[3] He continued: "This argument was rudely countered by Jeremy Waldron, an Englishman who emigrated to teach law in the United States."[4] And he quoted a passage from a 2006 essay I wrote in the *London Review of Books,* discussing John Durham Peters's book *Courting the Abyss: Free Speech and the Liberal Tradition.*[5] In that review I said:

> [T]he costs of hate speech . . . are not spread evenly across the community that is supposed to tolerate them. The [racists] of the world may not harm the people who call for their toleration, but then few of *them* are depicted as animals in posters plastered around Leamington Spa [an English town]. We should speak to those who are depicted in this way, or those whose suffering or whose parents' suffering is mocked by [the Skokie neo-Nazis], before we conclude that tolerating this sort of speech builds character.[6]

Having quoted me, Lewis retorted that something like this view of mine had earlier "animated a movement, in the 1980s and 1990s, to ban hateful speech on university campuses." And he said that that movement had led to all sorts of "foolishness" and political correctness. "Even a sense of humor seemed endangered."[7]

With this provocation, I thought it appropriate to write a mildly critical review of Lewis's book in the *New York Review of Books*. I focused my critical comments on this issue of racist speech, expressing some misgivings about the arguments commonly used by Mr. Lewis and others in America to condemn what we call hate speech regulation. An expanded version of that review is included as Chapter 2 in the present volume.

Let me interrupt this tale with a word about definitions. By "hate speech regulation," I mean regulation of the sort that can be found in Canada, Denmark, Germany, New Zealand, and the United Kingdom, prohibiting public statements that incite "hatred against any identifiable group where such incitement is likely to lead to a breach of the peace" (Canada);[8] or statements "by which a group of people are threatened, derided or degraded because of their race, colour of skin, national or ethnic background" (Denmark);[9] or attacks on "the human dignity of others by insulting, maliciously maligning or defaming segments of the population" (Germany);[10] or "threatening, abusive, or insulting . . . words likely to excite hostility against or bring into contempt any group of persons . . . on the ground of the colour, race, or ethnic or national or ethnic origins of that group of persons" (New Zealand);[11] or the use of "threatening, abusive or insulting words or behaviour," when these are intended "to stir up racial hatred," or when "having regard to all the circumstances racial hatred is likely to be stirred up thereby" (United Kingdom).[12] As is evident, there are similarities and differences between these various instances of hate speech regulation. We shall discuss some of the details later. But all of them are concerned with the use of words which are deliberately abusive and/or insulting and/or threatening and/or demeaning directed at members of vulnerable minorities, calculated to stir up hatred against them. (Also, some of these laws, in an evenhanded spirit, threaten to punish insulting words directed at *any* racial group in the community even when the group is a dominant or majority group.)[13] Racial and ethnic groups are prime examples of the kinds of groups that are supposed to be protected by these laws, but more recently the protection has been extended to groups defined by religion as well.[14]

That was the kind of legislation Anthony Lewis and I were talking about. He was mostly opposed to it, though he said he wasn't as sure now about this opposition as he once was.[15] In my review, I ventured the suggestion that there was perhaps more to be said in favor of this legislation than Lewis was indicating. I didn't make any very strong assertion. As I have said, Lewis's book was, on the whole, a thoughtful contribution to this debate and I wanted to review it in that spirit. I did say that it wasn't clear to me that the Europeans and the New Zealanders were mistaken in their conviction that a liberal democracy must take affirmative responsibility for protecting the atmosphere of mutual respect against certain forms of vicious attack. And I ended the piece quite reasonably (I thought), saying that "[t]he case is . . . not clear on either side," and repeating (more elaborately) the sentiments that had annoyed Mr. Lewis earlier:

> [T]he issue is not just *our* learning to tolerate thought that *we* hate—we the First Amendment lawyers, for example. The harm that expressions of racial hatred do is harm in the first instance to the groups who are denounced or bestialized in pamphlets, billboards, talk radio, and blogs. It is not

harm ... to the white liberals who find the racist invective
distasteful. Maybe we should admire some [ACLU] lawyer
who says he hates what the racist says but defends to the
death his right to say it, but ... [t]he [real] question is about
the direct targets of the abuse. Can their lives be led, can
their children be brought up, can their hopes be maintained
and their worst fears dispelled, in a social environment polluted by these materials? Those are the concerns that need
to be answered when we defend the use of the First Amendment to strike down laws prohibiting the publication of racial hatred.[16]

I thought that sounded all very measured and moderate. Until ...

"YOU ARE A TOTALITARIAN ASSHOLE" screamed one
of the emails I received after the piece was published. Other messages called me human garbage and a parasite on society. The
emails left me a little bit bruised, and so when I was invited to
deliver some lectures at Harvard—the 2009 Holmes Lectures,
dedicated to the memory of Oliver Wendell Holmes, who himself at one time or another took both sides on most free-speech
issues—I decided I would take the opportunity to explain myself. The three Holmes Lectures were delivered in Cambridge,
Massachusetts, on October 5, 6, and 7 under the title "Dignity
and Defamation,"[17] and were published in 2010 as an article in
the *Harvard Law Review*.[18] The published lectures correspond
(roughly) to Chapters 3, 4, and 7 of this book, though some ideas
set out briefly in the third lecture are also developed in Chap-

ters 5 and 6. Chapter 8, which is more historical in character, was presented originally as an Amnesty International Lecture at Oxford in June 2010.

My Modest Intention

My purpose in putting all this in front of you is not to persuade you of the wisdom and legitimacy of hate speech laws. My in-box can't take too many more of those hateful emails. Still less is it my aim to make a case for the constitutional acceptability of these laws in the United States. I will refer to the American debate from time to time, mostly suggesting ways in which it might be enriched by more thoughtful consideration of the rival positions. But as things stand, I think it is unlikely that legislation of the kind I set out above will ever pass constitutional muster in America. That's alright: there are many different kinds of laws, regarded as enlightened in other parts of the world, that do not satisfy this test—gun control laws, for example. The point is not to condemn or reinterpret the U.S. constitutional provisions, but to consider whether American free-speech jurisprudence has really come to terms with the best that can be said for hate speech regulations. Often, in the American debate, the philosophical arguments about hate speech are knee-jerk, impulsive, and thoughtless. Like Mr. Lewis's title, they address the case for hate speech legislation as though it consisted of certain do-gooders' disliking speech of a certain kind (speech that expresses "thought that we hate") and trying to write their likes and dislikes into law. We can do better than that, I think; *I* will certainly try to do better.

The hope is that even if my readers end up continuing to support the current constitutional position in the United States, they will at least understand—rather than impatiently dismiss—the more thoughtful arguments that can be mustered in favor of these laws.

Mostly what I want to do in this book, then, is to offer a characterization of hate speech laws as we find them, in Europe and in the other advanced democracies of the world. I also want to characterize hate speech regulations as we have found them, too, in America from time to time—because we must remember that opposition to these laws in the United States is by no means unanimous or monolithic. Apart from the legal academy, which is definitely divided on the matter, there is division among our lawmakers. There were state, municipal, and village ordinances enacted and waiting to be struck down in *Virginia v. Black*,[19] in *R.A.V. v. City of St. Paul*,[20] and in *Collin and the National Socialist Party v. Smith (Village President of Skokie)*,[21] and there was a state law enacted in Illinois, waiting to be upheld by the Supreme Court in *Beauharnais v. Illinois*.[22] Not everyone in America is happy with the constitutional untouchability of racist leaflets in Chicago, Nazi banners and uniforms in Skokie (Illinois), and the burning of crosses in Virginia; not everyone thinks that lawmakers must be compelled to stand back and let this material deface their society. There has been an honorable impulse among some legislators in America to deal with this problem; and what we need to do—before rushing to constitutional outrage on behalf of the First Amendment—is to understand that impulse.

Outside the United States, we know that legislation of this

kind is common and widely accepted (though it is certainly not uncontroversial). For us, that gives rise to a question about what the European or Canadian or New Zealand legislators think they are doing with these laws. Why have most liberal democracies undertaken to prohibit these manifestations of hatred, these visible defamations of social groups, rather than permitting and tolerating them in the name of free speech? How do they characterize these prohibitions, and how do they position them in relation to concerns—to which they also subscribe—about individual rights and freedom of expression?

One obvious point is that many countries see these laws not as violations of rights but as something which may be permitted or even required in a human-rights context. For one thing, their constitutions acknowledge that basic rights, including freedom of expression, are legitimately subject to restriction. The Canadian Charter and the South African Constitution say this of all the rights and freedoms set out in the Charter: they may be subject "to such reasonable limits prescribed by law as can be demonstrably justified in a free and democratic society."[23] Prohibitions on hate speech are seen as satisfying that provision. Moreover, there are the affirmative requirements of the International Covenant on Civil and Political Rights (ICCPR) to consider. It is sometimes said that these provisions prohibit hate speech. That's not quite right; what they do is obligate countries to pass legislation prohibiting it. Article 20(2) of the ICCPR requires that "[a]ny advocacy of national, racial or religious hatred that constitutes incitement to discrimination, hostility or violence shall be prohibited by law."[24] So does the International Convention on the

Elimination of All Forms of Racial Discrimination (ICERD).[25] No doubt, states vary in the extent to which they allow their national legislation to be guided by international human-rights law; but this aspect of the international human-rights consensus cannot be lightly dismissed.[26]

These prohibitions are not just a matter of obligation. Many advanced democracies willingly embrace the idea of restrictions on hate speech. Unless we understand how that embrace might be motivated—what deeper values of dignity, respect, equality, democracy, and social peace might be involved—we will not understand the thinking behind the international-law position.

Equally, it is important to have a sense of the best that can be said against these provisions, whether it is said in terms of constitutional rights or not. Again, the case against hate speech restrictions is not made simply by treating the free-speech icon as a monstrance. Hate speech is speech, no doubt; but not all forms of speech or expression are licit, even in America, and we need to understand why there might be a particular problem with restricting speech of this kind. My book is not an evenhanded survey of the arguments for and against. But I try to come to terms with and respond to what I think are the best arguments that can be made against the regulation of hate speech.

In Chapter 5, I shall respond to some arguments by the late C. Edwin Baker which assert that hate speech regulation (or almost any restriction on free speech) poses a threat to the ethical autonomy of the individual. Baker does not simply use "autonomy" as a slogan. He explains why it is a crucial part of a person's autonomy to be able to disclose her values to others, and he approaches the issue of hate speech through that lens. I engaged in oral argument with Baker on this issue on a number of occasions, and I believe his argument deserves a published answer.

The same is true of another powerful argument against hate speech laws—one made by Ronald Dworkin. Like a number of free-speech advocates, Dworkin is interested in the effect that restrictions on free expression may have on the legitimacy of other laws that we want to be in a position to enforce.[27] He thinks that suppressing hate speech undermines the legitimacy of anti-discrimination laws by depriving people of the opportunity to oppose them. I have a great deal of respect for Professor Dworkin's work on this issue, as on many others. But I believe that in regard to hate speech, his legitimacy argument can be answered. I will consider this in Chapter 7.

In addition to these specific responses to Baker and Dworkin, I also devote some additional pages—in Chapter 5—to the distinction between offending people and attacking their dignity. I accept the point, which many critics make, that offense is not something the law should seek to protect people against. I have argued this elsewhere in connection with the furor that accompanied the publication of Salman Rushdie's novel *The Satanic Verses* in 1988.[28] But the case made in the present book is about dignity, not offense, and I try to explain the distinction between the two.

The chapters in the first half of the book are less defensive in character. As I have said, I want to develop an affirmative characterization of hate speech laws that shows them in a favorable light—a characterization that makes good and interesting sense of the evils that might be averted by such laws and the values and principles that might plausibly motivate them. The core of my argument—the best and most favorable account of hate speech laws that I can give—is in the second half of Chapter 4, beginning with the section entitled "Assurance."

Talk of hate speech is never particularly pleasant: opponents as well as defenders of this legislation find such speech distasteful. But we need to go beyond the description of the speech itself as hateful to an understanding of the way it pollutes the social environment of a community and makes life much more difficult for many of those who live in it. In Chapter 4, I will argue that the issue is about what a good society looks like, and what people can draw from the visible aspect of a well-ordered society in the way of dignity, security, and assurance, as they live their lives and go about their business. I shall argue that this can be understood as the protection of a certain sort of precious public good: an open and welcoming atmosphere in which all have the opportunity to live their lives, raise their families, and practice their trades or vocations. In Chapter 3 I shall sketch some background for this, arguing that it may be helpful to view hate speech laws as representing a collective commitment to uphold the fundamentals of people's reputation as ordinary citizens or members of society in good standing—vindicating, as I shall say, the rudiments of their *dignity* and social status. These chapters, 3 and 4, are the affirmative core of the book.

The book ends with an essay of a different kind. Though there is a bit of history in Chapters 2, 3, and 4, my focus there is mainly on contemporary discussions. Chapter 8, however, takes us from twentieth-century and twenty-first-century debates about hate speech legislation into seventeenth- and eighteenth-century debates about religious toleration. I have long suspected that these debates were connected, but in the legal and philosophical literature they are often pursued as though they had nothing to do with each other. In this final chapter, I try to bring them together with a discussion of the way in which Enlightenment *philosophes*, from Locke to Voltaire, dealt with the question of expressions of religious hatred as threats to the character and viability of a tolerant society.

2   Anthony Lewis's *Freedom for the Thought That We Hate*

The United States, says Anthony Lewis, is the most outspoken society on earth: "Americans are freer to think what we will and say what we think than any other people" (ix).[1] They can do so without fear of official retaliation. If I had written, for example, in 2008 that George W. Bush was the worst president we had ever had, and that his vice president and former secretary of defense were war criminals, I would not have expected to be arrested for my impudence. That's just business as usual in America. "Today," says Lewis, "every president is the target of criticism and mockery. It is inconceivable that even the most caustic critic would be imprisoned for his or her words" (x).

It wasn't always so. In 1798 Colonel Matthew Lyon, a Republican member of Congress, sent a letter from Philadelphia to a newspaper called the *Vermont Journal* in which he conveyed to readers and constituents his low impression of President John Adams and the current administration:

> As to the executive, when I shall see the efforts of that power bent on the promotion of the comfort, the happiness, and

accommodation of the people, that executive shall have my zealous and uniform support: but whenever I shall, on the part of the executive, see every consideration of the public welfare swallowed up in a continual grasp for power, in an unbounded thirst for ridiculous pomp, foolish adulation, and selfish avarice; . . . when I shall see the sacred name of religion employed as a state engine to make mankind hate and persecute one another, I shall not be their humble advocate.

Shortly before this letter was published, Congress had passed a Sedition Act making it an offense to bring the president or Congress into disrepute or "to excite against them . . . the hatred of the good people of the United States."[2] Colonel Lyon was arrested and indicted under this legislation for seditious libel. At his trial, he disputed the constitutionality of the Sedition Act—a plea that was peremptorily struck out by the judge (Supreme Court Justice Paterson, riding circuit as Supreme Court justices did in those days). In the early 1800s, the First Amendment was understood by some as admonitory rather than as a legally enforceable restraint upon state and federal lawmakers. Or if it was seen as mandatory, it was thought to prohibit only prior restraints on publication, not criminal proceedings for seditious libel after publication had taken place.

In a curious proceeding, Colonel Lyon then called on the judge himself to testify to the extravagance of President Adams's household, for truth was a defense against charges of seditious libel under the 1798 Act. The judge replied angrily that the fare was plainer at the president's dinner table than at the Rutland Tavern.

The jury convicted Lyon, and the judge sentenced him to four months' imprisonment, from which he could not be released until he had also paid a $1,000 fine.[3]

The marshal charged with Colonel Lyon's imprisonment was a man called Fitch, who seems to have nurtured a long-standing grudge against him. Fitch had Lyon thrown into a tiny, filthy cell reserved mostly for horse thieves and runaway slaves. When Lyon's supporters heard about the conditions of his imprisonment, they rioted and almost tore down the prison. In 1800, the *Vermont Gazette* published an article describing Marshal Fitch as "the oppressive hand of usurped power" and "a hard-hearted savage, who has, to the disgrace of Federalism, been elevated to a station where he can satiate his barbarity on the misery of his victims." This, too, enraged the (Federalist) authorities. The editor of the *Gazette,* Anthony Haswell, was likewise convicted of seditious libel; he was fined $200 and imprisoned for two months.[4]

Why did locking these critics up seem like an appropriate thing to do in the early years of the republic? I am sure no explanation would be complete if it did not mention the volatile combination of wounded vanity and—for the time being—legally unlimited authority. But it would also be a mistake to omit the point that political institutions are sometimes a lot more fragile than they look. This entity—the state—which to us appears so powerful and self-sufficient, depends crucially on the opinion of those over whom it rules, and it requires for its operation a modicum of deference and respect. (Think of the way we still enforce laws against direct contempt of court—against ridiculing judicial officers in their courtrooms.) Murmurings of discontent are one thing. But if expressions of contempt and denunciations of oppression and corruption by officials become standard features of the public landscape, then the government's authority is shaken and citizens may start to think they can refuse to cooperate with the authorities or to comply with their directives unless compelled to do so. There is a danger, in other words, that the state will be thrown back on its meager resources for sheer coercion, without any goodwill or voluntary support or any sense of obligation on the part of its citizens. No democratic government in this predicament can do much or last long.

To many people, federal authority seemed weak and precarious in 1798. Public agitation by Colonel Lyon's supporters led to a brief uprising in Vermont, and there was a threat of considerable political violence elsewhere. George Washington was denounced as a thief and a traitor; John Jay was burned in effigy; Alexander Hamilton was stoned in the streets of New York; our hero, Matthew Lyon, attacked a Connecticut Federalist with fire tongs when the fellow spat on him in the House of Representatives; and Republican militias armed and drilled openly, ready to stand against Federalist armies.[5] Over everything, like a specter, hung news of the Jacobin terror in France. It was by no means obvious in those years—though it seems obvious to us now—that the authorities could afford to ignore venomous attacks on the structures and officers of government, or leave the publication of such attacks uncontested in the hope that they would be adequately answered in due course in the free marketplace of ideas. That a government could survive the published vituperations of the governed seemed more like a reckless act of faith than like basic common sense.

That is the premise of making seditious libel an offense, but the fact that such a law is open to abuse is equally obvious. Pomposity is a standard hazard of political life; and the pain experienced by a politician when his inflated self-esteem is publicly punctured is likely to be out of all proportion to any real danger posed to the viability of the state. Government cannot last long if most people believe it is a criminal kleptocracy; but accusations of malfeasance are standard fare in electoral politics—standard criticisms which politicians in power will go to any lengths to avoid. So a tool designed to protect government as such from public contempt is almost certain to be used for partisan political advantage. That's the dilemma.

It wasn't just political criticism that was punished in the early years of the republic. In 1823, a man was jailed for sixty days in Massachusetts for writing an essay in the *Boston Investigator* that denied the existence of God, affirmed the finality of death, and declared that "the whole story concerning [Jesus Christ] is as much a fable and a fiction as that of the god Prometheus."[6] At the time of the founding of the United States, William Blackstone's position—that "[b]lasphemy against the Almighty, . . . denying his being or providence, or uttering contumelious reproaches on our Saviour Christ . . . is punished, at common law by fine and imprisonment"[7]—was regarded as part of our heritage of common law, not just as a peculiarity of the English establishment. "Christianity," said a state court judge in 1824, "is and always has been a part of the common law of Pennsylvania." And that judge went on to suggest that Christianity could not do its work of holding society together if it was exposed to public denunciation. He added that prosecutions for blasphemous libel were perfectly compatible with freedom of conscience and freedom of worship, which the law of Pennsylvania also protected, since such prosecutions were directed not at belief but only at the most malicious and scurrilous public revilings of religion.[8]

How did we get from there to here? Anthony Lewis has taught law at Harvard and Columbia, but he does not fall into the lawyer's trap of ascribing the end of the offenses of seditious and blasphemous libel to the heroic actions of the judiciary. The Sedition Act did not last long; it was repealed in 1801. And its abuses were so clear to a subsequent generation that Congress in the 1840s passed bills to repay with interest the fines that Colonel Lyon and Anthony Haswell had incurred. But federal judges seemed perfectly happy to enforce it as long as it lasted. Its demise was the work of elected legislators. When something like seditious libel was revived in an Espionage Act passed in 1917 upon the entry of the United States into the First World War, once again the judges were by no means unenthusiastic. Oliver Wendell Holmes compared the publication of a leaflet denouncing conscription as slavery to a false shout of "Fire!" in a crowded theater, and the Supreme Court unanimously upheld a ten-year prison sentence for the author of the leaflet.[9] The premise was the same: the necessary tasks of government—in this case, military recruitment for war in Europe—could not be performed in an atmosphere polluted by public denunciation.

According to Lewis, it was not until 1931—in other words, 140 years after the passage of the First Amendment—that the Supreme Court began enforcing the constitutional guarantee of freedom of speech (Lewis, 39). It struck down a California law that had forbidden the display of a red flag "as a sign, symbol, or emblem of opposition to organized government."[10] Of course, even before that year, there had been dissenting voices on the bench in favor of free speech and freedom of the press. Justice Holmes began the long process of reversing his preposterous equation—that criticizing the military was comparable to shouting "Fire!" in a crowded theater—as early as 1919, when he dissented from a Supreme Court decision upholding a twenty-year prison sentence imposed upon Jacob Abrams for throwing leaflets from a building in New York condemning President Woodrow Wilson's dispatch of troops to Russia to fight the Bolsheviks.[11] But there were dissenters in the legislature as well—legislators who opposed the Espionage Act or who spoke out against the Smith Act, passed in 1940 (and still on the books today), which was used in subsequent decades to punish advocates of Marxism-Leninism. If justices like Holmes and Louis Brandeis are now glorified for their dissents, it is because their opinions are cited by a more rights-conscious Court many decades later, not because free speech was safe in the hands of the judiciary at the time.

What do we believe now about free speech that most American judges and politicians did not believe in 1798 or 1823 or 1919? What do we now believe that has made the United States the safest country on earth in which to criticize political leaders or denounce societal shibboleths?

Prosecutions for attacks on Christianity faded away much more quickly than prosecutions for political speech. The logic of prosecuting atheists always sat uncomfortably with the American position on religion. Christian belief might appear vulnerable to public denunciations, and it might seem in need of the law's support—but it wasn't clear that this was support that the law was entitled to give. The logic of blasphemous libel required courts to find ways of seeing the churches, or Christianity in general, as indispensable supports of government. By the middle of the nineteenth century, American courts found themselves unable to do this, and they struck out prosecutions for blasphemy not on free-speech but on anti-establishment grounds. Since Christianity could not be seen as part of the organized apparatus of social control, it would just have to fend for itself in the unruly marketplace of sacred and profane ideas.

So far as political speech is concerned, I suppose the crucial thing is that we now see the power of the state as much more of a threat to the individual than vice versa. In 1798, federal authority looked precarious; it was at the mercy of public opinion, and public opinion was looking well-nigh ungovernable. In the two centuries since then, we have learned that the state does not need our solicitude or legal protection against criticism. It is strong enough to shrug off our attacks, strong enough to dismiss our denunciations as not worth the effort of suppression. When Justice Holmes finally changed his mind on these matters in the 1919 case that I mentioned earlier, *Abrams v. United States,* he predicated his dissent on the derisory impotence of what he called the defendants' pronunciamentos. "Nobody," he said, "can suppose that the surreptitious publishing of a silly leaflet by an unknown man, without more, would present any immediate danger that its opinions would hinder the success of government arms" (Lewis, 29). Whatever threat was posed by these "poor and puny anonymities" would be better countered not by the suppression of speech but by more speech—by what Holmes called "the free trade in ideas."

As organized government came to seem less vulnerable, it also came to seem, itself, much more of a threat to the intellectual life of the country, to debate and deliberation among the citizenry and to the dignity and individuality of particular writers and dissenters. From this perspective, it is not the threat to social order that is alarming; it is the massive power that the government can deploy—that the government of this country has deployed in the past and the governments all over the world continue to deploy—to suppress dissent, deflect criticism, and resist exposure of its malfeasances. That is why the First Amendment has come to seem important. And to many people it has come to seem important as a counter-majoritarian device, because it is not just our rulers themselves who seek to suppress dissent. "It is, says Anthony Lewis, "a seeming characteristic of American society that it is periodically gripped by fear" (103)—panic about Jacobin terror in 1798, reactions against political radicalism and Bolshevism in 1919, hysteria about Communist infiltration in the 1940s and '50s, fear of radical Islam in more recent years. "[R]epeatedly, in times of fear and stress, men and women have been hunted, humiliated, punished for their words and beliefs" at the behest of a hysterical public (106). Those who call for these purges may think of themselves as patriots and as defenders of a free society; but their patriotism, in the words of one judge whom Lewis quotes,[12] is cruel and murderous. Like religious fanaticism, "it, too, furnishes its heresy hunters and its witch burners, and it, too, is a favorite mask for hypocrisy, assuming a virtue which it haveth not" (129–130).

Anthony Lewis is a defender of free speech, yet he is aware not only of the contingency of its development in the United States, but of a number of outstanding areas in which First Amendment freedoms remain controversial. Invasions of privacy, campaign finance, protection of the integrity of jury trials, and the regulation of hardcore pornography are all touched on and illuminated by Lewis's "biography" of the First Amendment. In some of these areas, Lewis is open to the arguments put forward by those who advocate limits on freedom of the press. For example, he is inclined to accept Justice Stephen Breyer's suggestion that sometimes protecting people from press intrusion can promote free speech: statutory restrictions on making private conversations public "encourage conversations that otherwise might not take place" (76).[13] In other cases, however, as in the argument that hardcore pornography is demeaning to women, he is much more dismissive (138).

One of the most difficult areas of modern controversy concerns what is sometimes called "hate speech"—that is, publications which express profound disrespect, hatred, and vilification for the members of minority groups. In 1952, the Supreme Court upheld an Illinois law prohibiting the publication or exhibition of any writing or picture portraying the "depravity, criminality, unchastity, or lack of virtue of a class of citizens of any race, color, creed or religion." The case was *Beauharnais v. Illinois*, and the Court refused an invitation on First Amendment grounds to overturn a fine of $200 imposed on the president of the White Circle League of America, who had distributed a leaflet on Chicago street corners urging people to "protect the white race from being mongrelized" and terrorized by the "rapes, robberies, guns, knives, and marijuana of the negro."[14]

Justice Felix Frankfurter, writing for the majority, described this pamphlet as a "criminal libel," and he thought this put it beyond the protection of the First Amendment. "Libelous utterances," he said, "are not within the area of constitutionally protected speech." Anthony Lewis doubts that this argument would be accepted today (159). Its basis, he says, has been undermined by the 1964 Supreme Court decision in *New York Times v. Sullivan*, where the Court held that public figures cannot recover damages for libel unless they can prove that a false statement of fact was made maliciously or recklessly. In that case, the *Times* had published an advertisement proclaiming that racist Southern officials were using lawless tactics against the civil rights movement. A city commissioner in Montgomery, Alabama, had sued the newspaper—saying that the advertisement implicitly accused him of lawlessness—and he was awarded $500,000 damages by an Alabama court. The Supreme Court struck down the award on the ground that the robust discussion of public issues, to which the United States has "a profound national commitment," is bound to include "vehement, caustic, and sometimes unpleasantly sharp attacks on government and public officials."[15] The idea was that when they take on public responsibilities, state and federal officials have a duty to develop a thick skin and sufficient fortitude to shrug off public attacks.

Lewis is right that the Court no longer regards libel per se as an exception to the First Amendment. But it is not at all clear that the reasoning in *New York Times v. Sullivan* would protect the defendant in the *Beauharnais* case. The African Americans libeled collectively in the "obnoxious leaflet"[16] that was at issue in *Beauharnais* were not public officials who had taken on the burden of office. They were ordinary citizens who may have thought they had a right to be protected from scattershot allegations of the most severe criminal misconduct—the "rapes, robberies, guns, knives, and marijuana of the negro." But Lewis is probably right that Joseph Beauharnais's conviction would not be upheld today. A 1969 decision of the Supreme Court,[17] reversing the conviction of an Ohio Ku Klux Klan leader, has held that hate speech, like seditious speech, is protected unless it is calculated to incite or likely to produce imminent lawless action.

Lewis notes that the United States differs from almost every other advanced democracy in the protection it currently gives to hate speech (157). The United Kingdom has long outlawed the publication of material calculated to stir up racial hatred. In Germany, it is a serious crime to display the swastika or other Nazi symbols. Holocaust denial is punished in many countries: the British author David Irving—a man who prides himself on having shaken more hands that shook the hand of Hitler than anyone else alive—was imprisoned until recently in Austria for this offense. New Zealand, Canada, France, and the Scandinavian countries—all use their laws to protect ethnic and racial groups from threatening, abusive, or insulting publications likely to excite hostility against them or bring them into public contempt. Moreover, these restrictions are not widely viewed as violations of individual rights; on the contrary, most countries have enacted them pursuant to their obligations under Article 20(2) of the International Covenant on Civil and Political Rights, which says that expressions of hatred likely to stir up violence, hostility, or discrimination *must* be prohibited by law.

Should the United States continue as an outlier in this regard? Our First Amendment faith is that the best response to a racist pamphlet is more speech, not less speech. But Lewis says, at the end of his book, that he is not as certain about this answer as he used to be: "In an age where words have inspired acts of mass murder and terrorism, it is not as easy for me as it once was to believe that the only remedy for evil counsels, in [Justice] Brandeis's phrase, should be good ones" (166). I believe he would still oppose anything along the lines of the British legislation which makes expressions of racial or interreligious hatred unlawful even when there is no immediate prospect of violence. But it is worth considering whether the arguments that have supported First Amendment protection in other areas really do support it for this case.

I said earlier that prosecutions for seditious libel began to seem inappropriate when we realized that the government had become so powerful that it did not need the support of the law against the puny denunciations of the citizenry. Does that apply to vulnerable minorities? Is their status as equal citizens in the society now so well assured that they have no need of the law's protection against the vicious slur of racist denunciation? I said earlier that prosecutions for blasphemous libel came to seem inappropriate when we realized that, however vulnerable the Christian religion may be, it was not something that the law had any business trying to protect. Does that apply to racial minorities? Is their position in society—the respect they enjoy from fellow citizens—a matter of purely private belief, with which the law should have no concern? It is not clear to me that the Europeans are mistaken when they say that a liberal democracy must take affirmative responsibility for protecting the atmosphere of mutual respect against certain forms of vicious attack.

In general, prosecutions for speech that threatened the good order of society came to seem inappropriate when we realized that we need not be so panic-stricken as the Federalists were in 1798 about public demonstrations and disorder. But is that true of the system of mutual respect among the members of racial groups? Can we complacently assume that it, too, is immune from serious disturbance, so that we need not worry about the cumulative effect of racist attacks? I have my doubts. The state and its officials may be strong enough, thick-skinned enough, well-enough armed, or sufficiently insinuated already into every aspect of public life, to be able to shrug off public denunciations. But the position of minority groups as equal members of a multi-racial, multiethnic, or religiously pluralistic society is not something that anyone can take for granted. It is a recent and fragile achievement in the United States, and the idea that law can be indifferent to published assaults upon this principle seems to me a quite unwarranted extrapolation from what we have found ourselves able to tolerate in the way of political and religious dissent. We sometimes say that the history of the United States is different in this regard from that of the European countries: their experience with the Holocaust necessarily flavors their attitude to hate speech, whereas Americans can afford to be more relaxed. But racial segregation, second-class citizenship, racist terrorism (lynchings, cross-burnings, fire-bombings of churches) are living memories in the United States—they are no less vivid than the memories of McCarthyism that haunt the defenders of the First Amendment—and those memories of racial terror are nightmarishly awakened each time one of these postings or pamphlets is put out into the public realm.

These hard questions are not intended to dispose of the matter. For the story of First Amendment freedom is not only that government came to seem so strong that it did not need the law's protection against criticism; the story of First Amendment freedom is that the government came to seem so strong that it constituted itself as a menace to individual freedom, and that is why it had to be restrained from interfering with free speech and freedom of the press. And I suppose the worry here is that a government equipped with hate speech codes would become a menace to free thought generally and that all sorts of vigorous dissenters from whatever social consensus the government was supporting would be, as Lewis puts it, "hunted, humiliated, punished for their words and beliefs" (106). Not only that, but as we saw earlier, campaigns against free speech tend to be motivated by public hysteria, and there is no telling what outbreaks of public hysteria would lead to if they had hate speech codes as one of the channels for their expression.

To me, it seems odd to concentrate only on *this* sort of manifestation of public hysteria, on the waves of majoritarian panic that could flow through the channels of the law, as opposed to other ways in which waves of public hysteria can threaten freedom in this society. Surely public hysteria is a danger to be recognized on *both* sides of this debate—both when it manifests itself in repressive laws and when it manifests itself in expressions of racial hatred. Why should we think that there needs to be protection only against the constraining laws and never against the racist expression?

Lewis's settled position, I think, is that we'd do better to swallow hard and tolerate "the thought that we hate" than open ourselves to the dangers of state repression. I am not convinced. The case is certainly not clear on either side, and Lewis acknowledges that. But it is worth remembering a couple of final points.

First, the issue is not the *thought* that we hate, as though defenders of hate speech laws wanted to get inside people's minds. The issue is publication and the harm done to individuals and groups through the disfiguring of our social environment by visible, public, and semipermanent announcements to the effect that in the opinion of one group in the community, perhaps the majority, members of another group are not worthy of equal citizenship. The old idea of group *libel*—as opposed to hateful thoughts or hateful conversation—makes this clear, and it is no accident that a number of European countries still use that term.

Second, the issue is not just *our* learning to tolerate thought that *we* hate—we the First Amendment lawyers, for example. The harm that expressions of racial hatred do is harm in the first instance to the groups who are denounced or bestialized in the racist pamphlets and billboards. It is not harm if I can put it bluntly—to the white liberals who find the racist invective distasteful. Maybe we should admire some lawyer who says he hates what the racist says but defends to the death his right to say it, yet this sort of intellectual resilience is not what's at issue. The question is about the direct targets of the abuse. Can their lives be led, can their children be brought up, can their hopes be maintained and their worst fears dispelled, in a social environment polluted by these materials? Those are the concerns that need to be answered when we defend the use of the First Amendment to strike down laws prohibiting the publication of racial hatred.

3 Why Call Hate Speech Group Libel?

Connotations of "Hate Speech"

What we call a thing tells us something about our attitude toward it, why we see it as a problem, what our response to it might be, what difficulties our response might cause, and so on. So it is with the phenomenon that we in America call "hate speech," a term that can cover things as diverse as Islamophobic blogs, cross-burnings, racial epithets, bestial depictions of members of racial minorities, genocidal radio broadcasts in Rwanda in 1994, and swastika-blazoned Nazis marching in Skokie, Illinois, with placards saying "Hitler should.have finished the job." When we call these phenomena "hate speech," we bring to the fore a number of connotations that are not entirely neutral.

First, the term "hate." The kind of speech whose regulation interests us is called "*hate* speech," and that word "hate" can be distracting. It suggests that we are interested in correcting the passions and emotions that lie behind a particular speech act. For most of us, the word highlights the subjective attitudes of the person expressing the views, or the person disseminating or publishing the message in question. It seems to characterize the problem as an attitudinal one, suggesting, I think misleadingly, that the aim of legislation restricting hate speech is to punish people's attitudes or control their thoughts. The idea of "hate speech" feels, in this regard, like the idea of "hate crimes"—offenses that are aggravated, in the eyes of the law, by evidence of a certain motivation.

In that connection, people may be excused for thinking that the controversy over the use of psychological elements like racist motivation as an aggravating factor in criminal law is also relevant to the controversy over racist expression.[1] In fact, though the two ideas—hate speech and hate crimes—do have a distant connection, they really raise quite different issues in our thinking about law. The idea of hate crimes is an idea that definitely does focus on motivation: it treats the harboring of certain motivations in regard to unlawful acts like assault or murder as a distinct element of crime or as an aggravating factor. But in most hate speech legislation, hatred is relevant not as the motivation of certain actions, but as a possible *effect* of certain forms of speech. Many statutory definitions of what we call hate speech make the element of "hatred" relevant as an aim or purpose, something that people are trying to bring about or incite. For example, the Canadian formulation that I mentioned in Chapter 1 refers to the actions of a person "who, by communicating statements in any public place, *incites* hatred against any identifiable group."[2] Or it is a matter of foreseeable effect, whether intended or not: the British formulation refers to speech that, in all the circumstances, is "*likely to stir up* hatred."[3]

Even once this distinction has been grasped, the phrase "hate speech" can also bog us down in a futile attempt to define "ha-tred." It is certainly not an easy idea to define. Robert Post takes a valiant stab at it in his essay in the collection *Extreme Speech and Democracy*, treating hatred as an extreme form of dislike. He identifies two crucial issues: "When do . . . otherwise appropriate emotions become so 'extreme' as to deserve legal suppression?"—notice how this still assumes we are aiming to suppress hate rather than punish the incitement of it—and "How do we distin-guish hatred from ordinary dislike or disagreement?"[4] Post says these questions involve profound conceptual difficulty (though he does not tell us exactly what the profundity consists in). I guess whatever difficulty there is here is going to arise whether hatred is regarded as a crucial motivation in the hate speech of-fense or as its crucial purpose or effect. But by giving the impres-sion that the laws in question are trying to "forbid expressions of 'extreme' intolerance or 'extreme' dislike," Post exaggerates the se-riousness (for instance, the possible unfairness) of our having to draw an *arbitrary* line between hatred and ordinary dislike.

Also, Post's discussion conveys a misleading impression that it is *hatred as such* which the law is trying to target—that the law regards hating (in whatever context) as "a bad thing." He thinks, therefore, that the defender of hate speech laws is required to take issue with Edmund Burke (who advocated hatred of ty-rants), James Fitzjames Stephen (who advocated hatred of great crimes), and Lord Patrick Devlin (who advocated hatred of im-morality).[5] According to Post's account, the defenders of hate speech regulation think hatred is always unhealthy, whereas Burke, Stephen, and Devlin denied that. But this is a distortion.

Advocates of hate speech legislation do not infer the wrongness of stirring up hatred against vulnerable minorities from the badness of hatred in general. That's not what they are interested in. They are concerned about the predicament of vulnerable people who are subject to hatred directed at their race, ethnicity, or religion; apart from that predicament, advocates of hate speech legislation may have little or no interest in the topic of hatred as such.

Second, the term "speech." If we say we are interested in restrictions on hate *speech*, we convey the idea that the state is proposing to interfere with the spoken word, with conversation,[6] and perhaps with vocabulary (interference that will result in our use of epithets being controlled by political correctness). We make it sound as though we are treating *what people say out loud* as a problem that calls for legislation—words that are blurted out, as Justice Robert H. Jackson once put it, "when the spirits are high and the flagons are low."[7] I think this creates a misleading impression. Speech, in the sense of the spoken word, can certainly be wounding.[8] But the sort of attacks on vulnerable minorities that elicit attempts to regulate and suppress "hate speech" include attacks that are printed, published, pasted up, or posted on the Internet —expressions that become a permanent or semipermanent part of the visible environment in which our lives, and the lives of members of vulnerable minorities, have to be lived. No doubt a speech can resonate long after the spoken word has died away— and I will say a little more in Chapter 4 about the audible as opposed to the visible aspect of a society which permits hate speech. But to my mind, it is the enduring presence of the published word or the posted image that is particularly worrying in this connection; and this is where the debate about "hate speech" regulation should be focused.

I don't want this shift away from "speech" to be understood as a maneuver in First Amendment jurisprudence. The U.S. Constitution protects freedom of speech as well as freedom of the press, and the former protection has been interpreted generously enough that the word "speech" will certainly cover the phenomena that I want to focus on. First Amendment scholars do debate an alleged difference between speech and action; I will touch on that in Chapter 5 and there take the position, which I think is unassailable, that calling something speech is perfectly compatible with also calling it an action that may be harmful in itself or that may have harmful consequences. In Catharine MacKinnon's blunt formulation, "Speech acts."[9] But that important point is not what I am trying to get at here, in my reservations about the term "hate speech." All I want to do is shift the focus somewhat from (for example) shouted epithets to more enduring artifacts of racist expression.

I said in Chapter 1 that all this began with my reviewing a book by Anthony Lewis (the review reproduced in Chapter 2). Lewis called the book that I reviewed *Freedom for the Thought That We Hate*, and this, too, is misleading in its suggestion that what is at stake is some sort of thought control, as though defenders of hate speech laws wanted to get inside people's minds: we want to restrict "thought"; he wants to emancipate it. That's moving in the wrong direction from the idea of speech control, back toward the idea of attitude control; whereas what we should really be talking about restricting are the *products* of people's attitudes, particularly the visible manifestation of the printed word. The restrictions on hate speech that I am interested in are not restrictions on thinking; they are restrictions on more tangible forms of message. The issue is publication and the harm done to individuals and groups through the disfiguring of our social environment by visible, public, and semipermanent announcements to the effect that in the opinion of one group in the community, perhaps the majority, members of another group are not worthy of equal citizenship.

Notice also the double reference to hate in Lewis's title. The thought in question is assumed to be full of hatred—i.e., it embodies or it is motivated by or it is intended to stir up hatred against minorities. And it is also assumed to be *hated* thought: liberals hate it; they don't like the thought of people who hate minorities in this way. So Lewis's premise is that we all hate thought that is imbued with hatred, but his argument is that we should not allow our hatred of hate-filled thought to justify restrictions on people's liberty. These convolutions quickly multiply and, though I will keep on using it for familiarity, I sometimes think it would be better if we dropped the phrase "hate speech" altogether.

Group Defamation

In many countries, a different term or set of terms is used by jurists: instead of "hate speech," they talk about "group libel" or "group defamation." Sometimes this is how legislation describes itself; it is the terminology used, for example, in section 130 of Germany's Penal Code. That section prohibits "attacks on human dignity by insulting, maliciously maligning, or defaming part of the population." Article 266 of the Danish Criminal Code forbids public defamation aimed at a group of persons because of their race, color, national or ethnic origin, religion, or sexual inclination. Section 251 of Norway's General Penal Code authorizes "the public authorities [to] prosecute a defamatory statement that is directed against an indefinite group or a large number of persons if it is so required in the public interest." In other European countries, "group libel" and "group defamation" are terms used in judicial doctrine, and among the jurists and lawyers of the legal system in question, to describe restrictions of the kind we would call hate speech restrictions. There is a specific French provision that prohibits defaming a group: Article 29 of the Law on the Freedom of the Press passed July 29, 1881, prohibits group as well as individual defamation. But some French jurists use the term "group defamation" or "racial defamation" to characterize all laws of this kind.[10] And such terminology extends beyond Europe. In Canada, Manitoba has a defamation statute which punishes "[t]he publication of a libel against a race, religious creed or sexual orientation."[11]

The term "group libel" used to be common in the United States as well. In the 1950s, American scholars would frequently observe that "group libel" or "group defamation" was the appropriate heading under which to describe the debate about the constitutionality and the desirability of legislation of this sort.[12] "Just a little more than a decade ago," wrote Harry Kalven in 1964, "we were all concerned with devising legal controls for the libeling of groups."[13] The idea of group libel was alluded to by the U.S. Supreme Court in characterizing the state law that it upheld in 1952 in *Beauharnais v. Illinois*.[14] (I shall say much more about that case later in this chapter.) Five years before *Beauharnais*, some scholars at Columbia had tried to crystallize debate by publishing a model group libel statute in the *Columbia Law Review*.[15] And it is worth remembering that—as its name suggests—the Jewish Anti-Defamation League took as its original mission "to stop, by appeals to reason and conscience, and if necessary by appeals to law, the *defamation* of the Jewish people."[16]

It is worth dwelling on these points of terminology, for I suspect we might get a better understanding of hate speech laws and of why people of good will have favored them if we consider them under this heading. Nadine Strossen of the American Civil Liberties Union disagrees: she tells us that since 1952 "[t]he group defamation concept has been thoroughly discredited."[17] I think that is too hasty. Certainly, group defamation is a complex and difficult idea, but the complications slow us down in a salutary way. They help to correct some of the simplicities fostered by the term "hate speech"; and an awareness of the difficulties, both conceptual and forensic, may make us more thoughtful on this issue, more open to new ways of thinking it through (whether or not we want to end up ultimately on the side that Strossen advocates). I hope people on all sides of the dispute will have some patience with this; it may be productive.[18]

Varieties of Libel

When we think about group libel, it is tempting to see it as an extension of individual defamation: we start with the idea of defaming a person, and with liability in tort law for libel and slander, and then we extend this to encompass liability for attacks on the reputation of a group.[19] But this is an oversimplification. Libel may be best-known today as a tort, but in the past it has often been understood also as a criminal offense. I think we should consider first the history of criminal libel.

Criminal libel laws have come in various flavors over the years. The best-known are laws against seditious libel—of which, for Americans, the most notorious example is the Sedition Act, passed by Congress in 1798. The Sedition Act made it a criminal offense to publish "false, scandalous, and malicious writing" bringing the president or Congress into disrepute or "to excite against them . . . the hatred of the good people of the United States."[20] (In the previous chapter, I discussed some of the prosecutions that occurred under the Sedition Act.) This spectacularly ill-considered piece of legislation has given criminal libel a bad name in the United States ever since.[21] It is worth noting, however, that at the time of its initial enactment and enforcement, the courts summarily refused to strike it down.[22] This is partly because, in the early 1800s, free-speech clauses were understood sometimes as admonitory rather than as legally enforceable restraints upon state and federal lawmakers; or if they *were* seen as mandatory, they were thought to prohibit only prior restraints on publication, not criminal proceedings for seditious libel after publication had taken place.

Or consider *blasphemous* libel. William Blackstone observed that "blasphemy against the Almighty, . . . denying his being or providence, or uttering contumelious reproaches on our Saviour Christ, . . . is punished, at common law by fine and imprisonment, for Christianity is part of the laws of the land."[23] For many years, this doctrine was accepted in the United States, notwithstanding the constitutional commitment to religious freedom. In 1823, a man was jailed for sixty days in Massachusetts for publishing an essay in the *Boston Investigator* that denied the existence of God, affirmed the finality of death, and declared that "the whole story concerning [Jesus Christ] is as much a fable and a fiction as that of the god Prometheus."[24] The Blackstone position on blasphemous libel was adopted explicitly by an American state court judge in 1824: "Christianity," he said, "general Christianity, is and always has been a part of the common law of Pennsylvania."[25] The judge said that prosecutions for blasphemous libel were compatible with freedom of conscience and freedom of worship, which the law of Pennsylvania also protected, since the prosecutions were directed not at belief but only at the most malicious and scurrilous revilings of religion.

There was also something called obscene libel—an offense which covered the publication of any pornographic material. In 1727, in England, Edmond Curl was found guilty as the author of a book called *Venus in the Cloister,* about lesbian love in a convent.[26] Obscene libel wasn't just restricted to books and pamphlets: in the 1826 case of *R. v. Rosenstein,* a man was convicted for offering for sale a snuffbox displaying an indecent painting when you lifted the lid.[27]

Notice that in these various senses of "libel," we are not really dealing with offenses that have a whole lot to do with defamation. Some of the prosecutions under the Sedition Act did involve defamation of those in power.[28] But others involved general subversion of government. In *U.S. v. Crandell* (1836), an indictment was laid against Reuben Crandell for publishing "libels tending to excite sedition among the slaves."[29] Sometimes, in these older uses, "libel" conveys the sense of "untruths," as in the title of one little book listed in the NYU Law Library Catalogue: *"A Libell of Spanish Lies . . . discoursing the . . . the death of Sir Francis Drake."*[30] But often the term just goes back to the neutral meaning of the Latin word *libellus,* meaning a little book. For much of its history, "libel" could be used to refer to any old published pamphlet, without conveying a judgment about its content. We mostly think of libel as a species of defamation; and those with a smattering of law know that libel is distinguished from slander by being written rather than just spoken. But in its original meaning, a "libel" could be any published declaration by an individual, printed in a pamphlet or nailed up on a church door. Inasmuch as it had a technical legal meaning, the term referred to the statement of claim commencing a lawsuit. But it could be any declaration purporting to have legal effect. John Wycliffe's *New Testament,* from the end of the fourteenth century, translated Matthew 5:31 as "Forsooth it is said, Whoever shall leave his wife, give he to her a libel, that is, a little book of forsaking." Libels often had an accusatory character, which I guess is the source of the association with defamation. One started a lawsuit or pasted a declaration up on a tree in the public square when one wanted to take someone or something to task. But the term's negative connotations went well beyond defamation: there could also be seditious libels, blasphemous libels, obscene libels, and libels (most notably blood libels) making accusations against whole groups in the community.

When we do focus on defamation, what is consistently emphasized, both in the law of torts and in the law of libel more generally, is the distinction between calumnies that are put about in *spoken* form—i.e., as speech, through gossip, rumor, or de-nunciation—and those that have the more enduring presence of something written or committed to paper, something published, as a number of U.S. civil codes put it, "by writing, printing, effigy, picture, or other fixed representation to the eye."[31] Defamation disseminated as speech is slander; defamation committed to pa-per is libel. The thought is that libel is much the more serious of the two, because the imputations it embodies take a more perma-nent form. "What gives the sting to the writing," said a New York court in 1931, "is its permanence of form. The spoken word dis-solves, but the written one abides and perpetuates the scandal."[32]

I believe this is important for our inquiry. When it comes to racist or religious attacks, this issue—what we might think of as the half-life of defamation—may help us to understand the spe-cific evil that the legislation we're considering is directed against. It is not the immediate flare-up of insult and offense that "hate speech" connotes—a shouted slogan or a racist epithet used in the heat of the moment. (Some campus hate speech codes may be directed at this, and also some workplace codes, but it is not usually the primary concern of what we call "hate speech legis-lation.") It is the fact that something expressed becomes estab-lished as a visible or tangible feature of the environment—part of what people can see and touch in real space (or in virtual space) as they look around them: this is what attracts the attention of the criminal law.[33]

Criminal Libel and Disorder

Until recently, many countries had laws relating to criminal defa-mation that was aimed at ordinary individuals. Until 1993, the

New Zealand Crimes Act specified a year's imprisonment as the penalty for any "matter published, without lawful justification or excuse . . . designed to insult any person or likely to injure his reputation by exposing him to hatred, contempt, or ridicule."[34]

Why, you may ask, would the criminal law concern itself with libel at all, in the specific sense of defamation, when there was no public issue of sedition or obscenity or blasphemy? Why not leave it to private law?

One possibility is that certain forms of defamation might be seen as an attack on public order. It is a matter of keeping the peace, avoiding brawls and so on, because egregious libel might flow over into fighting words. No doubt this is important. But we should bear in mind also that preventing fighting from breaking out—that very narrow sense of *keeping the peace*—is only one dimension of public order. Public order might also comprise society's interest in maintaining among us a proper sense of one another's social or legal status. In aristocratic societies, this meant securing the standing of great men or high officials—with laws of *scandalum magnatum* set up to protect nobles and great men from scandalous imputations on their breeding, their status, their honor, or their office.[35] I know the United States abolished titles of nobility in 1787, but maybe we should not regard Americans as having abandoned all concern for status. Think of it this way. Just as an aristocratic society might be concerned with the status of nobles, a democratic republic might be concerned with upholding and vindicating the elementary dignity of even its nonofficials as citizens—and with protecting that status (as a matter of public order) from being undermined by various forms of obloquy. Immanuel Kant observed that, in a republic, even the lowliest person may have the dignity of citizenship, and we should not expect this to be affected by our ban on titles of nobility.[36]

And just to anticipate: *that* is what I think laws regarding group defamation are concerned with. They are set up to vindicate public order, not just by preempting violence, but by upholding against attack a shared sense of the basic elements of each person's status, dignity, and reputation as a citizen or member of society in good standing—particularly against attacks predicated upon the characteristics of some particular social group. I am going to argue that group-libel laws aim at protecting the basics of each person's reputation against attempts (for example) to target all the members of a vulnerable racial or religious group with some imputation of terrible criminality—an imputation which, if sustained on a broad front, would make it seem inappropriate to continue according the elementary but important status of citizenship to the members of the group in question.

Beauharnais v. Illinois (1952)

Earlier I commented that the characterization of hate speech as group libel is not unknown in the United States. In 1952, what we would now call a hate speech law (an Illinois ordinance dating from 1917) was upheld by the Supreme Court of the United States as a law of criminal libel. What was in question was an Illinois statute prohibiting the publication or exhibition of any writing or picture portraying the "depravity, criminality, unchastity, or lack of virtue of a class of citizens of any race, color, creed or religion."[37] The case was *Beauharnais v. Illinois*,[38] and the Supreme Court refused an invitation on First Amendment grounds to overturn a fine of $200 imposed on Joseph Beauharnais, the president, founder, and director of something called the White Circle League of America, who had distributed a leaflet on Chicago street corners urging people to protect the white race from being "mongrelized" and terrorized by the "rapes, robberies, guns, knives, and marijuana of the negro."

The leaflet had as its headline: "Preserve and Protect White Neighborhoods! From the Constant and Continuous Invasion, Encroachment and Harassment of the Negroes." It said: "We are not against the negro; we are for the white people and the white people are entitled to protection." It went on: "The white people of Chicago MUST take advantage of this opportunity to become UNITED. If persuasion and need to prevent the white race from becoming mongrelized by the negro will not unite us, then the aggressions . . . rapes, robberies, knives, guns and marijuana of the negro, SURELY WILL." It alternated between a self-pitying and a triumphalist tone. On the one hand, it declared that "THEY CANNOT WIN! IT WILL BE EASIER TO REVERSE THE CURRENT OF THE ATLANTIC OCEAN THAN TO DEGRADE THE WHITE RACE AND ITS NATURAL LAWS BY FORCED MONGRELIZATION." But on the other hand, it complained, in tones of pathos designed to awaken the voice of the white race, that "[t]he Negro has many national organizations working to push him into the midst of the white people on many fronts. The white race does not have a single organization to work on a NATIONAL SCALE to make its wishes articulate and to assert its natural rights to self-preservation. THE WHITE CIRCLE LEAGUE OF AMERICA proposes to do the job."[39] The leaflet provided a tear-off application form, which, if submitted with a dollar, would enable the sender to become a member of the White Circle League of America (provided he or she promised to try and secure ten other members as well).

On March 6, 1950, Joseph Beauharnais was indicted on charges "that . . . on January 7, 1950, at the City of Chicago, [he] did unlawfully publish, present and exhibit in public places, lithographs, which publications portrayed depravity, criminality, unchastity or lack of virtue of citizens of Negro race and color and which exposed citizens of Illinois of the Negro race and color to contempt, derision, or obloquy." He was convicted by a jury and fined the sum of $200. His conviction was upheld on appeal in Illinois,[40] and upheld, too, by the Supreme Court of the United States by a majority of five to four.

From today's perspective, it is remarkable that the Supreme Court did not intervene to vindicate free speech in the form of this leaflet.[41] There were powerful dissents—"This Act sets up a system of state censorship which is at war with the kind of free government envisioned by those who forced adoption of our Bill of Rights," said one of the justices[42]—but they did not persuade the majority. The dissenting justices noted that the leaflet did not threaten violence, nor did it seem particularly likely that it would incite disorder. But the majority observed that it was enough that the leaflet was just hateful and defamatory: "Illinois did not have to look beyond her own borders or await the tragic experience of the last three decades to conclude that wilful purveyors of falsehood concerning racial and religious groups promote strife and tend powerfully to obstruct the manifold adjustments required for free, ordered life in a metropolitan, polyglot community." Justice William O. Douglas, even in dissent, noted that the Nazis were an example of "how evil a conspiracy could be which was aimed at destroying a race by exposing it to contempt, derision, and obloquy."[43] He said that, in principle, he "would be willing to concede that such conduct directed at a race or group in this country could be made an indictable offense." The decision and these statements indicate an openness in First Amendment jurisprudence that has not often been seen since.[44]

Nadine Strossen, of the American Civil Liberties Union, says that before we get too enthusiastic about the ordinance upheld in *Beauharnais,* we should remember that prior to its use against this white supremacist group, it was a weapon for the harassment of Jehovah's Witnesses, "a minority," as she says, "very much more in need of protection than most."[45] In fact, the Jehovah's Witnesses were prosecuted for what a federal court described as "bitter and virulent attacks upon the Roman Catholic Church" and "accusations which in substance and effect were charges of treasonable disloyalty."[46] In terms of the values attributed to the state by the Supreme Court justices, the prosecution was warranted. The fact that contempt, derision, and obloquy are directed at minority group X by members of another minority group, Y, does not mean we should not be concerned about the defamation of X. Defamation by a minority against a minority may constitute the same sort of obstacle to "free, ordered life in a metropolitan, polyglot community" as defamation by members of the dominant majority against a minority group.

The point about *Beauharnais* that I find most interesting is the terminology that the Supreme Court of Illinois used,[47] terminology that Justice Frankfurter endorsed when describing the statute as "a form of criminal libel law." Said Justice Frankfurter:

> No one will gainsay that it is libelous falsely to charge an-other with being a rapist, robber, carrier of knives and guns, and user of marijuana. . . . There is even authority . . . that such utterances were also crimes at common law. . . . [I]f an utterance directed at an individual may be the object of criminal sanctions, we cannot deny to a State power to pun-ish the same utterance directed at a defined group, unless we can say that this is a wilful and purposeless restriction unre-lated to the peace and well-being of the State.[48]

If the pamphlet could be described as a "criminal libel," Frank-furter thought that it would be beyond the protection of the First Amendment. "Libelous utterances," he said, "are not within the area of constitutionally protected speech."

Three of the four dissenters in *Beauharnais* acknowledged this point. Justice Stanley Reed, in his dissent, assumed "the constitu-tional power of a state to pass group libel laws to protect the pub-lic peace." His objection to the decision was based on the vague-ness of the terms of the ordinance. Justice Robert Jackson noted that "[m]ore than forty State Constitutions, while extending broad protections to speech and press, reserve a responsibility for their abuse and implicitly or explicitly recognize validity of crim-inal libel laws."[49] Only Justice Hugo Black disputed this premise outright, and for him the problem was precisely the *group* as-pect of group libel: "[A]s 'constitutionally recognized,' [criminal libel] has provided for punishment of false, malicious, scurrilous charges against individuals, not against huge groups. This limited scope of the law of criminal libel is of no small importance. It has confined state punishment of speech and expression to the narrowest of areas involving nothing more than purely private feuds."[50]

I think this was a mistake. And I would like now to consider and criticize Justice Black's argument in detail, before addressing a different criticism that could be made after 1964—namely, that the decision in *New York Times v. Sullivan* has removed (or—for non-American readers—indicated a good reason for removing) the whole category of libel from the list of exceptions to the protection of free speech.

Individuals and Groups

Justice Black claimed that criminal libel provides for the "punishment of false, malicious, scurrilous charges against individuals, not against huge groups." But in fact the law has traditionally pursued two complementary concerns in this domain. On the one hand, there is the concern for personalized reputation in civil cases. On the other hand, there is a concern for the fundamentals of *anyone's* reputation or civic dignity as a member of society in good standing. The latter has been the concern of the law of criminal libel. Unlike civil libel, criminal libel has traditionally been interested not in protecting the intricate detail of each individual's personalized reputation and that person's particular position in the scale of social estimation, but in protecting the foundation of each person's reputation. No doubt the foundation of a person's dignity might be attacked in different ways that vary from case to case. But the elementary aspects of civic dignity that are protected are the same in every case. People are assumed to be basically honest and law-abiding; it is assumed that their basic attributes—for example, that they are men rather than women, black rather than white, Jewish rather than Christian—do not in and of themselves dispose them to endemic criminality or anti-social character. In these ways, the civil law of libel and the criminal law of libel may be thought to work together—to cover the field, as it were. In the case of a civil action for libel, there must be a defamation of a particular person, or of a group so confined that the allegation descends to particulars. But—so the argument goes—this does not mean that the law is unconcerned with defamation on a broader front; it means only that that problem now becomes the concern of the criminal law rather than the civil law. And when we are dealing with the broad foundations of each person's reputation, rather than its particularity, the law might seek to deal with this by protecting large numbers of people, thought of as a group, against attacks on the fundamental reputation of all persons of that kind. When this is the law's interest, there is little point to insisting—as Justice Black thinks we should—upon focusing on the impact on individuals considered one by one. We should deal with the insult or libel at the level at which it is aimed and at the level at which damage to reputation is sustained.

Indeed, it is possible that a court might proceed more directly in a case like this, simply under the heading of public order. This is what happened (according to some reports) in the English case of *Osborne* (1732), a case I will discuss in more detail in the final chapter of this book. Mr. Osborne was charged with publishing a blood libel against Jews in London.[51] There was an objection at his trial that the allegation he had made "was so general that no particular Persons could pretend to be injured by it." But the court responded: "This is not by way of Information for a Libel that is the Foundation of this Complaint, but for a Breach of the Peace, in inciting a Mob to the Distruction of a whole Set of People; and tho' it is too general to make it fall within the Description of a Libel, yet it will be pernicious to suffer such scandalous Reflections to go unpunished."[52]

Now, case reports were not well organized or entirely consistent in the eighteenth century. Other reports of the same case say that it *was* decided as a matter of criminal libel, but they agree that the public-order dimension was key to that characterization.[53] Either way, it seems to me a viable or at least arguable position. As a matter of public order, assaults on the reputation of a group cannot be neglected. As Joseph Tanenhaus put it, "Since criminal libel is indictable at common law because it tends so to inflame men as to result in a breach of the peace, there is no rational basis for the exclusion of group defamers from liability to prosecution in common law jurisdictions."[54]

We find the same approach taken in an American decision from 1868. In *Palmer v. Concord,* accusations of cowardice were made against a company of soldiers who had been engaged in the Civil War. The New Hampshire court that heard the case said this:

As these charges were made against a body of men, without specifying individuals, it may be that no individual soldier

> could have maintained a private action therefor. But the
> question whether the publication might not afford ground
> for a public prosecution is entirely different. . . . *Indictments*
> for libel are sustained principally because the publication of
> a libel tends to a breach of the peace, and thus to the distur-
> bance of society at large. It is obvious that a libellous attack
> on a body of men, though no individuals be pointed out,
> may tend as much, or more, to create public disturbances as
> an attack on one individual.[55]

The court added that the number of people defamed might well
add to the enormity of the libel. It cited the 1815 New York State
case of *Sumner v. Buel,* where a majority held that a civil action
could not be maintained by an officer of a regiment for a publication reflecting on the officers generally, unless there was an aver-
ment of special damage; in that case, Chief Justice Smith Thomp-
son insisted that "the offender, in such case, does not go without
punishment." He said: "The law has provided a fit and proper
remedy, by indictment; and the generality and extent of such libels make them more peculiarly public offences."[56]

Unfortunately, Justice Black's dissent in *Beauharnais* takes all
this in exactly the wrong direction, with its perverse implication
that the larger the number of people defamed, the less likely it is
that the leaflet can be subject to any sort of regulation, because
large-scale defamations enjoy constitutional protection in a way
that the defamation of a single person or a small number of persons would not.

Someone might venture a separate contention that no real
harm or injury is done in large-group defamation. Maybe defa-

mation mostly loses its force when it is applied to groups: "the injury is lost in the numbers." But this is precisely *not* the case when a vicious slur is made against all the members of a group with reference to some ascriptive group characteristic. Perhaps if the defendant says "*Some* of the members of group X are guilty of criminality," with the implication that it may be an unknown dozen among millions, then the injury to the dignity and reputation of members of X generally is "lost in the numbers." And the disorder that such a diluted insult is likely to occasion may, by the same token, be slight or nonexistent. But that is not what happens when the libel is associated ascriptively with group membership as such—as it was in the Illinois leaflet. There, it does seem reasonable to say both that the group libel reflects seriously on all members of the group and, as the Illinois court observed, that "[a]ny ordinary person could only conclude from the libelous character of the language that a clash and riots would eventually result between the members of the White Circle League of America and the Negro race."[57]

Assaulting Group Reputation

How does one libel a group? What aspects of group reputation are we trying to protect with laws against racial or religious defamation? The first thing to note is that it is not the group as such that we are ultimately concerned about—as one might be concerned about a community, a nation, or a culture. The concern, in the end, is individualistic. But as I have already said, group-defamation laws will not concern themselves with the particularized reputations of individuals. They will look instead to the basics of social standing and to the association that is made—in the hate speech, in the libel, in the defamatory pamphlet, poster, or blog—between the denigration of that basic standing and some characteristic associated more or less ascriptively with all members of the group.

So, first of all, that association might take the form of a factual claim. That was important in *Beauharnais*, with its imputation that guns, crime, and marijuana were somehow typical of "the negro." Putting about such factual imputations and getting them accepted at a general level can have a profound effect on all members of the group: "[A] man's job and his educational opportunities and the dignity accorded him may depend as much on the reputation of the racial and religious group to which he willy-nilly belongs, as on his own merits. This being so, we are precluded from saying that speech concededly punishable when immediately directed at individuals cannot be outlawed if directed at groups with whose position and esteem in society the affiliated individual may be inextricably involved."[58] We could say something similar about a claim that Muslims are terrorists: a general imputation of dangerousness has a direct impact on the standing and social relations of all members of the group

Second, group libel often involves a characterization that denigrates people—a characterization that probably falls on the "opinion" rather than "fact" side of the distinction sometimes made in U.S. constitutional law.[59] Consider the statements complained of in the landmark Canadian case of *R. v. Keegstra:* James Keegstra was a high school teacher in Eckville, Alberta, who taught his classes that Jewish people seek to destroy Christianity and that they "created the Holocaust to gain sympathy."[60] Here, the fac-

tual imputation is damaging specifically to social and cultural
reputation, which can still isolate and stigmatize individuals.
Catharine MacKinnon—whose organization, the Woman's Legal Education and Action Fund, intervened in the *Keegstra*
case—put it this way: "We argued that group libel . . . promotes
the disadvantage of unequal groups; . . . that stereotyping and
stigmatization of historically disadvantaged groups through
group hate propaganda shape their social image and reputation,
which controls their access to opportunities more powerfully
than their individual abilities ever do."[61]

Third, a group libel may go directly to the normative basis of
equal standing, damning the members of the group with vicious
characterizations that dehumanize their ascriptive characteristics
and depict them as insects or animals. We believe that all hu-
mans, whatever their color or appearance, are equally persons,
with the rights and dignity of humanity. But I remember seeing
a racist agitator sentenced to a short prison term in England in
the late 1970s, under the Race Relations Act, for festooning the
streets of Leamington Spa with posters depicting Britons of African ancestry as apes. After his conviction by the jury, he was
sentenced by a crusty old English judge, who (one might have
imagined) would have little sympathy with this newfangled hate
speech legislation. But the judge gave the defendant a stern lecture to the effect that we cannot run a multiracial society under
modern conditions if people are free to denigrate their fellow
citizens in bestial terms. There was some shouting from the gal-
lery as the defendant was taken away. The case made a deep impression on me.[62]

Finally, there are libels that go even beyond opinion and moral characterization, but that denigrate the members of a group by embodying slogans or instructions intended implicitly to degrade (or signal the degradation of) those to whom they are addressed. It might be something as crude as "Muslims Out!" Or a group and its members can be libeled by signage, associating group membership with prohibition or exclusion. "No Blacks Allowed." Ontario's Racial Discrimination Act prohibited the publication or display of "any notice, sign, symbol, emblem or other representation indicating discrimination or an intention to discriminate against any person or any class of persons for any purpose because of the race or creed of such person or class of persons." And that is quite apart from the prohibition on discrimination itself. Or consider that in the early days of the Jewish Anti-Defamation League (ADL) in the United States, one of the aims of the League was to put a stop to the poisoning of the social environment by published declarations of racial and religious hostility. When the ADL campaigned for legislation against stores and hotels that denied their business to Jews, it was not just the discrimination they wanted to counter—it was the *signage:* "Christians Only." What concerned the organization was the danger that anti-Semitic signage would become a permanent feature of the landscape and that Jews would have to live and work and raise their families in a community whose public aspect was disfigured in this way.[63]

Singly or together, these reputational attacks amount to assaults upon the *dignity* of the persons affected—"dignity," in the sense of their basic social standing, the basis of their recognition as social equals and as bearers of human rights and constitutional entitlements. Dignity is a complex idea, and there is much more to say about it than I can say here: Chapters 4 and 5 will contain some further discussion.[64] For the moment, please note that dignity, in the sense in which I am using it, is not just a philosophical conception of immeasurable worth in (say) the Kantian sense of *würde*.[65] It is a matter of status—one's status as a member of society in good standing—and it generates demands for recognition and for treatment that accords with that status. Philosophically, we may say that dignity is inherent in the human person—and so it is. But as a social and legal status, it has to be established, upheld, maintained, and vindicated by society and the law, and this—as I shall argue in Chapter 4—is something in which we are all required to play a part. At the very least, we are required in our public dealings with one another to refrain from acting in a way that is calculated to undermine the dignity of other people. This is the obligation that is being enforced when we enact and administer laws against group libel.

In all of this, though we are talking about group dignity, our point of reference is the individual members of the group, not the dignity of the group as such or the dignity of the culture or social structure that holds the group together.[66] The ultimate concern is what happens to individuals when defamatory imputations are associated with shared characteristics such as race, ethnicity, religion, gender, sexuality, and national origin.[67] Ascription of the shared characteristic is what membership of the group amounts to—though once ascribed, the membership may be valued or not valued by the persons concerned; it may be a source of pride or something to which they, as individuals, prefer to remain indifferent. We might even say that protection against group libel (and thus protection of "group dignity" in the sense in which I am using the term here) is mainly a negative idea. The South African Constitutional Court came close to this position in *President of the Republic v. Hugo,* when it said "the purpose of our new constitutional and democratic order is the establishment of a society in which all human beings will be accorded equal dignity and respect *regardless of their membership of particular groups.*"[68] But I certainly don't mean that group membership is, in and of itself, a liability. Group defamation sets out to *make* it a liability, by denigrating group-defining characteristics or associating them with bigoted factual claims that are fundamentally defamatory. A prohibition on group defamation, then, is a way of blocking that enterprise. Whether we want to go further and uphold the affirmative dignity of the group (as a group) would be quite another matter, and that is not the concern of hate speech legislation. Affirmatively, what hate speech legislation stands for is the dignity of equal citizenship (for all members of all groups), and it does what it can to put a stop to group defamation when group defamation (of the members of a particular group) threatens to undermine that status for a whole class of citizens.

Beauharnais versus *New York Times v. Sullivan*

It is time to return to the case of Joseph Beauharnais. In the sixty years since it was decided, *Beauharnais v. Illinois* has never explicitly been overturned by the Court. In one or two cases, lower courts have expressed misgivings about the precedent,[69] and among First Amendment scholars there is some considerable doubt as to whether the Supreme Court would nowadays accept the idea of group libel as an exception to First Amendment protection. Many jurists—better informed than I am in the ways of the justices—say they probably would not.[70]

Anthony Lewis says that the basis of *Beauharnais* has been undermined by the 1964 Supreme Court decision in *New York Times v. Sullivan,* where the Court held that public figures cannot recover damages for libel unless they can prove that a false statement of fact was made maliciously or recklessly.[71] The Supreme Court argued that the sort of robust discussion of public issues to which the United States has "a profound national commitment" is bound to include "vehement, caustic, and sometimes unpleasantly sharp attacks on government and public officials."[72] The idea was that when they take on public responsibilities, state and federal officials have a duty to develop a thick skin and sufficient fortitude to shrug off public attacks.

Anthony Lewis is right that the Court no longer regards libel per se as an exception to the First Amendment. But it is not at all clear why the reasoning in *New York Times v. Sullivan* should protect Joseph Beauharnais or anyone else in his position. The African Americans libeled as a group in Beauharnais' "obnoxious leaflet"[73] were not public officials who had taken on the burden of office. They were ordinary citizens who may have thought they had a right to be protected from scattershot allegations of the most severe criminal misconduct—the "rapes, robberies, guns, knives, and marijuana of the negro." Justice Arthur Goldberg said in his concurrence that it does not follow from the decision in *Sullivan* "that the Constitution protects defamatory statements directed against the private conduct of a . . . private citizen."[74] Allegations of rape, robbery, and drug use by "the negro" are exactly statements of this kind, and it seems to me obvious that laws prohibiting defamation of this type are not affected by laws whose purpose is to protect public criticism of public officials.

Indeed, the court in *Beauharnais* itself indicated—and the court in *Sullivan* noted and approved of its making—just such a distinction between the defamation of private persons (individually or in large numbers) and the defamation of politicians and government officials. Justice Frankfurter said that protecting African Americans from group libel was quite different from protecting public figures. "Political parties," he said, "like public men, are, as it were, public property." He said there would be no difficulty blocking an extrapolation from the decisions he was making in *Beauharnais* to a decision that would interfere with political speech.[75] So there is a carelessness about the consensus of modern First Amendment jurists that *Sullivan* implicitly overturns *Beauharnais,* a carelessness that I suspect is really the product of nothing more scholarly than wishful thinking. To actually sustain an argument—as opposed to a hope—that *Sullivan* undermines *Beauharnais,* one would have to separate the Court's endorsement of the importance of robust public debate in *New York Times v. Sullivan* from the public-figure doctrine in which its conclusion was couched, arguing that if public debate is this important it must be protected even when the reputations of nonpublic figures (like ordinary African Americans living in Illinois) are at stake. Maybe that's what the Supreme Court now believes, but it certainly doesn't follow from the reasoning in *Sullivan.* Or—even less convincingly—one would have to argue that a group of citizens counts as a public figure even if the individual members of the group do not. And that just seems silly.

Still—who knows?—the naysayers are probably right to teach

their students that Joseph Beauharnais's conviction would not be upheld today. The reasoning I have been criticizing is common, and if constitutional scholars are taken in by it, there is no reason to suppose the present justices are immune. Judge Richard Posner is probably right when he said in 2008 that "though *Beauharnais* . . . has never been overruled, no one thinks that the First Amendment would today be interpreted to allow group defamation to be prohibited."[76] So we shouldn't rely too heavily on *Beauharnais*.[77] However, as I said in Chapter 1, my argument in this book is not about constitutional strategy, but about what might be involved as a matter of principle in thinking that group defamation is a problem, and what insights may be available from this characterization for those willing to take the risk of appearing thoughtful in these matters.

4 The Appearance of Hate

It is now time to turn attention to the social harm that hate speech does and to the substantive purpose of the legislation that aims to suppress it. In keeping with my emphasis on group libel, the approach I take will focus on the visual aspect of a society contaminated by posters or publications that deprecate the dignity and basic citizenship of a certain class of people in society. I want to contrast the ugly visual reality of a society defaced by racist or homophobic or Islamophobic slogans with what we would hope to see in a society that was open to the lives, opportunities, and expectations of members of every group. So let us begin with that contrast.

What Does a Well-Ordered Society Look Like?

I don't want this to be read as a technical question, though many philosophers will recognize "well-ordered society" as a term of art from John Rawls's political philosophy[1]—particularly in his book *Political Liberalism*. Rawls calls it "a highly idealized" abstraction.[2] Briefly: he wanted to consider the possibility of a society whose basic structure was regulated (and known to be regulated) by certain principles of justice and inhabited by people who took the idea of justice seriously; and he wanted to ask certain questions about such an imagined possibility—for example, whether it could exist as a stable entity under conditions of religious and philosophical diversity (*PL,* 35ff.). He used the term "well-ordered society" to refer to this entity that he was imagining. I am not going to go into any of the technical detail of Rawls's theory. But I do want to use an element of Rawls's conception to cast some light on the *non*-abstract and *non*-technical problem that I addressed in Chapter 3—the problem of what to do about hate speech, when it takes the form of group defamation—that is, the publishing of calumnies expressing hatred and contempt for some racial, ethnic, or religious group.

A society which permits such publications may *look* quite different from a society that does not. Its hoardings and its lampposts may be festooned with depictions of members of racial minorities characterizing them as bestial or subhuman. There may be posters proclaiming that members of these minorities are criminals, perverts, or terrorists, or leaflets saying that followers of a certain religion are threats to decent people and that they should be deported or made to disappear. There may be banners and swastikas celebrating or excusing the genocidal campaigns of the past. There may be signs indicating that the members of the minority in question are not welcome in certain neighborhoods or in polite society generally, and flaming symbols intended to intimidate them if they remain. That is what a society may look like when group defamation is permitted. And my question is: Is that what a *well-ordered* society would look like?

I ask because it is assumed by many liberal constitutionalists, particularly in the United States, that a free society—and a well-ordered society is certainly supposed to be a free society—will not permit laws or ordinances prohibiting stuff like this, on the ground that any such prohibition is precluded by our commitment to something like the First Amendment principle of free speech. The constitutionalists may acknowledge that the social environment resulting from their toleration of hate speech *looks* unpleasant; they may say that they don't like the look of these billboards, placards, blogs, or flaming crosses any more than we do. But, they say, the society that permits them and that presents this ugly appearance may still count as well-ordered, precisely because it is a society in which racists are allowed to speak their mind like everyone else. Some go further and are inclined to celebrate the diversity and unruliness of the various messages and speeches milling around visibly in the marketplace of ideas. They will mention that the objectionable placards and leaflets are likely to be opposed by hundreds of other published tracts and banners celebrating equality and affirming the equal dignity of all members of society. Even if this is not a matter of ideal balance, still they love the richness and untidiness of the marketplace of ideas: let a thousand flowers bloom, they say, even the poisonous ones. For of course some of the ideas are foul and distasteful. But if you blur your eyes a bit, what you see is a glorious splash of moving and variegated color—ideas interacting openly and unpredictably with one another in full public view. *That,* they will say, is surely a feature of a well-ordered society—even if the men, women, and children who are the targets of these foul and distasteful messages of hate have difficulty in maintaining this lofty perspective.

Of course, if the racist appearances correspond to a racist reality, then things are different. If the signs saying "Christians Only" —or, in the more discrete form that used to be seen in Miami, "Churches Nearby"—are accompanied by discriminatory practice against Jews, then there *is* something to worry about. Or if Muslims are actually beaten up in the street, if minority members are not protected against the discrimination advocated in racist posters, or if those in power treat people in the unequal and degrading ways that the racist leaflets call for—*that* would show that the society was not well-ordered. But if it's just signage, they say, there is nothing to worry about. And even if we act against the discrimination, the beatings, and the inequality, still—they will add—we should leave the signage in place.

That's the position I want to test in this chapter, by focusing on this issue of appearances. The question I have asked—what does a well-ordered society look like?—is not a coy way of asking what makes a society well-ordered, or what a well-ordered society is *like*. I am interested in how things literally look; I'm interested in the visible environment. How important is the look of things in a well-ordered society? Is it unimportant, compared to how things actually are? Or is it an important *part* of how things actually are? And if it is an important part of how things are, what in particular should we be looking for? The colorful, unruly diversity of a free market of ideas? Or the absence of visible features that are at odds with the fundamental commitment to justice with which a well-ordered society is supposed to be imbued? If it is the latter, then can we present that as a way of understanding restrictions on hate speech and group defamation—understanding such restrictions as being among the ways in which real-world societies try to make themselves visibly more well-ordered (better-ordered) than they would otherwise be?

I am not saying that those who enact hate speech legislation are familiar with Rawlsian ideas, but I am interested in whether hate speech restrictions amount *in effect* to an embrace of Rawls's idea of a well-ordered society, particularly in regard to one element of that conception. The element that interests me is this: Rawls stipulates that in a well-ordered society "everyone accepts, and knows that everyone else accepts, the very same principles of justice" (*PL*, 35). Now, this is an attractive idea, quite apart from its role in Rawls's argument. We like the idea of a society bearing its values on its sleeve, making clear to all comers the fundamental principles of liberty, equality, and dignity that it embraces. That's what I want to concentrate on: the assurance of a general commitment to the fundamentals of justice and dignity that a well-ordered society is supposed to furnish to its citizens as part of "the public culture of a democratic society."[3] I want to take the measure of this assurance and, to the extent that it is important, consider how comfortable we should be with public and semi-permanent manifestations of racial and ethnic hatred as visible aspects of the civic environment.

Rawls on Free Speech

I am not asking this Rawlsian question in order to get at John Rawls's own views in the free speech/hate speech debate. What Rawls says about free speech is set out mainly in an essay entitled "The Basic Liberties and Their Priority" (the final chapter of *Political Liberalism*), but it is not particularly interesting for our purposes. It does not address the specific issue of hate speech or group libel. And it does not follow up on the implications of his own characterization of a well-ordered society in the way that I want to. Also it is a bit confusing because, unlike almost everything else in *Political Liberalism*, "The Basic Liberties and Their Priority" is focused on real-world constitutions, with all their flaws and messiness, rather than on the idea of a well-ordered society as a stipulated abstraction. Rawls's method for developing a list of basic liberties is to "survey the constitutions of democratic states and put together a list of liberties normally protected, and . . . examine the role of these liberties in those constitutions which have worked well" (*PL*, 292–293). And in fact he draws mainly upon the American experience, though he has acknowledged elsewhere that the United States certainly cannot be regarded as a well-ordered society, as things stand.[4]

There is some speculation in the Rawls literature about what his view on hate speech might have been, or what implications his other more abstract views might have for this issue. But that discussion is mostly inconclusive.[5] The closest Rawls gets to the issues we are addressing in this book is in a discussion of seditious libel, where he insists—in line with American free-speech orthodoxy—that a well-ordered society will be one in which anything and everything may be published, even things which tend to question the basic principles of a given society. Subversive advocacy, he says, must be permitted. But I am not sure whether Rawls thinks this should extend even to advocacy against the fundamentals of justice—for example, to attempts to advocate publicly for the exclusion or subordination of a given group, or their disenfranchisement, segregation, enslavement, concentration, deportation, or whatever. He does not discuss this; he does not consider the status of speech or publication that, in its content and tone, runs counter to the assurances that citizens are supposed to have of one another's commitment to equality. But I suspect Rawls would not have dissented from First Amendment orthodoxy on this regard; certainly that is what his admiration of the work of Harry Kalven intimates.[6]

So when I ask what a well-ordered society should look like, I am using a Rawlsian idea and running with it in a direction that may be quite different from that in which Rawls would have run.

Political Aesthetics

What should a well-ordered society look like? We might ask with equal sense: What should a well-ordered society *sound* like? On the one hand, we might bring to mind the flat, steady drone of an interminable but well-ordered exercise of what Rawls calls public reason—respectful and mutually comprehensible speech, on matters of common concern, in the vocabulary common to all (analytic philosophers). On the other hand, we might contrast that with darker images of the sounds protected under expansive doctrines of free expression: the marching feet and the chants of neo-Nazis in Skokie, a Grand Wizard's speech at a Ku Klux Klan rally, or the incessant anti-Tutsi radio broadcasts—"You are cockroaches! We will kill you!"—of Radio Télévision Libre des Mille Collines (RTLM) in Rwanda in 1994, broadcasts that my NYU colleague Ted Meron, American representative on the International Criminal Tribunal for Rwanda, sought to privilege as free speech in his dissenting judgment in the *Nahimana* case.[7]

I said in Chapter 3 that an emphasis on speech is an emphasis on the ephemeral. There I had in mind the occasional angry and politically incorrect use of one or another racial epithet, and I contrasted that—using the figure of slander versus libel—with the relatively enduring expression of visible signage or the published word. But it is true, on the other hand, that the accepted vocabulary of a culture can become part of its established environment. And certainly the broadcast word can be as much a matter of enduring concern, especially when it insistently and repeatedly demonizes a minority as cockroaches and vermin, day after day.

So there is the visible and the audible. We might round out the picture with the emphasis by Richard Delgado and Jean Stefancic on tangible aspects of a society's self-presentation. Their book *Understanding Words that Wound* has a chapter entitled "When Hate Goes Tangible: Logos, Mascots, Confederate Flags, and Monuments." And the authors say this:

> [S]tatues, monuments, and the like . . . perhaps because they are intended to be seen by a large audience, . . . contribute to a climate of opinion that is injurious to members of the group singled out. . . . [T]angible symbols have a quality that words—at least of the spoken variety—do not: They are enduring. Words disappear as soon as they are spoken. They may resonate in the mind of the victim, causing him or her to recall them over and over again. But a flag [or a] monument . . . is always there to remind members of the group it spotlights of its unsolicited message.[8]

Delgado and Stefancic do not advance the discussion much beyond this in their short book; but I am trying to proceed in the spirit of the concerns they raise. The tangible, or, as I would put it, the visible and semipermanent audible aspects of racist and sectarian display—these are the manifestations of hate speech and racist attitude that I want to consider in relation to Rawls's idea.

Another body of work that addresses the same topic negatively—What does a *disordered* society look like?—is the work of Catharine MacKinnon on pornography. MacKinnon is interested in the look, the sound, and the feel of a society saturated with pornography. For some, what it looks like is what it feels like: for men, she says, "pornography is masturbation material,"[9] only not just in a mental fantasy, but in the public environment, everywhere you look. And for women? There is public portrayal of them (or women like them, or women they are supposed to be like) everywhere: open, vulnerable, visible, violated. What it sounds like is a silenced scream. And for people generally,

> As society becomes saturated with pornography, what makes for sexual arousal, and the nature of sex itself . . . , change. What was words and pictures becomes, through masturbation, sex itself. As the industry expands, this becomes more and more the generic experience of sex, the woman in pornography becoming more and more the lived archetype for women's sexuality in men's, hence women's, experience. In other words, as the human becomes thing and the mutual becomes one-sided and the given becomes stolen and sold, objectification comes to define femininity, and one-

sidedness comes to define mutuality, and force comes to define consent as pictures and words become forms of possession and use through which women are actually possessed and used.[10]

Mine is not a book about pornography and the two issues are mostly independent of each other, but the shape of the concerns expressed here about hate speech is similar to the shape of the concerns (the anger, the outrage) that MacKinnon expresses in the case of pornography. Pornography is not just an image beamed by a sort of pimp-machine directly into the mind of a masturbator. It is world-defining imagery, imagery whose highly visible, more or less permanent, and apparently ineradicable presence makes a massive difference to the environment in which women have to lead their lives. And similarly, racist or religious defamation is not just an idea contributed to a debate. In its published, posted, or pasted-up form, hate speech can become a world-defining activity, and those who promulgate it know very well—this is part of their intention—that the visible world they create is a much harder world for the targets of their hatred to live in.[11]

A *general* consideration of what a well-ordered society looks like, sounds like, smells like, and feels like might be an exercise in political aesthetics—the sort of thing we find in Edmund Burke's observation that "[t]o make us love our country, our country ought to be lovely," and in his talk about "the pleasing illusions, which [make] power gentle and obedience liberal, . . . the superadded ideas, furnished from the wardrobe of a moral imagination, which the heart owns, and the understanding ratifies, as necessary to cover the defects of our naked, shivering nature, and ... raise it to dignity in our own estimation."[12] Political aesthetics invites us to think about such things as monuments, cenotaphs, public statues, public architecture. Or ceremonies (coronations, inaugurations, armistice day, etc.) and the settings and choreography for public or political events. Or costumes, like wigs, gowns, and uniforms in the administration of justice. We can think about the visible display of power, including the presence and bearing and uniforms of police and security forces, about flags and banners, and civil and military parades. Above all, we can think about publicly visible signage as subsumed under this heading of political aesthetics, from official posters and warnings to advertising hoardings to posters pasted up by citizens. I think that, in political philosophy, we need to pay more attention to all such issues than we do at present.[13]

Notice that these examples—monuments, ceremonies, uniforms, etc.—are mostly a matter of official or publicly sponsored appearances. But in any discussion of hate speech, it is speech and publication by private persons, not by the state, that we are concerned about. Sometimes, of course, there is a messy interface between public and private, which shows up (for example) in the United States in the First Amendment jurisprudence of church-and-state: I mean, for example, legal issues about the permitted presence of religious symbols—crosses, crèches, menorahs, depictions of the Ten Commandments—in town squares or in courthouses, or at any rate on public property. Also, we know that it is possible for a society to *look* religious, without in any official or governmental sense *being* religious.[14] There may be temples, steeples, churches, mosques, and synagogues as far as the eye can see, and many of us think this can be so without any message being conveyed that the society as a whole is committed to any religion. All this may be compatible with a society being well-ordered in the sense of religiously neutral. Sometimes we have to be able to separate, in our view of a well-ordered society, the look of civil society from officially sponsored appearances.

Sometimes, indeed, we have to separate the questions of what the state and civil society, respectively, look like from a third question about how individuals present themselves. This is at the heart of the debate, in countries like France, over Muslim women appearing in public with headscarves or veiled or with the full covering of the burqa.[15] And it is a version of the question we are asking: What should a well-ordered society look like—for example, in the appearance that people present to one another? I am not a supporter of the proposal to ban the burqa; I think people should be allowed to follow the rules prescribed by their religion for modest dress; women should not be forced to uncover their heads and wear what they consider immodest garments, just so the world can see that we are not a society of religious conservatives.[16] But it is a complicated issue: it is partly about the presentation in public of our division between the public realm and the private realm. We are accustomed to such division being visible in the form of the doors and walls of private homes. But the burqa offers a slightly different view: it might be compared to a sort of portable private realm carted around in public, like an Edwardian bathing machine. And perhaps it is this aspect that opponents object to—the visible presentation of a doctrine that women may not really appear in public at all, and that when they do have to go out into what the rest of us regard as public space, they must take the blocking and obscuring aspect of the private realm with them.

At any rate, the arguments that are used to support a burqa ban are not a million miles from the arguments that I am pursuing in this book. What individuals do, how they present themselves, can add up to an impression that matters from the point of view of the dignity and security of others. The burqa may be a bad example. But think about the appearance of masked men in white sheets and pointy hats in Georgia or Mississippi, and the effect that has on the lives and the security of members of the African American community in that state. The Georgia Criminal Code makes it an offense to wear in public "a mask, hood, or device by which any portion of the face is so hidden, concealed, or covered as to conceal the identity of the wearer," and several other American states do as well.[17] Free-speech advocates sometimes criticize such laws as attacks on free expression.[18] The expressive aspect of wearing Klan hoods and robes is undeniable. But as with the more articulate hate speech that I am concerned with, the question is whether the law should be indifferent to its impact on what our society looks like and what it is for the members of certain groups to have to try and make a life in a society that looks like that.

Hatred and Law in a Well-Ordered Society.

Will hate speech be tolerated by law in a well-ordered society? We have already considered one response: yes, it will be tolerated as part of the energizing diversity of a free market of ideas. Another response goes as follows: a society cannot *be* well-ordered if people are advocating racial or religious hatred. The idea of a well-ordered society is the idea of a society being fully and effectively governed by a conception of justice. In technical terms, it is full-compliance theory rather than partial-compliance theory.[19] On this account, discussion of a society with sufficient rancor and division to generate hate speech cannot be discussion of a well-ordered society (in John Rawls's sense), since both the hatred this speech expresses and the hatred it is calculated to drum up are incompatible with the attitudes whose prevalence among the citizenry—indeed, whose universal adoption—is supposedly definitive of a well-ordered society. We don't call a society "well-ordered" unless these attitudes have died out and been replaced by sentiments of justice.

So compare what Rawls says about illiberal religions. Intolerant religions—Rawls says—"will cease to exist in the well-ordered society of political liberalism" (*PL*, 197). Religions that demand the suppression of other religions, that insist upon constitutional establishment, or that demand the adoption of a certain comprehensive conception of the good by the whole society—a society cannot be well-ordered unless such religions have, so to speak, died out. Accordingly, the question of what to do about such religions in a well-ordered society will not arise. Similarly, a society cannot become well-ordered unless the bigots and racists give up their mission and accept the basic principles of justice and equal respect that were formerly anathema to them. And so the question of what to do about hate speech and group defamation in a well-ordered society does not arise. A well-ordered society will definitely not look racist, on this account. But, it may be said, this will not be because there are laws against that sort of thing. It will be because the citizens—being citizens of a well-ordered society—have no wish or motivation to express themselves in these terms.

Taking this response one step further, our well-ordered respondent may also say: even if it is true that Rawls's ideal society would not be festooned with racial signage, Islamophobic leaflets, and ethnically prejudiced billboards, *still* nothing of interest follows from this for our debate about hate speech laws or group-defamation laws. A well-ordered society would not need such laws, because there would be no impulse to do what they forbid. Maybe the lesson for us, in our much-*less*-than-well-ordered society, is that we must hope that hate speech dies out, just withers away, not because of coercive laws limiting free speech, but because of changes of heart brought about perhaps by public education and (not least) by effective answers to hate speech in the free marketplace of ideas.

It is an interesting argument. But I think that this response—which I am not attributing to anyone in particular—is misconceived at a number of levels. Most notably, it misconceives the role of law in a well-ordered society. It is true that Rawls's conception of a well-ordered society is part of what he calls "strict-compliance theory." But, for one thing, it is not at all clear how we are supposed to get there. Consider again the case of intolerant religions. They don't feature in a well-ordered society. Why? Presumably because they have died out. But Rawls says a little more than that: he says that the basic institutions of a just society "inevitably encourage some ways of life and discourage others, or even exclude them altogether" (*PL,* 195). That is an ambiguous formulation. What does "discourage" mean here, in terms of the operation of institutional arrangements? And what does it mean to "exclude" certain ways of life altogether?

One thing is for sure. We should not think of a well-ordered society as a utopian fantasy, in which laws are unnecessary because everyone's attitudes are now utterly just. No one supposes that law can be eliminated from the basic structure of a well-ordered society, or that we can drop the laws about murder or burglary because, by definition, no one in a just society would ever be motivated to engage in those crimes. Rawls's society is not utopian in that fantasy sense; it is steadfastly located in the circumstances of justice, which include subjective circumstances of anxiety and limited strength of will among the citizens.[20] Rawls himself gives us a fine discussion in *A Theory of Justice* of the role of law, including the role of coercive law and sanctions, in a well-ordered society. He says there that

> even in a well-ordered society the coercive powers of government are to some degree necessary for the stability of social cooperation. For although men know that they share a common sense of justice and that each wants to adhere to the existing arrangements, they may nevertheless lack full confidence in one another. . . . [T]he existence of effective penal machinery serves as men's security to one another.[21]

Maybe in a well-ordered society "sanctions . . . may never need to be imposed."[22] But this doesn't mean that their existence or the laws providing for them are unnecessary or redundant. Apart from anything else, as Emile Durkheim argued, penal laws have an important expressive as well as a coercive function; and one would expect that expressive function to be at the fore in a well-ordered society, particularly in connection with the public and visible assurance of just treatment that a society is supposed to provide to all of its members.[23]

In any case, even if a well-ordered society could dispense with laws prohibiting group defamation, it would be a mistake to infer from this that the societies we know must be prepared to dispense with those laws, as a necessary way of becoming well-ordered. Societies do not become well-ordered by magic. The expressive and disciplinary work of law may be necessary as an ingredient in the change of heart within its racist citizens that a well-ordered society presupposes. And anyway, as with all issues of justice, the necessity of such laws is a matter of the goods to be secured and the likelihood that they can be secured in the ab sence of legal intervention. If, as I am going to argue, the good to be secured is a *public* good, a general and diffuse assurance to all the inhabitants of a society concerning the most basic elements of justice, then it is natural to think that the law would be involved—both in its ability to underpin the provision of public goods and in its Durkheimian ability to express and communicate common commitments. This is particularly likely to be true in the case of societies, like European societies (and I think also the United States), which have not yet entirely shaken off histories of murderous racist terror and oppression.

Assurance

Why does it matter what a well-ordered society *looks* like? Why do appearances count? The answer has to do with security and assurance. As I said earlier, I want to build on an insight of Rawls's that a well-ordered society is one "in which everyone accepts, and knows that everyone else accepts, the very same principles of justice" (*PL*, 35). The idea is that the look of a society is one of its primary ways of conveying assurances to its members about how they are likely to be treated, for example, by the hundreds or thousands of strangers they encounter or are exposed to in everyday life.

The content of the assurances conveyed in this way might vary. In Rawls's philosophical ideal, a well-ordered society is defined by reference to the whole detailed array of principles that characterize his conception of justice as fairness: what people know, and what they assure each other of, is their joint allegiance to the "Principle of Basic Liberties," the "Difference Principle," and the exact balance between the Difference Principle and the "Equal-Opportunity Principle," along with the various priority rules and so on. These are the principles constitutive of Rawls's own conception of justice, and he is using the idea of a well-ordered society to imagine what a society would be like if it and all its members were imbued with respect for principles of this kind. He is of course right to note that one of the reasons we cannot describe the United States as a well-ordered society in this sense is that there is nothing approaching a consensus about justice at this level of detail. But in the real world, when people call for the sort of assurance to which hate speech laws might make a contribution, they do so not on the controversial *details* of someone's favorite conception of justice, but on some of the fundamentals of justice: that all are equally human, and have the dignity of humanity, that all have an elementary entitlement to justice, and that all deserve protection from the most egregious forms of violence, exclusion, indignity, and subordination.[24] Hate speech or group defamation involves the expressed denial of these fundamentals with respect to some group in society. And it seems to me that if we are imagining a society on the way to becoming well-ordered, we must imagine ways in which these basic assurances are given, even if we are not yet in a position to secure a more detailed consensus on justice.

So far as these fundamentals are concerned, in a well-ordered society, "[c]itizens accept and know that others likewise accept those principles, and this knowledge in turn is publicly recognized" (*PL*, 66). Why, exactly, is the public and visible conveyance of this knowledge important? I referred earlier to political aesthetics: the decent drapery celebrated by Edmund Burke; the notion that to make us love our country, our country must be lovely; and so on. But when we ask about the public conveyance of these assurances, we are not just talking about justice on show for the sake of an impressive or pretty display (in the way that a society might display the glories of its power or the splendor of its culture or the prowess of its athletes). We are not even talking about a society displaying pride in its achievements on the front of equality or diversity, touching though such displays sometimes are. We are talking about displays that matter to the individuals whose ordinary conduct of life and business relies on widespread acceptance of the fundamentals of justice. We are talking about the security that such individuals have and need in connection with that reliance. In a well-ordered society, where people are visibly impressed by signs of one another's commitment to justice, everyone can enjoy a certain assurance as they go about their business. They know that when they leave home in the morning, they can count on not being discriminated against or humiliated or terrorized. They can feel secure in the rights that justice defines; they can face social interactions without the elemental risks that such interaction would involve if one could not count on others to act justly; there is security, too, for each person's proper pride and dignity against the soul-shriveling humiliation that a discriminatory rebuff can give rise to. David Bromwich once quoted a remark that President Lyndon Johnson made in response to a question about the moral necessity of the 1964 Civil Rights Act. The president's response? "A man has a right not to be insulted in front of his children."[25] It is a telling image of the ugliness and distress that the details of discrimination inflict upon people;[26] and it is security against interactions of this kind in the ordinary dailiness of life, as much as the upholding of any grander constitutional right, that is at stake when we ask about the assurances that a well-ordered society holds out for its citizens.

In a landmark case that we have already mentioned, *R. v. Keegstra* (1990), the Canadian chief justice Brian Dickson said this about the effect that public expressions of hatred may have on people's lives:

> The derision, hostility and abuse encouraged by hate propaganda . . . have a severely negative impact on the individual's sense of self-worth and acceptance. This impact may cause target group members to take drastic measures in reaction, perhaps avoiding activities which bring them in contact with non-group members or adopting attitudes and postures directed towards blending in with the majority. Such

consequences bear heavily in a nation that prides itself on tolerance and the fostering of human dignity through, among other things, respect for the many racial, religious, and cultural groups in our society.[27]

The point of the visible self-presentation of a well-ordered society, then, is not just aesthetic; it is the conveying of an assurance to all the citizens that they can count on being treated justly.

However, when a society is defaced with anti-Semitic signage, burning crosses, and defamatory racial leaflets, that sort of assurance evaporates. A vigilant police force and a Justice Department may still keep people from being attacked or excluded, but they no longer have the benefit of a general and diffuse assurance to this effect, provided and enjoyed as a public good, furnished to all by each.

Focusing for a moment on the assurance itself, notice how it connects to dignity and reputation in the sense discussed in Chapter 3. A person's dignity is not just a decorative fact about that individual. It is a matter of status, and as such it is in large part normative: it is something about a person that commands respect from others and from the state. Moreover, one holds a certain status not just when one happens to have a given set of entitlements, but when the recognition of those rights or entitlements is basic to how one is in fact dealt with. The element of *assurance* that one will be dealt with on this basis is an intrinsic part of what dignity requires. So it is with the fundamentals of social reputation. (Remember how we distinguished the fundamentals of an individual's reputation as a person, a member of society in good standing, from the details of personal reputation

which it might be the function of tort law to enforce.) We accord
people dignity on account of the sorts of beings human persons
are, and we are gravely concerned when it is said publicly that
some people by virtue of their membership in a racial, ethnic, or
religious group are not really beings of that kind and so are not
entitled to that basic dignity. Such hateful claims are not just an-
thropological speculations; they intimate that the people concerned should expect to be treated in a degrading manner if the
person making the hateful claim and the fellow-travelers that he
is appealing to have their way.

Does this mean that individuals are required to accord equal
respect to all their fellow citizens? Does it mean they are not
permitted to esteem some and despise others? That proposition
seems counterintuitive. Much of our moral and political life involves differentiation of respect. People respect those who obey
the law and do good, while withholding their respect from those
they regard as wrongdoers. Democrats respect President Barack
Obama, while some conservatives despise him; most Republicans
have a great deal of respect for former president George W. Bush,
while some of his political opponents want him tried as a war
criminal. Many people despise bankers after the recent financial
crisis. So are we now saying that these distinctions of respect are
impermissible and that everyone has a duty to respect everybody
else? Not quite.

It is important to distinguish between two senses of "respect"
that might be in play here—what Stephen Darwall has called
"appraisal respect" (which varies in one's estimation of a person
by their virtues, vices, crimes, views, merits, and so on) and "recognition respect" (which is fundamental to the dignity of persons

and which is invariant, even governing how they are to be treated when they are guilty of terrible crimes).[28] It is recognition respect that we are talking about here: one's entitlement "to have other persons take seriously and weigh appropriately the fact that they are persons in deliberating about what to do."[29] The fact that we might subscribe to different estimations of different persons as a matter of appraisal respect does not show that we may not reasonably be required to play our part in society's accordance of recognition respect for one another.

Let us come back now to the assurance that people need from one another in a well-ordered society. How is this assurance conveyed? I don't think Rawls imagines that there will be billboards proclaiming the principles of justice as fairness or even the fundamentals of recognition respect. The creepy totalitarian flavor of that makes us uneasy, and rightly so. There may be some affirmative efforts: I think of the public proclamation of a new constitution, like the South African constitution, seeking to focus people's attention on the fact that they all now have these rights; or just the mundane business of pamphlets and advertisements ensuring that people know their rights and know how to claim them. I saw a sign recently on the New York subway, in English and Spanish, telling people that they do not have to put up with unwanted sexual touching in a crowded subway car.

Mostly, however, the assurance is implicit, as though the underlying status of each person as a citizen in good standing goes without saying. Various forums of social, political, and commercial interaction are just open to all, as a matter of course; no one has to say "Muslims Welcome" or "African Americans Allowed." Indeed, if they do, that in itself is evidence of a problem, now or in the recent past. It is tremendously important that assurance be conveyed in this implicit way so that it can be taken for granted, and so that people who might otherwise feel insecure, unwanted, or despised in social settings can put all that terrible insecurity out of their minds, and concentrate on what matters to them in social interaction: its pleasures and opportunities.

At the same time, the necessary implicitness of this assurance makes it tremendously vulnerable. Suppose that a spate of discriminatory signs appear; maybe they bespeak a real intention to discriminate, or maybe they do not. But suddenly the stakes have changed for those to whom they are directed. Or think of this: suppose that after a 9/11-type attack, hateful signs go up intimating that Muslims should be accosted as terrorists, and suddenly taxicabs in New York City start sporting American-flag decals. One could read the presence of those flags as a sign not of pride or patriotism, but of fear—that cabs without them will have their Muslim-looking drivers beaten up.

This helps us to see what hate speech is about. The point of the bigoted displays that we want to regulate is that they are not just autonomous self-expression. They are not simply the views of racists letting off steam. The displays specifically target the social sense of assurance on which members of vulnerable minorities rely. Their point is to negate the implicit assurance that a society offers to the members of vulnerable groups—that they are accepted in society, as a matter of course, along with everyone else; they aim to undermine this assurance, call it in question, and taint it with visible expressions of hatred, exclusion, and contempt. And so it begins: what was implicitly assured is now visibly challenged, so that there is a whole new set of calculations for a minority member to engage in as he sets out to do business or take a walk in public with his family.

The Analogy with Pornography

I spoke earlier about an analogous application of this sort of analysis to the related issues of pornography, sexist advertising, and the demeaning depiction of women—things we find in more or less inescapable form all over the visible (and the virtual) public environment of our society. Even if we focus just on advertising, we can ask questions similar to those I have been asking about hate speech. Can we characterize as well-ordered a society decorated—on advertising billboards, subway placards, and innumerable television screens—in ways that demean one large class of its citizens, ways that convey a degrading message about their sexuality, ways that highlight a particular range of opportunities and activities presented as appropriate for them to the exclusion of a large number of other activities and opportunities, or ways that portray as normative a kind of subordination in relationships that is at odds with the idea of an autonomous person working out her own destiny under conditions of justice and dignity? And this is to say nothing of the deeper disgrace of what Catharine MacKinnon calls a society "saturated with pornography," and the degradation that pornography depicts in the real and virtual neighborhoods that it dominates.[30]

The case against pornography has its own integrity, and it should not be hijacked here. But we learn all the time from analogy with others' work. I have found the emphasis by Catharine MacKinnon and others on pornographic spectacle as visible sexism a helpful way of informing my more abstract thought about this question of how a well-ordered society presents itself, about the cumulative effect on the visible environment of numerous individual defacements, and about the contribution that might reasonably be demanded from citizens to the maintenance of a respectful atmosphere. (I don't mean abstract for its own sake, but abstract so that similar insights can be applied elsewhere.) MacKinnon's discussion, for example, about the entrenched spectacle of "the hundreds and hundreds of magazines, pictures, films, videocassettes, and so-called books now available across America in outlets from adult stores to corner groceries, [representations in which] women's legs are splayed in postures of sexual submission, display, and access" for all to see—this has been useful in crystallizing my thoughts about what it is for a society to embody fundamental disrespect in its visible appearance.[31] And though I know she has misgivings about using the logic of defamation as the whole basis of the case against pornography, I have found MacKinnon's insights on the connection between the defamation of women and the indignity and insecurity they face in everyday life hugely helpful in thinking through similar connections in the realm of hate speech: "Construed as defamation in the conventional sense, pornography says that women are a lower form of human life defined by their availability for sexual use. Women are dehumanized through the conditioning of male sexuality to their use and abuse, which sexualizes, hence lowers, women across the culture, not only in express sexual interactions."[32] Something of the same is true of racially or ethnically demeaning signs and posters, which not only intimate an intention to discriminate in particular areas, but bespeak a whole mentality abroad in society that is incompatible with the aspiration of ordinary members of racial and religious minorities to live their lives in this society on the same terms as others.

Of course there are differences. The visibly pornographic aspect of our society has a pedagogical function that dwarfs in its scale and intensity the attitudes that racist hate speech tries to inculcate. Not only does pornography present itself as undermining society's assurance to women of equal respect and equal citizenship, but it does so effectively by intimating that *this is how men are taught, around here,* on the streets and on the screen, if not in school, about how women are to be treated:

> Through its consumption, [pornography] further institutionalizes a subhuman, victimized, second-class status for women by conditioning men's orgasm to sexual inequality. When men use pornography, they experience in their bodies, not just their minds, that one-sided sex—sex between a person (them) and a thing (it)—is sex, that sexual use is sex, sexual abuse is sex, sexual domination is sex. This is the sexuality that they then demand, practice, purchase, and live out in their everyday social relations with others. Pornography works by making sexism sexy. As a primal experience of gender hierarchy, pornography is a major way in which sexism is enjoyed and practiced, as well as learned. It is one way that male supremacy is spread and made socially real.[33]

Proponents of free speech in the areas of pornography and hate speech have indicated that they are not prepared to consider any of this unless it is shown to be connected with, respectively, sexual or racial violence. MacKinnon has risen admirably to this challenge, in *Only Words* and elsewhere. But the advantage of the assurance-versus-defamation framework that I am using is that it does not allow the issue to be presented *simply* as a matter of the causation of violence, important though that is. There is also the deeper issue of public order that I spoke about in Chapter 3—the dignitary order of society. And it seems to me that women are entitled to ask whether official legal tolerance of pornography and of its pervasive public display is consistent with our commitment to the dignity and equality of women. I think the connection between dignity and defamation is as important here as it is in the case of hate speech (though the relationship is also more complicated). In both cases, a well-ordered society ought to be conveying, at least implicitly, the assurance that members of a vulnerable group can live their lives gracefully and in a dignified manner, in routine interactions with others— friends, colleagues, and strangers; in both cases, the purveyors of hate and degradation do their best to undermine any assurance that has been given to this effect; in both cases, their efforts involve the twisted portrayal of attributes shared by members of the vulnerable group. I wish there were space to pursue these analogies further. I have taken this opportunity to indicate the connectedness between hate speech and pornography in the hope that this will enrich our sense of what is at stake on both sides of the analogy.

Rival Public Goods

Let us return now to the issue of assurance in a well-ordered society. Provision of the assurance that I am talking about is like a public good, albeit a silent one. It is implicit rather than explicit, but it is nonetheless real—a pervasive, diffuse, general, sustained, and reliable underpinning of people's basic dignity and social standing, provided by all to and for all.

A well-ordered society, it seems to me, has a systemic and structural interest in provision of this public good—that is, in the general and diffuse furnishing of this assurance and the recognition and upholding of the basic dignity on which it is predicated. It has a powerful interest in each person's having the ability to rely on such an assurance. This public good of assurance certainly has a collective aspect, like the good of a cultured or a tolerant society.[34] But like street lighting (a common and mundane example), the assurance I am talking about is a public good that redounds to the advantage of individuals—millions of them—namely, those whose dignity is affirmed when its social underpinnings might be otherwise in question and those whose reliance is vindicated by a sense that there doesn't have to be anything explicit on which to rely.

However, unlike street lighting, which can be provided by a central utility company, the public good of assurance depends on and arises out of what hundreds or thousands of ordinary citizens do singly and together. It is, as John Rawls puts it, a product of "citizens' joint activity in mutual dependence on the appropriate actions being taken by others" (*PL*, 204). It may not affirmatively require a great deal from the ordinary citizen; this fact is part of what it means to say that this is an implicit good. But just because assurance is a low-key background thing, the prime responsibility for its provision that falls upon the ordinary citizen is to refrain from doing anything to undermine it or to make the furnishing of this assurance more laborious or more difficult. *And this is the obligation that hate speech laws or group defamation laws are enforcing.*

Those who publish or post expressions of contempt and hatred of their fellow citizens, those who burn crosses and those who scrawl swastikas, are doing what they can to undermine this assurance. Their actions may not seem all that significant in themselves; an isolated incident here, a forlorn Nazi procession there, some ratty racist little leaflet. But as I've said, precisely because the public good that is under attack is provided in a general, diffuse, and implicit way, the flare-up of a few particular incidents can have a disproportionate effect. I will say a little more at the conclusion of this chapter about social and historical contexts. For now, it is worth considering this observation by William Peirce Randel, a historian of the Ku Klux Klan, about an isolated incident of cross-burning. "Such is the symbolic power of the fiery cross," said Randel, "that people in many parts of the country still talk in subdued voices about the cross that was burned one night years ago in the field across the road or on a local hilltop."[35] And he added this about the isolated incident of the burning cross: "What [a cross-burning] is commonly taken to mean is that neighbors one sees every day include some who are Klan members, and that Klaverns supposedly extinct are only dormant, ready to regroup for action when the Klan senses that action is needed. It casts a shadow on many a neighborhood to know that it harbors a potentially hostile element which at any moment may disrupt the illusion of peace."

Hate speech doesn't just seek to undermine the public good of implicit assurance. It also seeks to establish *a rival public good* as the wolves call to one another across the peace of a decent society.

The publication of hate speech, the appearance of these symbols and scrawls in places for all to see, is a way of providing a focal point for the proliferation and coordination of the attitudes that these actions express, a public manifestation of hatred by some people to indicate to others that they are not alone in their racism or bigotry. Frank Collin, the leader of the Nazis who sought to march through Skokie, put it this way: "We want to reach the good people—get the fierce anti-Semites who have to live among the Jews to come out of the woodwork and stand up for themselves."[36] Accordingly, hate speech laws aim not only to protect the public good of dignity-based assurance, but also to block the construction of this rival public good that the racists and Islamophobes are seeking to construct among themselves.

It is sometimes objected that such laws simply drive hate underground. But in a way, that is the whole point: we want to convey the sense that the bigots are isolated, embittered individuals, rather than permit them to contact and coordinate with one another in the enterprise of undermining the assurance that is provided in the name of society's most fundamental principles. True, there is a cost to this: such laws may drive racist sentiment out of the marketplace of ideas into spaces where it cannot easily be engaged. But the notion that what we most need for expression and publication of this kind is a great debate in which Nazis and liberals can engage one another honestly and with respect for each other's points of view is a curious one. Of course we ought to be able to speak out in favor of our most fundamental commitments. But presenting them as propositions up for grabs in a debate—as opposed to settled features of the social environment to which we are visibly and pervasively committed—is exactly what the speech in question aims for. Its implicit message to the members of vulnerable minorities is something like this: "I know you think you are our equals. But don't be so sure. The very society you are relying on for your opportunities and your equal dignity is less than whole-hearted in its support for these things, and we are going to expose that half-heartedness and build on that ambivalence every chance we get. So: think about it and be afraid. The time for your degradation and your exclusion by the society that presently shelters you is fast approaching." If this is the message of hate speech, then it is not at all clear that public engagement is the sole appropriate response; nor is it at all clear that driving this message underground is altogether a bad thing.

Clear and Present Danger?

In a way, we are talking here about an *environmental* good—the *atmosphere* of a well-ordered society—as well as the ways in which a certain ecology of respect, dignity, and assurance is maintained, and the ways in which it can be polluted and (to vary the metaphor) undermined. The environmental analogy has another advantage: it changes the terms of the conversation about public disorder. Many who are open to these concerns about societal assurance say that the law should not be brought in to protect such assurance, except when there is a clear and present danger of its collapse. This is similar to the concern about violence which we considered above, at the end of section on pornography: unless there is a demonstrable and immediate causal connection with violence against women (say MacKinnon's opponents), so that

each act of consuming pornography makes a discernible difference to a man's propensity to rape or assault women, we should
not contemplate restricting freedom of expression.

Imagine if we took that attitude toward environmental harms
—toward automobile emissions, for example. Suppose we said
that unless someone can show that *my automobile* causes lead poisoning with direct detriment and imminent harm to the health
of assignable individuals, I shouldn't be required to fit an
emission-control device to my car's exhaust pipe. It would be irresponsible to reason in that way with regard to environmental
regulation; instead we figure that the tiny impacts of millions of
actions—each apparently inconsiderable in itself—can produce a
large-scale toxic effect that, even at the mass level, operates in-
sidiously as a sort of slow-acting poison, and that regulations
have to be aimed at individual actions with that scale and that
pace of causation in mind. An immense amount of progress has
been made in consequentialist moral philosophy by taking causation of this kind, on this scale and at this pace, properly into account,[37] and it is odd and disturbing that older and cruder models
of social harm remain dominant in the First Amendment arena.

The Rule of Law and the Role of Individuals

I have said that dignity-based assurance is a public good provided
to all by all, and that unlike the benefit of street lighting it cannot
be provided by a central utility. I am sure some readers will balk
at this and say that it is a mistake for me to saddle private citizens
with what is surely a responsibility of government. Is not the

manifestation of commitment by government much more important than the manifestation of the attitudes of citizens to one another?

This gives me one last objection to answer: maybe, in the end, it doesn't matter what a well-ordered society *looks* like. Surely what is important, in the end, is upholding the principles of justice, not the visible display of citizens' attitudes. Shouldn't the primary vehicle of assurance be the government's resolution to uphold the laws? Isn't the most important thing the government's manifestation of attitude and commitment in this regard? If laws against discrimination are upheld and if people are confident that they will be upheld, what does it matter what private signage is out there? If laws protecting people from violence or from being driven out of their neighborhoods are upheld and if people are confident that they will be upheld, what does it matter whether the odd cross is burned on somebody's lawn? If the laws protecting people against violence and mass murder are upheld and if people are sure that they will be upheld, what does it matter what neo-Nazis say on the placards that they carry through Jewish neighborhoods in an Illinois suburb? It is law enforcement that matters, not the cardboard signs. That is the objection.

But this is a false contrast. In no society is the state able to offer these guarantees on its own account without a complementary assurance that ordinary citizens will play their part in the self-application of the laws.[38] Think of the administration of anti-discrimination laws. The law does not have the resources to provide an armed escort for every minority member who wants to approach and enter a school, or university, or other public accommodation without fear of being turned away and humiliated on racial grounds. We know exactly what that looks like: the spectacle of the National Guard being deployed to desegregate a school in Little Rock, Arkansas, in 1957. States don't have the coercive resources to do this in any but a very few cases, and anyway it is hardly a satisfactory provision of justice when an individual has to proceed under armed escort. Even routine enforcement efforts by the Department of Justice against routine discrimination can handle only a handful of cases. By and large, the law has to rely in this area—as in almost every area—on self-application by ordinary citizens. And this means that any citizen who relies upon the *law* is, in the last analysis, relying indirectly on the voluntary cooperation of his or her fellow citizens.

That's the reliance we are talking about when we talk of the assurance that is furnished in the visible aspect of a well-ordered society. And that's the concern about the public expression of racist attitudes by members of the public: they are intimations that certain members of the public (and those they are trying to influence) will not play their necessary part in the administration of the laws, if they can get away with it. What's more, they are playing a competing assurance game: they are using public and semipermanent displays to assure those who are disinclined to play their part in upholding laws against violence and discrimination that they are not alone, that there are plenty of others like them.

Ronald Dworkin takes the view that all this is a matter for the government. The government is the entity which is required to show and display equal concern and respect for its citizens.[39] But the citizens themselves have no such obligation: Dworkin thinks they are permitted to show respect for some and concern for others—respect for their parents and concern for their children—in ways that differ from the concern and respect that they manifest to strangers. There may be something in this division of private and public responsibility. But as stated, it is too simple. Government is not an entity separate from the people, not in the formation of its policies or the enactment of its laws, and certainly not in the discharge of its distinctive responsibilities. The discharge of some governmental responsibilities is impossible without the whole-hearted cooperation of members of the public, and the discharge of other public responsibilities is certainly vulnerable to what private people do in public. Many of the responsibilities of justice are of the former sort, and clearly the responsibility of providing the assurance that Rawls tells us will be a feature of a well-ordered society is of the latter sort. We must not be misled into regarding hate speech and group defamation as essentially private acts with which governments are perversely trying to interfere in the spirit of mind control. Hate speech and group defamation are actions performed in public, with a public orientation, aimed at undermining public goods. We may or may not be opposed to their regulation; but we need at least to recognize them for what they are.

Transition and Assurance

In this chapter, I have taken up John Rawls's suggestion that in a well-ordered society, citizens should have and be able to rely upon public assurance of one another's commitments to justice, and that this reliance should be public knowledge, publicly conveyed. I have argued that one way of thinking of the point of group-defamation laws is that they protect these assurances against egregious forms of denigration, subversion, and coordinated defiance. People need these assurances and they need protection against displays and manifestations whose point is to undermine them and to begin constructing an assurance of exactly the opposite kind—an assurance that, whatever the constitution and the laws say, those who discriminate or those who try to drive minorities out of majority neighborhoods will be in good and supportive company. I argued that people have a responsibility to participate in the provision of the first kind of good, at least to the extent of not participating in undermining it; and that society cannot do what is necessary to uphold this good unless it is permitted to enforce that responsibility.

I suspect that one could make a case along these lines *in the abstract,* applicable to any society, based entirely on the circumstances of justice, which, as Rawls has insisted, are characteristic of even the most well-ordered society: moderate scarcity, social pluralism (which may include cultural inscrutability), limited strength of will, and so on.[40] In any such society, people will stand in need of the assurances which, in Rawls's account, it is the function of a well-ordered society to provide.

But the case becomes particularly pressing when we think not just of the abstractions of political philosophy, but of real-world societies here on earth, and the chances of their becoming anything like well-ordered. For us, the question is not just an abstract need for assurance that people might have even in the best of social circumstances, but a need for assurance in relation to the history of their society, which in most cases has been far from well-ordered—indeed, hideously ill-ordered—so far as the basic elements of justice and dignity are concerned.

It is often said that there is a historical reason for the fact that, compared with Americans, people in European countries are more receptive to laws prohibiting group defamation. This is half true: European countries do have to think about these matters against the background of Nazism and the Holocaust (still within living memory). But it is false—and egregiously so—if this is supposed to suggest that Americans have no such burden. Many Americans and the parents of many Americans suffered in the Holocaust. And even on its own shores, the United States has historical memory within the past two centuries of one of the most vicious regimes of chattel slavery based on race that the world has ever known, upheld by the very Constitution that purported then and still purports to guarantee individual rights; the United States has living memory of institutionalized racism, segregation, and the denial of civil rights in many of its states; living experience—here and now—of shameful patterns of discrimination and racial disadvantage; and above all, living memory of racial terrorism—lynchings, whippings, church-bombings, cross-burnings and all the paraphernalia of Klan symbolism—from 1867 to the present.

This is the background against which people—especially members of formerly subordinated minorities—have to situate public manifestations of race hate, group libel, and the like. It is not merely that the tone and content of such displays is at odds with the guarantees supposedly afforded as a public good by the members of a well-ordered society to the members of a well-ordered society. It is that these manifestations intimate a *return* to the all-too-familiar circumstances of murderous injustice that people or their parents or grandparents experienced. Such intimations are directly at odds with the assurances that a well-ordered society is supposed to provide. So it is important that we remember: these assurances are sought not just in the abstract, but in relation to precisely the history that hate speech nightmarishly summons up.

As I said in Chapter 1, my aim is not directly to advocate hate speech laws in the United States, but to understand the case for them in the societies that have them. And certainly whatever case I am making is not Rawlsian, really. As I said, I imagine that Rawls, like many of his close friends, was opposed to laws of this kind. But I have used a Rawlsian framework because I think that his abstract conception of a well-ordered society is very useful for deepening our understanding, in the American case, of what might be at stake on one side of the hate speech debate. What is helpful about his conception—what we can take and use perhaps beyond the context of his particular body of work—is that it is not enough that a society be effectively regulated by a conception of basic justice and equal dignity. What is important is that citizens have a public assurance that this is so, and that this public assurance be provided not just by the government and the laws, but by citizens assuring one another of their willingness to cooperate in the administration of the laws and in the humane and trustful enterprise that elementary justice requires.

As I say, it is not just a matter of protecting people from sporadic insult, offense, and wounding words. It is a matter of securing, in a systematic fashion, a particular aspect of social peace and civic order under justice: the dignity of inclusion and the public good of mutual assurance concerning the fundamentals of justice. It is important to secure this in any community, but it is particularly important for a community burdened by a history like ours that aspires now to become a just and well-ordered society.

5 Protecting Dignity or Protection from Offense?

Are hate speech laws supposed to protect people from being offended? I think not, and in this chapter I shall set out the basis of a distinction between undermining a person's dignity and causing offense to that same individual. It may seem a fine line to draw, but in this chapter I shall argue that offense, however deeply felt, is not a proper object of legislative concern. Dignity, on the other hand, is precisely what hate speech laws are designed to protect—not dignity in the sense of any particular level of honor or esteem (or self-esteem), but dignity in the sense of a person's basic entitlement to be regarded as a member of society in good standing, as someone whose membership of a minority group does not disqualify him or her from ordinary social interaction. That is what hate speech attacks, and that is what laws suppressing hate speech aim to protect.

The Distinction between Indignity and Offense

I have said several times in this book that laws restricting hate speech should aim to protect people's dignity against assault. I am referring to their status as anyone's equal in the community they inhabit, to their entitlement to basic justice, and to the fundamentals of their reputation. Dignity in that sense may need protection against attack, particularly against group-directed attacks which proclaim that all or most of the members of a given group are, by virtue of their race or some other ascriptive characteristic, not worthy of being treated as members of society in good standing. That was the burden of my argument in favor of hate speech laws or group-defamation laws in Chapters 3 and 4. It understands dignity as a status sustained by law in society in the form of a public good.

However, I do not believe that it should be the aim of these laws to prevent people from being offended. Protecting people's feelings against offense is not an appropriate objective for the law. In this chapter I shall try to show how a dignitarian rationale for legislation against hate speech or group defamation differs from an approach based on the offense that may be taken by the members of a group against some criticism or attack. And I will defend the claim that the law can hold a line between indignity and offense.

The distinction is in large part between objective or social aspects of a person's standing in society, on the one hand, and subjective aspects of feeling, including hurt, shock, and anger, on the other. A person's dignity or reputation has to do with how things are with respect to them in society, not with how things feel to them. Or at least that is true in the first instance. Of course an assault on one's dignity will be felt as hurtful and debilitating. And no doubt those who assault another's dignity in this way will be hoping for certain psychological effects—hoping to cultivate among minority members a traumatic sense of not being trusted, not being respected, not being perceived as worthy of ordinary citizenship, a sense of being always vulnerable to discriminatory and humiliating exclusions and insults. Those feelings will naturally accompany an assault on dignity, but they are not the root of the matter.

Offense, on the other hand, is inherently a subjective reaction. The *Oxford English Dictionary* gives this as the main definition of "offend": "To hurt or wound the feelings or susceptibilities of; to be displeasing or disagreeable to; to vex, annoy, displease, anger; (now esp.) to excite a feeling of personal upset, resentment, annoyance, or disgust in (someone)." The dictionary indicates that this is the main modern use of the word (in its transitive sense),[1] although it acknowledges some other obsolete usages, including "to cause spiritual or moral difficulty," to assault or assail, to wound or harm, and to attack (as in "go onto the offensive"). And it defines the relevant meaning of "offense" in a similar way: "The action or fact of offending, wounding the feelings of, or displeasing another (usually viewed as it affects the person offended). . . . Offended or wounded feeling; displeasure, annoyance, or resentment caused (voluntarily or involuntarily) to a person." So, to protect people from offense or from being offended is to protect them from a certain sort of effect on their feelings. And that is different from protecting their dignity and the assurance of their decent treatment in society.

In insisting on this distinction, I do not mean to convey indifference to the felt aspect of assaults on dignity. Dignity is not just decoration; it is sustained and upheld for a purpose. As I emphasized in Chapter 4, the social support of individual dignity furnishes for people the basis of a general assurance of decent treatment and respect as they live their lives and go about their business. Any assault on this is bound to be experienced as wounding and distressing; and unless we understand that distress, we don't understand what is wrong with group defamation and why it is appropriate to prohibit it by law. Protecting people from assaults on their dignity indirectly protects their feelings, but it does so only because it protects them from a social reality—a radical denigration of status and an undermining of assurance—which, as it happens, naturally impacts upon their feelings. That someone's feelings are hurt is more or less definitive of offense, but it is not definitive of indignity. Shock, distress, or wounded feelings may or may not be symptomatic of indignity, depending on the kind of social phenomenon that causes these feelings or that is associated with their causation.

We can see this in the way that dignity used to work, when it was associated with hierarchical office or differential status. Something was an assault on the dignity of a judge, for example, not simply because the judge's feelings were hurt, but because the action complained of tended to lower the esteem in which the judge was held and diminish the respect accorded to him, so that it fell below the threshold that would sustain his authority and enable him to do his job. Even if a judge was distressed at some expression of contempt, it was not the distress we sought to protect him from; it was the diminution of his (socially necessary) dignity. And so, too, for the dignity of basic citizenship (in the sense that being a "citizen" means being a member of society in good standing), which is something we accord as high status now to everyone.[2] A democratic society cannot work, socially or politically, unless its members are respected in their character as equals, and accorded the authority associated with their vote and their basic rights. An assault on a person's status undermines his or her dignity, whether or not it is also associated (as it ordinarily would be) with hurt and distress.

Something similar happens with the concept of degrading treatment, which derives from the idea of dignity. The prohibition on degrading treatment in the International Covenant on Civil and Political Rights, Article 7, and in Article 3 of the European Convention on Human Rights (ECHR), is designed to protect people against being treated in ways that diminish their elementary status as persons. In almost every case, degrading treatment will be experienced as humiliation and will be felt as deeply distressing. This is because human dignity almost always has a conscious component, if only because it is linked to aspects of our being such as reason, understanding, autonomy, free will, and normative self-regard. So, in most cases, degradation may not be possible without some conscious impact. But not as a matter of definition. In unusual cases—the treatment of the very old, for example—where a person's awareness of how he or she is being treated is necessarily limited, degradation may be possible without the typical mental impact.[3] As the English High Court put it in a recent discussion of treatment of the aged,

> Treatment is capable of being "degrading" within the meaning of article 3 [of the ECHR], whether or not there is awareness on the part of the victim. However unconscious or unaware of ill-treatment a particular patient may be, treatment which has the effect on those who witness it of

degrading the individual may come within article 3. It is enough if judged by the standard of right-thinking bystanders it would be viewed as humiliating or debasing the victim, showing a lack of respect for, or diminishing, his or her human dignity.[4]

In any case, the distress is not the essence of degradation even when we would expect it to be present. Unlike offense, insults to dignity are not about wounded feelings, at least not in the first instance.

We see this, too, in the way the law of defamation works. Whether something is defamatory depends on the effect that it tends to have on a person's reputation—that is, on the view that others have of him or her. Of course a libel is wounding, and people are greatly distressed when they are defamed. But that is a consequence of what the law of defamation is supposed to protect people against; it is not itself what the law of defamation is supposed to protect people against.

There are areas of law where people *can* be held liable for something like hurting others' feelings. I have in mind the tort of intentional infliction of emotional distress. In the nineteenth century, the legal position was that "mental pain or anxiety" was not something the law could value for the purpose of awarding damages, at least not when it stood alone apart from other grounds of liability: this was one of the holdings in *Lynch v. Knight* (1861), in which a woman was distressed by a slander on her moral character communicated to her husband.[5] But since the beginning of the twentieth century, the common law in England and in many American states has permitted plaintiffs to recover for emotional distress suffered as a result of a defendant's negligent action, and, in certain cases, for conduct intended to cause mental shock (such as falsely telling someone that his loved ones have been injured or killed in an accident).[6] The idea, then, that it might be unlawful to wound people's feelings is not an incoherent one, and we know how to recognize legal principles whose aim it is to protect people from this sort of harm. But such principles are a distraction in the present context—a distraction, I might add, which is introduced gratuitously into the discussion of hate speech laws by those intent on discrediting them.[7] It is not the function of racial or religious hatred laws to protect against hurt feelings, and the rationale for doing so would have to be quite different from the dignitary rationale elaborated in Chapters 3 and 4 of this book.

Complexities

The basic distinction, I think, is reasonably well understood. But its application may be more difficult, for several reasons. One we have already mentioned. Assaults on people's dignity, on their status as members of society in good standing, are normally experienced as distressing. And the distress associated with these assaults is not unimportant. We protect people's basic dignity because it matters: it matters to society in general, inasmuch as society wants to secure its own democratic order and its character as a society of equals; and dignity matters of course to those whose dignity is assaulted. That it matters to them will certainly be indicated by their very considerable distress and grave fear and apprehensions about what may be done to them, what is to become of them, and how they and their family members are to navigate life in society under the conditions that the hate-speakers are striving to bring about. The importance of this subjective aspect of indignity should not be suppressed, even though the price of emphasizing it is to open the way for critics of hate speech laws to say—I think, with studied obtuseness—that the only purpose of such laws is solicitude for people's hurt feelings.

Second, the ordinary meanings of terms like "dignity," "hurt," "distress," and "offense" may be looser than the analytic distinctions outlined in the previous section. "Hurt" can comprise a variety of phenomena ranging from physical injury to emotional suffering, from the violation of rights to the undermining of a person's social standing. In many contexts, it is not important to make these distinctions. But in the justification of hate speech laws, it is. When we describe hate speech as hurtful, we may—depending on the context—be registering the damage it does to people's social status or using the term "hurtful" to refer to that damage, by metonymy, via the subjective consequences that are normally associated with it. And "offense," too, can be ambiguous. In the section above, I emphasized its primary meaning in terms of hurt feelings, but there is a deeper, more abstract sense that may also be in play: the sense in which something may be an offense against a person's standing, quite apart from the distress that that offense occasions. In this sense—but in this sense only—hate speech laws do protect people against offense; but if we say that they do so, we have to take special care to emphasize that it is not offense in the sense of hurt feelings that is the primary concern.

Third, we have to deal with the complexity of psychological

phenomena, which are not always as tidy as our verbal taxonomy promises. The phenomenology of the reaction by a minority member to any particular incident of hate speech is likely to be complex and tangled. As a man walking with his family turns a corner and sees a swastika or a burning cross or posters depicting people of his kind as apes, he will experience a plethora of thoughts and emotions. It will not be easy to differentiate terror from outrage, from offense, from insult, from incredulity, from acutely uncomfortable self-consciousness, from the perception of a threat, from humiliation, from rage, from a sense that one's world has been up-ended, from sickening familiarity ("Here we go again"), from the apprehension of further assaults or worse, and all these from the shame of having to explain to one's children what is going on.[8] In the gestalt that these roiling emotions compose, it will be difficult, and sometimes may seem futile and insensitive, to start picking and choosing to see whether we can separate out those feelings that are not appropriate for legislative concern from those which are or from those that accompany other phenomena that are. And critics of hate speech laws will say, "How are we supposed to make this distinction in real-life cases?"

The answer is actually easier than the psychological complexity indicates. For, first, we do not make decisions about the lawfulness and unlawfulness of certain speech acts on the basis of a case-by-case analysis of the emotions of particular victims. Instead, we identify categories and modes of expression that experience indicates are likely to have an impact on the dignity of members of vulnerable minorities. If we pay attention to the hurtfulness of this kind of speech—in order to convey how much it matters to those on the sharp end of it—we can indicate certain kinds of suffering and apprehension that are likely to be involved, whatever other emotions are also occasioned. We don't have to dissect any of this and present it in a pure form in order to understand the wrongness of hate speech and the wisdom of legislating against it.

Let me add one last thing. On my account, legislators do have to be vigilant that those who demand solicitude for their dignity and for their group reputation do not also succeed in securing protection against offense. A situation in which someone is gravely offended by what another says may involve an emotional reaction which, as a conglomerate, might look quite similar to the complex emotional reaction that we just considered. A religious person confronting an offensive image of Jesus, for example, like Andres Serrano's *Piss Christ* or the poem by James Kirkup that was the subject of prosecution in the U.K. in *Whitehouse v. Lemon* (1976),[9] may experience the same thoughts and feelings we listed a few paragraphs ago: outrage, offense, insult, incredulity, uncomfortable self-consciousness, the perception of a threat, humiliation, rage, a sense that his or her world has been up-ended, and so on, all the way through to the shame of having to explain what is going on to one's children. And someone may ask or complain: If legislative action is appropriate in response to a minority member's welter of emotions in the case of cross-burning or the daubing of swastikas, why isn't it also appropriate in response to a similar welter of emotions generated by *Piss Christ* or by some other blasphemous publication? We should not try to answer this question by pointing to some key item whose presence distinguishes the one emotional gestalt from the other.

We should answer it by saying that the primary concern in the hate speech case is with the assault on dignity and the public good of assurance, which we spoke about in Chapter 4. With this object in mind, we are in a position to parse the emotional complex differently in one case from the way we parse it in the other, even though the psychological aspect of the two cases may seem quite similar to an impatient observer.

These are not simple matters, and in my experience opponents of hate speech laws will pretend to be exasperated by their subtlety. But I am not proposing a complicated legal test for distinguishing hate speech from speech that merely offends. I am only suggesting that in defending (or arguing about) such a distinction, we should be willing to come to terms with psychological complexity.

Some will say that the lines I am defending in this chapter are difficult lines to draw. And so they are. But I do not infer from this that we should give up the position. Legislative policy is often complicated and requires nuanced drafting and careful administration; outside the United States, the world has accumulated some experience of how to draft these regulations and how to administer these distinctions. Some people believe that no position can be valid in these matters unless it is presented with rule-like clarity, uncontroversially administrable, requiring nothing in the way of further moral judgment or careful thought and discretion. I do not belong to that school. I belong to a school of thought that accepts that the tasks assigned to courts and administrators in matters of fundamental rights (rights to free expression, rights to dignity) will often be delicate and challenging, often involve balancing different goods and essaying difficult value judgments.[10] I do not think people should defect from this school of jurisprudence just because they perceive some advantage in doing so for their position in the hate speech debate.

Racial Epithets

Some of the complexity here can be illustrated by reference to issues about racist or homophobic abuse. In American discussions of hate speech, it is often assumed that restrictions on hate speech will attempt not only to protect people's dignity and the social assurance on which their dignity depends, but also to protect people from having vicious epithets concerning their race or sexuality directed at them. There can be no doubt about the wounding effect of racial and sexual epithets. Charles Lawrence has done a tremendous amount to convey the trauma that such wounding words might cause, and I can imagine an honorable legislative attempt to protect people from this and to prohibit the infliction of this harm.[11] But that project is different from mine, different from the dignity-and-reputation rationale that I am considering here.

My argument depends partly on points I made in Chapter 3 concerning the legal distinction between slander and libel. I mean the distinction between the spoken word—words that are blurted out "when the spirits are high and the flagons are low"[12]—and the visible presence of that which is written or scrawled on a wall or otherwise published, and which becomes part of the environment in which all the members of society have to live their lives. My main interest in this book is the enduring impact of hate speech over and above the dynamics of any particular encounter.

Still, things may be complicated. In suggesting that a shouted epithet is relatively ephemeral, I don't mean that it doesn't linger in people's experience, nor do I mean that the bruise of its impact magically gets better as soon as the person who shouted it goes away. Under certain conditions, the echo of an epithet can linger and become a disfiguring part of the social environment. This is particularly true when there is reason to suppose that the license that permitted racist anger or contempt to express itself this way on one occasion is likely to be equally hospitable to its repetition, whenever the members of minorities came within range of the hatemongers.

So I don't want to draw the line too sharply. I can certainly understand the importance of restricting the use of racial and other abusive epithets on campuses and in the workplace, in an effort to maintain the atmosphere required for the particular enterprises pursued in these settings.[13] From one point of view, a prohibition on racial epithets in the workplace can be justified by reference to the exigencies of the business: most employers do not want their employees to be bullied, traumatized, distressed, and demoralized in this way. But also the language of "hostile environment" used when anti-discrimination law is applied to workplaces takes up, in microcosm, themes which we have been pursuing at the level of society in general. In the United States the logic of hostile environment seems to make great sense to people at this level, and they can easily see that concerns of this kind must be able to prevail over First Amendment considerations in the workplace.[14] For some reason, however, it is more difficult for them to recognize the compelling nature of the same or similar considerations when they are extrapolated out of the workplace to the level of society as a whole.

The other point to remember is that the shouted epithet seldom occurs in isolation. Often it is used in the context of the communication of a more extensive message which is more evidently an assault on dignity, as in "Niggers, go back to Africa!" Indeed, even without such explicit context, the epithet itself is capable of spitting out in its venomous way a message of radical denigration. Like a burning cross or a noose placed on someone's door, it intimates (even if it does not explicitly convey) the desirability of returning to a time when members of a racial minority were kept in their place by terrorizing threats, and it expresses and, more importantly, seeks to evoke the contempt on which such subordination was predicated. The conveying of that sort of message, even if it is done in a two-syllable word, is part of the target of my argument, provided it is capable of becoming a permanent—and thus a permanently damaging and permanently disfiguring—feature of the environment in which people have to live their lives.

Religious Hatred and Religious Offense

It is sometimes said that the distinction between offending people and assaulting their dignity is more difficult to sustain in the case of religious hate speech than it is in the case of racial hate speech. For example, a very distinguished former English Court of Appeal judge, Sir Stephen Sedley, says that he supports racial hatred laws but that the enactment of laws prohibiting incitement to religious hatred is "a much more contentious shift." The tendency of the latter prohibition, he suggests, is to try to insulate individuals or groups against religious insult and offense.[15]

Part of the problem that Sedley alludes to has to do with the particular circumstances in which the British Parliament enacted the Racial and Religious Hatred Act of 2006. I mentioned in Chapter 3 that the United States abandoned the category of blasphemous libel in the nineteenth century. Blasphemous libel was not understood as an attack on the believers or on their reputation or social standing; it was understood as an attack on Christian belief itself, following Blackstone's definition of it as an offense "against the Almighty, . . . denying his being or providence, or uttering contumelious reproaches on our Saviour Christ."[16] Britain maintained laws against blasphemy until very recently. In the last successful prosecution, blasphemy was defined as "any contemptuous, reviling, scurrilous or ludicrous matter relating to God, Jesus Christ or the Bible, or the formularies of the Church of England as by law established."[17] As these definitions indicate, the only body of religious belief protected by the blasphemy laws was Christian belief. The Islamic and Jewish faiths were not protected in this way, and occasional attempts to invoke the blasphemy laws to punish alleged attacks on Islam or on the character of its founder always failed.[18] Many thought this was unfair. After the passage of the Religious and Racial Hatred Act, which defined certain "offences involving stirring up hatred against persons on religious grounds,"[19] Parliament legislated to abolish the common law offenses of blasphemy and blasphemous libel altogether.[20] This could be seen as a move to promote fairness—a leveling down, so that Christian faith enjoyed no more protection than the others (i.e., none). But inevitably some people saw the definition of new offenses in the 2006 statute as a way of leveling up, a way of giving all faiths protection against the sort of attacks that only Christianity had been protected against until

that point. Or at least it was hoped that the act might be interpreted in that way: maybe the statutory definition of "religious
hatred"—"hatred against a group of persons defined by reference
to religious belief"[21]—might be extended to comprehend hatred
of the beliefs themselves, as well as hatred of the persons holding
them. Never mind that Parliament felt constrained to insert into
the statute a sharp distinction between words attacking believers
and words attacking religious beliefs: "Nothing in this Part shall
be read or given effect in a way which prohibits or restricts discussion, criticism or expressions of antipathy, dislike, ridicule, insult or abuse of particular religions or the beliefs or practices of
their adherents."[22] The hope was that this distinction might be
finessed via an understanding of "religious hatred" that would be
capacious enough to include the idea of giving offense. I think
that, with this background, it is possible to sympathize with Sedley's doubts about whether a line could be held between attacks
on dignity and giving offense in the context of Britain's laws
about the fomenting of religious hatred.

What I do not accept, however, is that the blurring of this line
is inevitable, given the sort of approach to dignity that I am taking in this book. Later in this chapter, I will consider whether
dignity is too vague or mushy a concept to be relied on in this
context. But the basic distinction between an attack on a body of
beliefs and an attack on the basic social standing and reputation
of a group of people is clear. In every aspect of democratic society,
we distinguish between the respect accorded to a citizen and the
disagreement we might have concerning his or her social and political convictions. Political life always involves a combination of
the sharpest attacks on the latter and the most solicitous respect

for the former. I think the views held by many members of the Republican "Tea Party" right are preposterous and (if they were ever put into effect) socially dangerous; but Tea Party members are entitled to stand for office, to vote, and to have their votes counted. Denying any of these rights would be an attack on them; but attacking or ridiculing their beliefs is business-as-usual in a polity in which they, like me, are members in good standing. Moreover, it would be inconsistent with the respect demanded by their status as citizens to publish a claim, for example, that Tea Party politicians cannot be trusted with public funds or that they are dishonest. I don't know whether the Tea Party people could navigate the byzantine complexities of American free-speech and defamation laws so as to hold someone liable for such an imputation; but in my view they ought to be able to do so, because that would be a scurrilous attack on what I have called their elementary dignity in society. It would be group defamation of exactly the kind we have been considering. But at the same time, there is no affront to their dignity in "expressions of antipathy, dislike, ridicule, insult or abuse" directed at their economic views. We draw this distinction all the time in democratic politics, and there seems no reason why it should not be drawn also in the context of religious life. True, in the religious life of a society there is nothing resembling voting or candidature which could give vivid content to the socially protected dignity of every individual. But there are free-exercise guarantees, which are quite compatible with the most scurrilous criticism of the doctrines and ceremonies that free exercise involves. And there are laws entitling believers of all faiths to go about their business as ordinary respected members of society in good standing, no matter how absurd their beliefs seem to others. Again, the ordinary understanding of religious freedom depends on our grasp of this distinction.

So why does the distinction seem so difficult to sustain in the case of laws against religious hate speech? There is the psychological similarity discussed earlier in this chapter, and it may seem that by ignoring a complex of anger, distress, and so forth when it can be categorized as mere "offense," we are failing in our concern and empathy for the feelings that believers actually have when their faith is put under attack. But my argument at this stage is simply that this distress is not, in and of itself, the evil that hate speech legislation seeks to address. This leaves open the possibility that the law may respond differently to it in other contexts—for example, in legislation prohibiting the disruption of religious services and in legislation prohibiting attacks on particular cherished religious symbols.[23]

Apart from the psychological similarities, there is also verbal confusion, particularly about the application of words like "defamation." I have assimilated hate speech laws in general to laws against group defamation. But when people speak of "religious defamation," they often mean defaming the religion or its founder, and not just defaming its adherents. When I wrote about "group defamation" in Chapter 3, I tried to make clear that the issue concerned defamation of individual members *via* group characteristics, not defamation of the group as such. If we talk about a religious group as such, considered apart from the individuality of its members, it may seem that there is nothing to defame—and nothing to be protected from defamation—except the beliefs which make the group what it is, and the reputation of the group's founder and its most venerated holy figures. Defaming the group that comprises all Christians, as opposed to defaming Christians as members of that group, means defaming the creeds, Christ, and the saints. Defaming the group that comprises all Muslims may mean defaming the Koran and the prophet Muhammad. I actually don't think this is an inappropriate use of the term "defamation," just as I do not think it is inappropriate to talk of the dignity of groups.[24] The only reason it is inapplicable in the present context is that the whole tendency of the hate speech laws that exist in the world is—and ought to be—to protect individuals, not groups as such. That is what I have been urging. It may be difficult to keep sight of this when what we are protecting individuals against is an attack centered around a group characteristic. But ultimately the concern of this book is for individual dignity—particularly for vulnerable individual members of minority groups that have attracted the rage and contempt of their fellow citizens in the past.

To sum up, then. Individual Christians, millions of them, are entitled to protection against defamation, including defamation as Christians. But this does not mean that any pope, saint or doctrine is to be protected, nor does it mean that the reputation of Jesus is to be protected (as Mary Whitehouse tried to protect it in the *Gay News* case).[25] By the same token, individual Muslims, millions of them, are entitled to protection against defamation, including defamation as Muslims. But that doesn't mean that the prophet Muhammad is to be protected against defamation or the creedal beliefs of the group. The civic dignity of the members of a group stands separately from the status of their beliefs, however offensive an attack upon the prophet or even upon the Koran may seem.

So we have to be careful with a term like "defamation of

religion"—careful with its use by those who want to extend the
ambit of hate speech legislation (and careful also with its use by
opponents of such laws). A recent incident will illustrate. The
United Nations General Assembly and its Human Rights Commission (UNHRC) have from time to time voted on resolutions
condemning religious defamation. For example, on March 26,
2009, a UNHRC resolution was passed condemning the "defamation of religion" as a human-rights violation. It is pretty clear
that these resolutions have been motivated more by a desire to
protect Islam from criticism (in the way that blasphemy laws
used to protect Christianity) than by a desire to prevent the denigration of Muslims and their exclusion from social life.[26] But
many commentators treat these resolutions as being on a par with
laws that ban the fomenting of racial hatred. The words of Jonathan Turley, a commentator in the *Washington Post*, are typical:

> Emblematic of the assault is the effort to pass an interna-
> tional ban on religious defamation supported by United Na-
> tions General Assembly President Miguel d'Escoto Brock-
> mann. . . . The U.N. resolution, which has been introduced
> for the past couple of years, is backed by countries such as
> Saudi Arabia, one of the most repressive nations when it
> comes to the free exercise of religion. Blasphemers there are
> frequently executed. . . . While it hasn't gone so far as to sup-
> port the U.N. resolution, the West is prosecuting "reli-
> gious hatred" cases under anti-discrimination and hate-
> crime laws. British citizens can be arrested and prosecuted
> under the 2006 Racial and Religious Hatred Act, which
> makes it a crime to "abuse" religion.[27]

The deliberate misrepresentation of religious hate speech laws is epitomized in the last sentence of this extract, particularly in the use of quotation marks around "abuse." The quotation marks make it seem as though Professor Turley is quoting from the penal provisions of the statute. But the word "abuse" is used only once in the Racial and Religious Hatred Act, and that is in the passage already cited which specifically *privileges* and *protects* "expressions of antipathy, dislike, ridicule, insult or abuse of particular religions."[28]

The U.N.'s moves against religious defamation were in large part a reaction to the "Danish cartoons" affair.[29] I mean the cartoons portraying the prophet Muhammad as a bomb-throwing terrorist that were published in a Danish newspaper in 2005.[30] The images led to a storm of protest around the world and many calls for legal (and, indeed, for extralegal) action against those who would defame the founder of a great religion in this way. In and of themselves, the cartoons can be regarded as a critique of Islam rather than a libel on Muslims; they contribute, in their twisted way, to a debate about the connection between the prophet's teaching and the more violent aspects of modern jihadism. They would come close to a libel on Muslims if they were calculated to suggest that most followers of Islam support political and religious violence. As one scholar notes, "[c]artoons that associate the prophet Muhammad with terror . . . tend to reduce the social status of Muslim identity as they enforce a negative stigma, according to which terror is part and parcel of Islam."[31] I have heard some Danish colleagues say that the language that surrounded the cartoon panel in the original publication sought to impute to Danish Muslims hostility to the liberal institutions under which they lived; in other words, it juxtaposed the bomb cartoon with text stating, in effect, "Some Muslims reject modern secular society."[32] So it might be a question of judgment whether this was an attack on Danish Muslims as well as an attack on Muhammad. But it was probably appropriate for Denmark's Director of Public Prosecutions not to initiate legal action against the newspaper. As I have argued throughout this book, where there are fine lines to be drawn the law should generally stay on the liberal side of them.

I do not mean that the newspaper's actions—or the actions of the publications in the West that also reproduced the cartoons—were admirable. In my view, there was something foul in the self-righteousness with which Western liberals clamored for the publication and republication of the Danish cartoons in country after country and forum after forum.[33] Often, the best they could say for this was that they were upholding their right to publish them. But a right does not give the right-bearer a reason to exercise the right one way or another, nor should it insulate him against moral criticism.[34] My view is that the exercise of this right was unnecessary and offensive; but as I have now said several times, offensiveness by itself is not a good reason for legal regulation.

Thick Skins

The position I am defending combines sensitivity to assaults on people's dignity with an insistence that people should not seek social protection against what I am describing as offense. I commend this sensitivity on the matter of dignity to the attention of our legislators, even as I try to steer them away from undertaking

any legal prohibition on the giving of offense. It is a fine line—
we have seen that—though I contend that it's a viable one. But
what motivates it? One can see that it makes sense tactically: I
am drawing this line between protecting dignity and protecting
against offense because laws protecting against offense are easy
to discredit. But does the combination of these attitudes make
sense intellectually? I believe it does.

Especially in a multifaith society, religion is an area where offense is always in the air. Each group's creed seems like an outrage to every other group: Christian trinitarianism seems like an
affront to Jewish or Islamic monotheism, while Islam's relegation
of Jesus to the status of a mere prophet, and Judaism's characterization of him as a deceiver, seem like affronts in the other direction. Even within faith communities, each person's attempt to
grapple with diverse beliefs in the circumstances of modernity is
likely to involve their saying things that seem blasphemous, he-
retical, irreverent, and offensive. I see no way around this. Persons
and peoples have to be free to address the deep questions raised
by religion the best way they can. For either these questions are
important or they are not. If they are, we know that they strain
our resources of psyche and intellect. They drive us to the limits
of linear disputation and beyond, for they address the ineffable,
the speculative, the disturbing, the frightening, the unknowable,
and the unthinkable. The religions of the world make their
claims, tell their stories, and consecrate their symbols, and all that
goes out into the world, as public property, part of the props and
furniture of culture. It is not always requisite, nor is it psychologi-
cally possible, to just tiptoe respectfully around this furniture in
our endeavor to make sense of our being and upbringing. We

have to do what we can with the hard questions, and make what we can of the answers that have been drummed into us since childhood.

I wrote about these issues many years ago in connection with the Salman Rushdie affair, and I gave the example of the relation between religion and sex.[35] I didn't just mean the various ecclesiastical prohibitions on fornication, adultery, homosexuality, and so on. I meant our deeper understanding of the issue. We all cast about for an understanding of ourselves, our bodies, and the intense experience of sexuality. We find in our culture tales of pure and holy men, like Muhammad, and even the claim that God has taken human form, flesh and blood, in the person of Jesus Christ. Incarnation itself is not a straightforward idea, and it beggars belief to say we are required to think about it without dealing with the fraught question of Christ's sexuality. In general, our view of the body—*the flesh,* as it is so often described—is so bound up with what we are taught about holiness that we cannot prohibit all associations of the sacred and the sexual in our attempt to come to terms with ourselves. Some may be able to hold the two apart, but their piety cannot clinch the issue of how others are to deal with this experience.

By the same token, we all cast about for an understanding of evil in the world. There is disease, there are great crimes, children are killed, the heavens are silent, and there seems no sense in it. We know the great religions address the issue shyly and indirectly, with a cornucopia of images and stories. Satan lays a wager with God that Job, a good and holy man, can be brought by misfortune to curse God to His face[36]—a story which, if it were not already in the Bible, might have earned its publisher a firebomb or two. The point is not a cute *Tu quoque:* it is that no one even within the religious traditions thinks this issue can be addressed without a full range of fantastic and poetical techniques. Once again, respect for the sensitivities of some cannot, in conscience, be used to limit the means available to others for coming to terms with the problem of evil. It is already too important for that.

The upshot of all this is, as I have said, that offense is likely to be endemic. Things that seem sacred to some will in the hands of others be played with, joked about, taken seriously by being taken lightly, fantasized upon, juggled, dreamed about backwards, sung about, and mixed up with all sorts of stuff. Storytelling will take on the hush of reverence or the hue of blasphemy. Sacraments and traditions will be clouded in incense and satirized in smoke-filled comedy clubs. History will contaminate theology as each faith nurtures its favorite grievances against the others. Inquiry will alloy with indignation. And those who have settled on a given set of answers, for the time being, to the deepest questions that humankind has ever posed will pretend to believe that alternatives are unthinkable and further questioning is an outrage.

There is nothing to be done about this. Neither in its public expression nor in an individual's grappling aloud with these matters can religion be defanged of this potential for offense. The deepest, most troubling feelings are involved, and mutual affront is pretty much the name of the game. Offense in these matters can spring up like wildfire. Some groups go out of their way to offend others, and then make the response of those others the ground of their own offense. But there is plenty of offense to go around, without its deliberately being cultivated. The key to the matter is not to try to extirpate offense, but to drive a wedge between offense and harm, while at the same time maintaining an intelligent rather than a primitive view of what it is for a vulnerable person to be harmed in these circumstances.

But precisely because religious differences can be offensive, there is a standing danger that people will be attacked—harmed or denigrated—for their modes of worship or for the things they believe. Protection against this harm is first and foremost a matter of mutual toleration. We forbid religiously motivated violence or attacks on people's freedom or property, and we stand together to protect people when their lives are threatened by people inside or outside their religious communities. But it would be a mistake to pretend that violence is the only threat. Those who are precluded from beating up the individuals whose faith they find offensive will try, if they can, to make the offenders into social pariahs, to disparage and disenfranchise them, and to get others to do the same. They will see this as an attractive alternative to the violence that is forbidden them, and they will think they can get away with it as "the exercise of their rights." The gist of my argument is that this danger must be recognized, too—the harm of denigration, defamation, and exclusion—along with the more familiar evils of terror, arson, and violence. I believe we can recognize it and legislate against it without taking on the impossible burden of protecting everyone from offense.

Religious freedom means nothing if it is not freedom to offend: that is clear. But, equally, religious freedom means nothing if it does not mean that those who offend others are to be recognized nevertheless as fellow citizens and secured in that status, if need be, by laws that prohibit the mobilization of social forces to exclude them.

The Perils of Identity Politics

People sometimes say they *identify* with their religious beliefs. When they say this, they make it difficult to distinguish between an attack on a belief and an attack on a person. When a belief reels under the impact of the "criticism or expressions of antipathy, dislike, ridicule, insult or abuse of particular religions"[37]—expressions that hate speech laws permit—those who adhere to the faith in question may feel that their very identity is at stake. They may be tempted to make a big deal of this in the context of "identity politics."

I think that what we call identity politics is largely an irresponsible attempt on the part of individuals, groups, and communities to claim more by way of influence and protection for their interests and opinions than they are entitled to. I have written about this elsewhere in relation to cultural identity.[38] Let me repeat the gist of that critique here.

In politics, everyone has to be willing from time to time to accept defeat. There is a plethora of opinion in society, and opinions other than my own may prevail now and then, in deliberation and in voting. People's interests often point in different directions, and public policy may favor your interests rather than mine or neglect my interests or set them back. We hope this doesn't happen too often or too consistently to any particular person or group, but we have to accept that it happens, and it is part of the discipline of ordinary democratic politics to accept these defeats and setbacks gracefully. However, it is also part of democratic politics to insist that, although sometimes my interests have to be sacrificed for what is perceived in collective decision-making as the greater good, *I myself* am not to be sacrificed. Although people inevitably have to bear some costs, risks, and disappointments for the sake of peace, justice, democracy, and the common good, still we should not enact laws or implement policies that require individuals to give up their very being to secure some social good. Each person has fundamental interests—we call these "rights"—and they impose constraints on the political decisions that are taken in the community and set limits on the defeats and setbacks that any person can expect to suffer. These interests mark the inviolability of the individual.

Now, if a conception of this kind is accepted, then of course there will be disputes about which individual interests fall into this category; that is, there will be disputes about what rights we have. Contributing to and resolving these disputes will be part of what civic participation involves. This, too, is a part that must be played responsibly: one of the things each of us should bear in mind as we advance our list of rights is the impact of that list on the overall civic enterprise of decision-making. Each individual must ask himself whether a given demand that he makes as a matter of *rights* will promote or preclude the decision-making and settlement that politics requires. In liberal thought, the assumption has been that only a very small number of such claims need to be put forward—that the inviolability of persons is not infinitely demanding, and that most individual preferences and interests can be dealt with on a fair basis that allows voting, negotiation, and trade-offs. There is a modest list of rights, but the idea of rights is not all there is to political morality, so far as the interests of individuals are concerned. True, we have to acknowledge that if the list is too modest, individuals may be required to

give up too much, in derogation of their fundamental personhood. (This has been my worry about the neglect of dignity,
as though it didn't really matter that some persons' basic social
standing was undermined.) But if the list of non-negotiable interests is too demanding, then politics will face an impasse as
each alternative decision seems to violate the rights of somebody.

It is in this context that we should understand the irresponsi-
bility of modern identity politics. When I say that I *identify* with
some opinion I hold, when I say it is part of my identity, then I
purport to elevate that opinion above the scrum of ordinary politics, into the realm in which protection is accorded to fundamental interests. I say: "I can give up many things for the social good,
but I will not give up my identity. I should not be required to sacrifice *who I am* for the sake of majority rule or benefit to others."
Identity links the opinion in question with the idea of certain
reservations which one is entitled to insist on for oneself and
which others have to recognize as constraints. By saying that
some issue is crucial to my identity, I present my view of that issue as politically non-negotiable: I imply that accommodating
my interests, needs, and preferences in this matter is crucial to
respecting me.

In earlier writing on this topic, I suggested that claims of cultural identity are particularly pernicious because "culture" has the
ability to expand and include many issues on which, as a matter
of fact, collective decisions have to be made.[39] For example: we
have to make decisions about environmental values, but if everyone "identifies" with one or other option regarding a given moun-
tain or wetland, then collective decision will face an impasse; it
will no longer be possible to settle on any policy without assault-

ing someone's identity. I think it is incumbent on people in this situation to think very carefully about the identity claims that they make, and to reconsider whether identifying *themselves* with some option that has to be examined and debated in society is actually necessary from the point of view of what the protection of personhood really requires.

I have no doubt that some needs and preferences relative to religion are among the individual interests that must receive non-negotiable protection in a modern liberal state. Free exercise of religion—freedom of worship—is one of those interests. No one should be required to compromise the demands of worship, as he or she understands it, for the sake of the greater good. To adapt a phrase of Ed Baker's: forcing people to give this up, to accept defeat on this front, is like requiring them to "take off their skin."[40] Even here, we debate the outer limits of this requirement, as we consider in U.S. constitutional law whether generally applicable laws which have no religious motivation should nevertheless be subject to strict scrutiny in the light of First Amendment values.[41] However, that problem pales into insignificance compared to the debate that would be required if each person, in a religiously plural society, identified so strongly with every element of his creed that he demanded protection from offense at the hands (or mouth) of any other believer. I believe that Jesus Christ is the Son of God and redeemer of mankind, and of course my right to believe that is one of the core interests that must be protected in society come what may. But can I plausibly demand—in the same non-negotiable spirit—a social environment in which this view is never contradicted or made fun of? Of course not. Many other creedal claims, held as fervently as mine, deny this belief about Jesus, and many religions (and certainly the views of many secularists) bolster this denial by making fun of what any objective observer has to recognize as an intrinsically absurd and implausible proposition. I may be distressed by these denials and this derision, and I may hope that when they are expressed they are expressed softly and tactfully (and preferably out of my hearing). But I have no right to demand the suppression of these views on the ground that they offend me. The administration of such a right would be impossible in a religiously plural society, for reasons I explained in the previous section. The rights that are recognized in society must be compossible; they must be able to be respected together. But the only way in which we could secure compossibility of individual rights and not be offended would be by suppressing any religious speaking, thinking, or consideration in public.

This argument cannot be evaded by associating religious beliefs with identity. On the contrary, it is identity politics that poses the difficulty here: recklessly presenting claims about offense as though they were non-negotiable, without regard to this important issue of their compossible administration. If I identify my *self* with my beliefs, then criticisms of them will seem like an assault on me. And that, I might say, is something I am entitled to protection against by the law. In my view, this implication or tendency of identity politics makes it much harder for a society to be administered in the midst of difference and disagreement. Better to reserve the idea of "an assault on me" for attacks on my person or attempts to denigrate or eliminate my social standing. Once we apply that phrase to any criticism of a belief that I hold, then we place the elementary duty of respect for persons in the way of any sort of public expression or meaningful debate.

Critics of what I wrote about cultural identity say that I exaggerate the claims that are made in the course of identity politics: they say that "recognizing the importance of identity to the intelligibility of reasons offered in the context of civic deliberation is the first step towards the kind of dialogue that democratic participation requires."[42] I hope that is right in the present context. I fear that identity politics contributes a lot to a muddying of the waters in the hate speech debate; but I hope I am wrong. Maybe it is more innocuous than I am saying. No doubt people will want to convey to one another how deeply they are hurt by various religious presentations, and, hopefully, respectful dialogue can soften some of the sharp edges that are involved in the coexistence of different faiths. I have no problem with the idea of "identity" as it might be used in such a dialogue. I developed a broader critique in this section because I was anxious to show (in the spirit of what I said at the beginning of the previous section) that limiting the legislative impact of identity claims in this context is not just an ad hoc strategy adopted to make the overall position here more defensible. It is part of an independently motivated position in political philosophy which requires caution and responsibility in the individual claims that we make.

Is the Concept of Dignity Too Vague?

Much of my discussion has been organized around the concept of dignity, and in this chapter I have tried to distinguish an attack by X on Y's dignity from Y's being merely offended at something that X says or does. That puts a lot of weight on the concept of dignity. Some have questioned whether the concept is capable of bearing that weight.[43] There are a number of concerns.

One concern is that dignity is a soft and mushy idea, and that invocations of it are often just "happy talk." "Dignity" is a feel-good word—who could be against it?—designed to elicit warm approval without analytic scrutiny for whatever normative proposals happen to be associated with it at a given time.[44] Schopenhauer referred to it scathingly as "the shibboleth of all perplexed and empty-headed moralists."[45] In a recent survey of the uses of dignity in human-rights law, Christopher McCrudden ventured the suggestion that the concept is often used in grand international conventions at places where everyone wants to sound deep and philosophical but is not quite sure what to say or what they can agree on: "Dignity was included in that part of any discussion or text where the absence of a theory of human rights would have been embarrassing. Its utility was to enable those participating in the debate to insert their own theory. Everyone could agree that human dignity was central, but not why or how."[46] The point is not that we lack a theory of dignity. We have many such theories—too many, perhaps, to allow the term to do any determinate work. There is Kant's theory that identifies dignity with moral capacity; there is Roman Catholic theology that associates it with men and women being created in the image of God; there is Ronald Dworkin's theory that associates it with the responsibility each person must take for his or her own life; there are theories that use dignity to capture something about the high status we accord every person in social and legal interactions.[47] My usage is like the last of these, but there is no denying that the other uses are also very prominent.

The proper response, however, is to point out that "dignity" is not being used legislatively in my account.[48] Nor am I proposing that we recognize a free-standing legal "right" to dignity, which might allow hate speech laws built on that foundation to compete with First Amendment considerations in a fair fight.[49] The proposal set out in Chapters 3 and 4 is not that we should interfere whenever speech compromises or affects something one could plausibly describe as dignity, or that a statute should be enacted to that effect. In those chapters, I developed an argument about the interest that people have in their elementary social reputation and their status as ordinary members of society in good standing. I proposed employing the term "dignity" to capture the importance of this interest, but I certainly did not use the term (in the way McCrudden thinks the framers of human-rights conventions used the term) to excuse myself from the obligation of explaining what was at stake. I used it in the course of making an argument about the desirability of certain legislation. It was not proposed as a legal principle, but as a value or principle embedded in political argument.[50]

Personally, I believe McCrudden's critique of the multiple uses of dignity and of its placeholder status in major human rights conventions is overblown.[51] But I am willing to concede the following. If some philosopher can identify a different kind of interest, which might also plausibly be characterized as "dignity," then, as things stand in the usage of "dignity," the case that I have made in favor of hate speech laws adds nothing to any case that that philosopher might be making. "Dignity" does have multiple uses, and dignity discourse is cursed by equivocation. So we do have to be careful to ensure that a case made for the importance of one set of considerations under the heading of "dignity" should not be conflated with the case made for the importance of another set of considerations under that heading. It may be that there are conceptions of the human-dignity principle which hold that dignity requires that people be protected from offense. I am not actually aware of any such conceptions, but the critics to whom I imagine myself responding in this section may try to convey the impression that "dignity" can be conceived in this way. After all, it's a mushy word; it might mean anything. Very well: if that is a serious problem, then I base nothing on the word. I rest my case on a particular argument developed over many pages and on the distinction between the values pursued here (whatever you call them) and the issue of offense, a distinction for which I have argued since the beginning of this chapter. If the association of all this with "dignity" is confusing, then I urge my readers to concentrate on the argument itself: an argument about reputation, status, standing in a society, and the damage that hate speech may do to it.

What should we say, secondly, about the fact that dignity might be cited on both sides of this argument? I have spoken about the damage done by hate speech and group libel to the dignity of members of vulnerable minorities. But the right of free speech is an aspect of dignity.[52] And hate-speakers might also complain about the indignity of having their speech censored and being told, like children, what they are and are not to say in public. Doesn't that in itself attest to the indeterminacy of the concept?[53] I think not. We are familiar in ordinary moral and political life not only with clashes and trade-offs between different values such as liberty and equality, but also with clashes and trade-offs between one and the same value represented perhaps in different ways in the same confrontation: my liberty may obstruct your liberty, for example, or my interest may clash with your interest. Such clashes do not by any means indicate that there is anything confused in the way each party's side of the story is represented; on the contrary, it may be impossible to accurately describe what is going on, except to say that it is X's liberty against Y's liberty and so on. Why should it not be the same with dignity?[54] Dignity is a complicated enough concept to have multiple applications in one and the same setting—and even without any conceptual confusion, there might be legitimate contestation about the extent or strength of its application on one side or the other. In Chapter 6, I will consider an argument by Ed Baker that hate speech legislation undermines the basic autonomy of self-disclosure, which he thinks is one of the most important functions of speech. I have no doubt that that could also be expressed in the language of dignity. What I argue in Chapter 6 is not that we should dismiss this interest, but that it must be balanced against other interests at stake in the situation—interests which, as it happens, can also be represented in dignitarian language. We should keep our heads. There is no paradox or contradiction in any of this.

Is there any other ground for concern about the introduction of the concept of dignity into this debate? It is true that using a term like "dignity" to sum up the force of an argument does indicate an openness to nuance and new insight in moral and political philosophy. Maybe this is a third concern: people may worry that once "dignity" is admitted to our discourse, we will no longer have on the blinkers that are constituted by narrower and sharper-edged concepts. We all know what it is for someone to be hit, and we are against violence. We know what it is for someone to be hurt, and, like good utilitarians, we are against pain. We know what it is for someone's movements to be blocked or threatened, and we are in favor of negative liberty. We know what it is for someone to be excluded from facilities otherwise open to the public, and we are against discrimination—at least if it is direct intentional discrimination. This is all straightforward. But if we introduce dignity into the picture, as something to be protected, something to be solicitous of, then things may get out of hand and there may be much more to be concerned about—concerns that are much more difficult to parse—than were dreamt of in our analytical philosophy.

There is nothing much to be said in response to this concern except "Get used to it!" The use of the notion of dignity in contemporary moral and political philosophy does indicate a willingness to notice new conceptions of value and principle, and new sources of concern. Like American government lawyers facing the supplementation of their familiar rule against cruel and unusual punishment with a prohibition on "inhuman and degrading treatment" of detainees, we now have to be alert—and we have to be aware that the world is alert—to the dehumanizing implications of some practices that we may not have thought much about. I believe "dignity" is a status term, and my use of it indicates the importance of paying attention to the way in which

a person's status as a member of society in good standing is affirmed and sustained. This concern is more diffuse than concerns
about their safety or negative liberty in several ways.

First of all, it looks at how things are for the person in question
in all the myriad interactions of social life—not that we want to
micromanage any of this, but that we understand the connection
between social status and living a life with others in a society.
Status is not just like citizenship, something that may be relevant
only at the passport counter or in the voting booth. It has to do
with the way one is received in society generally.

Second, the concern for the ordinary dignity of an individual
focuses on the ways his or her status is affirmed and upheld—and
the ways in which it might be endangered—as one person among
thousands or millions of others. We are interested in the affirming and upholding of people's status as a public good, accruing to individuals, to be sure—but provided uniformly and non-
crowdably to millions of people at a time. And we are concerned,
too, with ways in which this status might be endangered on the
basis of what hatemongers make of ascriptive group characteristics like race or religion. There is an interplay here between individuals, groups, mass characteristics, and mass provision which
may make traditional liberals a little nervous, conditioned as they
are to recoil from any form of collectivism. But like many social
goods, basic dignity and social standing are provided and affirmed en masse as public goods. And if we are concerned about
what it is like for people when they are led to feel that their very
status in a society is imperiled, we have no choice but to add an
understanding of these mass characteristics to our repertoire. In
these and other ways, the use of the concept of dignity does rep-

resent a perhaps disconcerting opening-up of our moral and political interests. But the disconcerting can sometimes be salutary, and I think that is the case here. It gives the hate speech issue, as I understand it, some interest not just for itself but for broader consideration about how we should approach things in political philosophy.

6 C. Edwin Baker and the Autonomy Argument

I turn now to the critics of hate speech legislation. In this chapter and the next, I will examine the views of two opponents whose work I have found particularly challenging: Ronald Dworkin and the late C. Edwin Baker. They both make powerful cases against any restriction on hate speech. But, more than that, each of their critiques is illuminating and insightful. I have learned a lot from them about what is at stake in this issue, and the best I can do in response is to show that there are insights to be gleaned from the other side as well.

Exceptions to the Free-Speech Principle

There are very few First Amendment absolutists. Ed Baker used to claim to be one of them,[1] and part of this chapter will be devoted to his argument. But most people who insist on the importance of free speech also accept that in some cases speech acts may be regulated or criminalized. Examples vary. There is a hoary saying, attributed to Oliver Wendell Holmes, that the principle of free speech inscribed in the First Amendment does not privilege a right to shout "Fire!" in a crowded theater (that one knows is not on fire).[2] This is a sort of abstract paradigm for the idea of an exception; it is not as though American free-speech jurisprudence has had to deal with multiple cases of thespian conflagration;[3] and Holmes's own use of the paradigm—suggesting that the publication of a pamphlet questioning conscription policy in the light of the Thirteenth Amendment is like shouting "Fire!" in a crowded theater—is an obvious abuse of the idea.

Other cases are more solid. Some emphasize the residue of genuine concerns about subversion and sedition that dominated American free-speech jurisprudence in the early years of the twentieth century. Some talk about "fighting words." Some emphasize incitement to violence. Others follow the doctrines of the criminal law in regard to verbal threats or the incitement or procuring of any criminal offense. Some say that obscenity and certain forms of hardcore pornography may be regulated in certain circumstances; almost everyone says this about child pornography. Some recognize an exception for defamation, at least defamation of private individuals. Not everyone recognizes all these exceptions, but almost everyone recognizes some of them. Our question is whether the stirring up of racial or religious hatred, or group defamation on racial or religious grounds, should be included in this catalogue.

The logic of the received exceptions is unclear. One approach —a balancing approach—emphasizes the importance of the free-speech principle but acknowledges that in these cases it is outweighed by other considerations having to do with the harm that such speech might cause. According to this account, we see two values in play in a case of subversion or obscenity: on the one hand, there is the value or the importance of the incitement as speech; on the other hand, there is the value of the state interests which the law of subversion protects, and the value of the community or individual interests which the law of obscenity protects. When interests of the latter kind outweigh interests of the former kind, then laws regulating speech are permissible. In order to mark the importance of the free-speech side of the balance, we may say that in these cases the harm to state or community or interests has to be particularly grave; the harm that would normally suffice to justify legislation when free speech was not stake will not be enough. That is a plausible-sounding approach.

An alternative method would be to say that the character of a speech act as a (grave) act of subversion or an (egregious) publication of child pornography or an (unjustified) act of defamation deprives it of any protection by the free-speech principle. So it is not a question of balance at all. It's simply that certain free-speech claims never really get off the ground, so far as the regulation of these speech acts is concerned. Sometimes this is indicated by the statement (rhetorical or fictitious) that pornography or subversion or threats or incitement or false shouts of "Fire!" are not really speech at all. Taken literally, the statement is obviously false; but what it means is that speech acts of this kind may not get any benefit from the free-speech principle.

This need not be a simple matter of assertion. The second approach may be based on a sense that the considerations which justify free speech in general do not extend in any shape or form to offensive cases like these. Or it may be based on a more abstract doctrine—associated with a sort of liberal perfectionism defended by Joseph Raz in the late 1980s—that autonomy (a consideration often cited in defense of the free-speech principle) has little or no value when its exercise is wrongful from a moral point of view.[4]

Which approach should the defender of hate speech legislation subscribe to? The second approach is tempting. But I believe it is more sensible to argue for hate speech regulation in terms of the first approach. We recognize, in general, that the considerations which argue in favor of the broad importance of free speech *do* extend to speech attempting to stir up racial or religious hatred; but we say that nevertheless such speech must be regulated, and in extreme cases prohibited, because of the harm that it does. And we acknowledge that the harm in prospect must be grave—more serious than the harm that would justify regulation where such speech was not an issue —on account of the value of free speech that has to be outweighed on the other side.[5]

Making an Honest Case

The great advantage of the first of the approaches I mentioned is its candor. We acknowledge that a restriction on racial or religious hate speech involves a trade-off, and we specify as clearly as we can the nature and importance of the values on each side of the balance.

Sometimes the opponents of hate speech legislation refuse to do this. In Chapter 7, we will consider a common maneuver which involves saying that because free speech is valuable, therefore any allegation about the harm that speech may do is necessarily overblown. More generally, opponents of hate speech legislation go out of their way to denigrate the terms in which claims about harm are phrased. They say, for example, that these claims are, by and large, inflated and absurd,[6] and no doubt they will say the same of my arguments about dignity. Rather than examining the evidence about the harm that hate speech does, and assessing that evidence in an impartial spirit, they proceed on the basis that the harm is most likely nonexistent or overblown, or that they are entitled to hope that it is nonexistent or overblown; and that in any case it is appropriate to denigrate claims of harm in terms that would be quite fatal if they were applied to the vague and airy considerations with which, on the other side of the balance, the principle of free speech is defended. The idea seems to be that we should give the supposed advantages of free speech the benefit of the doubt because free speech is a well-established liberal principle; but that we are entitled to raise the bar very high indeed in our assessment of the harms that racist speech might do, and that we are not required to pay attention to such evidence unless it is established beyond a scintilla of doubt. All those who call into question any aspect of free-speech orthodoxy have become familiar over the years with this asymmetry of assessment and the self-congratulatory evasions and platitudes that reinforce it.[7]

It would be wise not to echo this obtuseness from the other side. Defenders of hate speech regulation need to face up honestly to the moral costs of their proposals.[8] Obviously, restrictions of the kind we are considering are designed to stop people from printing, publishing, distributing, and posting things that they would like to say and that they would like others to read or hear. And let us remember that we are not just talking about casual epithets spoken in anger or racist conversation in a restaurant. The restrictions I have been talking about have a direct bearing on freedom to publish, sometimes on freedom of the press, very likely on freedom of the Internet. The point is to stop these messages from taking a publicly visible or audible form—to stop them from becoming part of the landscape, part of the evident stock of a people's ideas circulating in a society and looming over the environment in which people live their lives.

Statutory provisions of the kind I am talking about—for example, Parts 3 and 3A of the Public Order Act in the United Kingdom, or section 61(1) of the Human Rights Act in New Zealand, or section 130(1) of the German criminal code—make the public expression of ideas less free than it would otherwise be. Some defenders of hate speech restrictions toy with the idea that, since hate speech tends to silence minorities or exclude them from the political process, the net effect of restricting it may be to empower more expression than it denies.[9] Perhaps that is so; I do not want to rule it out. But I believe many countries would uphold their hate speech laws even if that wasn't the case.

So let us not flinch from the underlying concern. laws of the kind we are discussing make the public expression of ideas less free than it would otherwise be. And this matters to individuals. Ed Baker observes that "[t]ypically racist hate speech embodies the speaker's at least momentary view of the world and, to that extent, expresses her values."[10] Often the messages that racists or Islamophobes are stopped from expressing in public or punished for expressing in public are the very messages, out of all the things a person could express, which matter most to them. For them, other aspects of political expression pale into insignificance compared with their leaflets libeling Muslims as terrorists or their public portrayals of people of other races as apes or gibbons. It is not exactly true that *they themselves* are silenced. They can say what they like on innumerable other topics of public concern and, as we have noted already, the laws we are talking about generally permit them to restate their racism or their contempt for Islam in more moderate terms, less calculated to stir up hatred. But the vituperations that are banned are the very words they want to use in order to disclose themselves to others; this is the stuff that matters to them. It matters to them that they express racist ideas in a hateful form; and to that extent, we have to say that their autonomy is compromised—not fatally perhaps, but certainly compromised. So what we have to consider is how this compromise of individual autonomy stands in relation to the legislative enterprise of protecting the dignity and social standing of those who are targeted by the hate speech in question.

A "Content-Based" Restriction

It is important to acknowledge that the kind of restriction we have in mind operates and is envisaged explicitly as a limitation based on content. As such, it flies directly in the face of one of the pillars of American free-speech doctrine—namely, the principle that an exception may not be based on the content of what is said or published, or on the distance between what is said or published, on the one hand, and, on the other hand, some official orthodoxy which everyone in society is supposed to subscribe to in public. As Laurence Tribe put it, "[I]f the [First Amendment] guarantee means anything, it means that, ordinarily at least, 'government has no power to restrict expression because of its message, its ideas, its subject matter, or its content.'"[11] In this regard, content-based restrictions are contrasted with restrictions that affect only the time, place, and manner of the exercise of speech.

The distinction is no doubt a subtle one.[12] I have heard it argued that Oliver Wendell Holmes's famous example, the shouting of "Fire!" in a crowded theater, is not really prohibited on account of its content; it is prohibited for the likely effect of this content—as Holmes puts it, "causing a panic." One could engage in similar casuistry for the case of hate speech. One could argue that racist speech or the defamation of some racial, ethnic, or religious group is prohibited (where it is) not because of its content per se, but either because of the way it is expressed or because of the likely effect of what is said or published upon society's maintenance of the basic dignity of the members of the targeted group. One could make this argument if one wanted to take the American distinction between content-based and non-content-based prohibitions extremely seriously. But it does not sound right to me. If we start drawing such distinctions, then we will have to conclude that precious few proposals for content based restrictions will ever be oriented *purely* toward content, to the exclusion of any interest in what happens as a result of the publication of content. Better to admit that hate speech legislation is forbidden, where it is, because of the effect *of its content* in helping to undermine the assurance that members of vulnerable groups are supposed to be able to draw from the public affirmation of their dignity. No doubt the adverbial element is important: we want to catch only hate speech that is expressed in an abusive, insulting, or threatening way. But usually, as the British statute indicates, that adverbial element will be indicated by the content of the words or the written material itself, rather than by non-content-based elements such as tone, volume, shrillness, or other aspects of expression.[13]

Part of my reluctance to join this game has to do with the fact that this book is not intended as a study in American constitutional law. Who knows how hate speech regulation would now be accommodated within the principles, exceptions, and interstices of that jurisprudence if it were ever permitted by the courts? American First Amendment doctrine is mostly a tangled mess, as judges and legal scholars add byzantine epicycles to their basic principles in order to accommodate various exceptions that for one reason or another they are inclined to allow. Other countries have not allowed their free-speech doctrine to degenerate in this way, partly because their commitment to free speech is not presented as uncompromising in the first place, so that their departures from free speech are not the shamefaced lapses that Americans have to acknowledge. So I forgo any benefit from these doctrinal subtleties. Better to stay free of that entanglement, and stick with the policy argument; better just to acknowledge straight up that a restriction on hate speech or on group defamation is a restriction on speech on account of its content, and that it is the content that explains the restriction.

For not only does the argument I am making about hate speech confront the prohibition on content-based regulation—it also confronts what seem to be the most compelling reasons behind the doctrine. The best account of these reasons is given by Geoffrey Stone. Professor Stone says that one problem with content-based restrictions is that they are motivated by and reflect concerns on the part of the government about the impact that certain communications will have on the public. "Unlike content-neutral restrictions," he says, "content-based restrictions usually are designed to restrict speech because of its 'communicative impact'—that is, because of 'a fear of how people will react to what the speaker is saying.'" He says that this is not a respectable justification in the American constitutional tradition, because it indicates that "the government does not trust its citizens to make wise decisions if they are exposed to the expression."[14] And that is more or less precisely the case with hate speech or group-defamation laws. Legislatures that enact such laws are fearful of the consequences of the reception of this kind of content. They fear that members of vulnerable minorities will become convinced that they are not accepted as ordinary good-faith participants in social life. They fear that isolated racists will secure a heightened sense of the diffusion of their poisonous ideals. And they fear that ordinary people will think and act on the assumption that the place of minority members in ordinary life is up for grabs. These apprehensions may seem patronizing: Why can't government presume that people's sense of the place of minorities in social life is resilient, even in the face of a proliferation of hateful material proclaiming the opposite? But the question answers itself, particularly in the context of a society that has a history of racism or intercommunal conflict. Nobody knows when that heritage of hate and conflict is really over. Old fears die hard; old nightmares are never entirely put to rest; old antipathies can sometimes be awoken.[15]

So: in a way, Stone is right. Hate speech legislation would seem to indicate that government has apprehensions about how certain content will be received in a society. My position is that these apprehensions are not unreasonable. Our legislators are not indifferent to how people regard one another, at least so far as people's basic recognition of one another's dignity is concerned, because it is understood that one's dignity is partly a function of the actions performed and the attitudes expressed by one's fellow citizens. As I argued in Chapter 4, dignity and the assurance that comes with it are public goods, constituted by what thousands or millions of individuals say and do. Our society is heavily invested in the provision of those goods. The point of hate speech is to detract from that provision—to undermine it and establish rival public goods that indicate (to fellow racists, to members of vulnerable groups, and to society generally) that the position of some minority or other is by no means as secure as the rest of the world would like to affirm. The point of hate speech restrictions or laws against group defamation is to protect the first set of public goods from being undermined in this way.

Another thing that Geoffrey Stone says about content-based restrictions is that "[b]y definition, [they] distort public debate. . . . Such a law mutilates 'the thinking process of the community.'"[16] Perhaps words like "distort" and "mutilate" beg the question. But Stone is surely right to point out that restrictions on group defamation or hate speech are intended to change or modify the character of public debate. Without them, public discourse would be coarser, more intimidating, more demoralizing to the members of vulnerable groups: they would have to live and go about in a society festooned with vicious characterizations of them and their kind and with foul denigrations of their status. They would have to explain all that to their children. And as the Canadian chief justice pointed out in *Keegstra*,[17] the upshot might be that they would avoid much public life or participate in it without the security that the rest of us enjoy; either that, or they would have to summon up (from their own resources) extraordinary reserves of assurance as they went about their business, a burden that is not required of the rest of us.

The restriction of hate speech or group defamation represents an attempt to modify public debate, inasmuch as there is a chance of its taking on that sort of character. Should this count as a distortion? Such a description presupposes a privileging of what public debate would be like without intervention. But why should we privilege that? At any given time, public debate consists in an array of millions of contributions of various sorts, interacting and snowballing in various ways. At any given time, this heaving array has various effects on the beliefs held and attitudes adopted by millions of people, making some more enlightened and sophisticated, trivializing or degrading others, and so on. Is there any reason to suppose that this interaction or its effects are more valuable when they are not altered in any regard by legal regulation?

The Marketplace of Ideas

We might think something like that on the basis of an analogy with free markets in the economic sphere. Left to themselves, free markets can generate efficient outcomes by processes that economists say they understand. And analogously, we may say, in the long run the free marketplace of ideas, if it is left to its own devices, will generate the acceptance of truth and foster the eventual emergence of attitudes of mutual respect. The trouble is that, in the free-speech case, this is more superstition than analogy.[18]

Economists understand that economic markets are capable of producing some good things and not others; they may produce efficiency, but they may not produce, or they may undermine, distributive justice. In the case of the marketplace of ideas, is truth the analogue of efficiency or is it the analogue of distributive justice? I have never heard any proponent of marketplace-of-ideas imagery answer this question, mainly because such proponents admit that when they try to figure out how the marketplace of ideas might be expected to produce truth, they have no notion that is analogous to the economists' understanding of how markets produce efficiency (and undermine distributive justice).[19] They just teach their students in law school to spout the mantra "the marketplace of ideas," and fail to remind them that, although some government regulation is generally thought important in the economic marketplace, we have not developed any analogues for "the marketplace of ideas" that would be useful in the arguments for or against hate speech regulation.

So without further evidence, I am not convinced by the usual objection to content-based restrictions that they "distort" public debate. They are designed to *have an effect on* public debate in circumstances where it is reasonable to believe that, without some sort of restriction, public debate will have effects on people's lives that government has an obligation to be concerned about. We design and enforce restrictions on the economic market for this sort of reason, prohibiting certain transactions and regulating others, and we do so in other respects in the marketplace of ideas, too—in the restriction of child pornography, for example.

One useful effect of facing up to the character of hate speech regulation as a content-based restriction on individual freedom is

that it helps us face down some of the traditional myths and slogans of which free-speech "jurisprudence" is largely composed.
Since we do not buy into the assumption that truth will eventually prevail in the marketplace of ideas, or the assumption that
the best remedy for bad speech is more speech, or the assumption
that legislative attention to content-based impact is always a bad
thing, it is not necessary for us to try to force hate speech regulation into a framework of exceptions that have already been admitted into the interstices of these platitudes. Rather, we start
from the assumption that hate speech regulation is seen in most
parts of the developed world as a necessity or as a reasonable legislative enterprise, aimed at combating certain well-known evils
(evils outlined in Chapters 3 and 4 above). And we consider
whether an equally honest case can be made against such regulation in terms of the value of free speech or its importance to individuals.

Free Speech as Trump?

Hate speech restrictions are intended to avert certain evils—certain harms to individuals and to the public order of the community. But hate speech laws restrict free speech, and that counts
against them. *How much* does it count against them?

In the general introduction to their excellent edited volume
Extreme Speech and Democracy, Ivan Hare and James Weinstein
addressed some arguments I made in the book review discussed
in Chapter 1, about the damage hate speech can do to the fabric
of mutual respect on which advanced democracies depend. I argued that the damage is serious and that we cannot assume that

a social system can simply shrug it off. I said that it was wrong to ignore the harm to minorities in particular, since they may depend more than the rest of us on socially secured principles of mutual respect. Hare and Weinstein damned this with faint praise by saying that "Waldron's point has merit, as far as it goes" —a locution which is usually a prelude to pushing the point aside for the rest of the discussion. They went on to say that my analysis was

> deficient in its assumption that the test of the legitimacy of a speech restriction is exclusively, or even primarily, the need for such laws. While gratuitous restrictions on speech . . . are obviously illegitimate, the converse is not true. . . . [A] speech restriction is not legitimate just because it is actually needed to promote some important societal interest. . . . What Waldron's analysis omits is the crucial question of whether the restriction on speech is justified despite speakers' interests in expressing their views as well as the audience interest in hearing those perspectives.[20]

I am not sure whether to take this as a modest point (indicating what we have already acknowledged above: that the considerations that argue for restriction must be sufficiently strong to outweigh the considerations in favor of free speech), or whether the Hare-Weinstein comment amounts to a claim that free speech trumps any consideration of social harm. If the latter is the case, then the Hare-Weinstein view is that almost any showing of harm resulting from hate speech, harm that might be averted or minimized by its prohibition, will be insufficient to justify restrictions on free speech of the kind that we are talking about.

The idea of rights as trumps is familiar from Ronald Dworkin's political theory. According to Dworkin, if an individual has a right, then it is wrong for him to be denied the exercise of that right even when social utility would be advanced by the denials. His right to speak *trumps* the considerations of social utility that would be promoted by his being stopped from speaking. Even if the utilitarian considerations are very substantial, still the right prevails, just as the two of hearts prevails over the ace of diamonds when hearts are trumps in a hand of bridge. Of course it seems much easier to sustain this position when we just talk abstractly about "social utility" on the other side; it sounds a bit more dodgy when we have to say that A's right to speak trumps the protection of B from the harm that speaking might cause. Dworkin acknowledges that "[t]he institution of rights . . . is a complex and troublesome practice that makes the Government's job of *securing the general benefit* more difficult and expensive, and it would be a frivolous and wrongful practice unless it served some point."[21] But substitute, for the phrase I have emphasized, "protecting people from harm" and the burden of justification would have to be very strong indeed. (It is a fault of Dworkin's analysis that he does not say nearly enough about the idea of trumping the prevention of harm. Though he acknowledges that rights-as-trumps may be defeated, defeat is envisaged only in the case of a conflict with other rights or when there is some threat of moral catastrophe. Harm as such, or harm whose prevention is not the clear subject of a right, is not discussed.)[22]

Still, maybe the burden can be discharged. Stopping an individual from speaking his mind or from publishing what he wants to publish inflicts a sort of harm on him. Maybe the opponent of regulation can show that this harm is greater (in all cases or in most cases) than the individual harm that accrues from hate speech. This doesn't seem very likely, given the nature of the harms from hate speech that we have been describing: these include not just a heightened prospect of violence and discrimination, but also a jolting failure or undermining of the assurance that people need to rely on: the assurance that they can go about their daily life and their ordinary business without fear of being denigrated and excluded as subhuman or second-class citizens. Compared to the prospect of this sort of dignitary harm, the irritation and annoyance of having to replace a threatening, abusive, and insulting form of racist speech with some more moderate expression of one's social antipathies would seem quite mild. Of course, there is a check to autonomy; but we are unfree in all sorts of ways in modern society; and usually it is taken for granted that—unless more can be said—a slight loss of freedom is justified by the prospect of preventing real harm to other people. (Think of the way we organize our traffic laws, for example.)[23] If that is the standoff, perhaps the only basis for the trumping power of the right to free speech would be that the damage done to a speaker by hate speech regulation is immediate, whereas the damage accruing from hate speech is more a matter of long-term causality (and is, in any case, controversial).

Or maybe someone can show that free speech has *a special kind of importance* for individuals that at least matches the dignitary harm that hate speech regulations try to prevent. That, I think, is the core of the case against hate speech restrictions, and in the next section I will try to explain that case and answer it in its most persuasive form.

Ed Baker and Self-Disclosure

C. Edwin Baker, the Nicholas F. Gallicchio Professor of Law and Communication at the University of Pennsylvania, died suddenly in late 2009. His death deprived us of one of the most thoughtful advocates of the free-speech position and one of the most penetrating opponents of restrictions on hate speech.

A moment ago, I compared laws regulating speech to laws regulating traffic; both impact upon our freedom. But Baker argued forcefully that free speech is not like other exercises of freedom. When people speak, they are disclosing important aspects of themselves to the world, staking out their own place in a society that consists of millions of distinctive individuals, each defined by his or her principles, values, convictions, and beliefs. Historians sometimes talk about "the ideas of a society." But ideas are held by individuals, though often they are held in common among thousands or millions of them. Individual speech reveals the way in which ideas are connected to persons: it presents a person as the locus of ideas. When I hear another speaking, I am conscious that he or she is disclosing, and I am discovering, his or her place in the world of ideas. This, according to Baker, is one of the most important things that speech does. It presents the speaker to the world as the holder of a certain view or the adherent of a certain principle. And that is what distinguishes free speech from the sort of freedom regulated by traffic laws. We are, after all, not just little nodes of behavior, of the sort that traffic lights might regulate.[24] What each of us is—and what we want others to know us as—is the locus of a point of view, an outlook on the world. And we want to disclose ourselves as such.

I do not mean (and Baker does not mean) that all individuals feel an overwhelming need to reveal their innermost thoughts to the world. Individuals choose what and how to reveal; they choose what to disclose themselves as. Still, this does not affect the importance of self-disclosure; it merely indicates the special connection it has with autonomy. Self-disclosure is how individuals take an *autonomous* place in the world of others' hearing, seeing, and regard. This is not all there is to autonomy; Baker refers to it as "formal autonomy"—but he does not intend that as denigration, in a rush to move on to "substantial autonomy." He argues that formal autonomy in this sense is fundamental to respecting people as individual beings in a social world.

So far, Baker's formal autonomy sounds mostly like a mode of display. But Baker also understands it as interactive. I disclose my values not just so that the world can take notice of who I am, but also to interact with others in a world of value-disclosers. And, equally, I disclose myself autonomously in how I respond to others' self-disclosure. So the overall picture is this: "Respect for personhood, for agency, or for autonomy, requires that each person must be permitted to be herself and to present herself. She must be permitted to act in and sometimes affect the world by at least some means, in particular by trying to persuade or criticize others (that is, influence their values, knowledge, perspectives, or emotions)."[25] Others, in responding to the ideas they hear expressed, identify themselves as thinkers and valuers of a certain sort—either steadfast in the face of what others say, or amenable in various ways to their arguments or to shared reasoning. In general, the picture that Baker presents is an attractive image of something like a Kantian kingdom of ends,[26] an array of self-disclosing individuals choosing how to present themselves and their values to others, and choosing how to respond (and, in turn, reveal themselves by responding) to others' self-disclosure. Baker's position is that this is the foundation of a free, autonomy-respecting society, and that securing this—or at least not interfering with it or frustrating it—is one of the prime duties of government.[27]

I have paraphrased Baker's argument as it appears in a number of places.[28] But I have not set it out as he did, arguing first for a general right of autonomy, and then backing up to confine that claim to a right of autonomous expression. Thus, sometimes Baker took as his first premise that "the law must not aim at eliminating or suppressing people's freedom to make decisions about behavior or values," and then went on to argue that this has implications for speech.[29] But that premise goes too far and is too easy to discredit. Instead, I have cut to Baker's most interesting claim: that there is something special about speech, namely the element of autonomous self-disclosure. The idea of discriminating among different kinds of actions—different kinds of liberty —seeing some as more central to autonomy than others, is a familiar one. We do this, for example, when we give special weight to religious freedom—to our right to worship in accord with our beliefs—and to people's interest in conscientiously abiding by religious laws, even when they conflict with human laws.[30] We recognize that forcing people to abandon their autonomous convictions in this regard is not like forcing them to change clothes; it is like forcing them to "take off their skin."[31] And speech is similarly important, on account of the special disclosure function it serves with respect to value, to what people care about. Of course, value is disclosed in all sorts of ways, and we sometimes say that actions speak louder than words. But it is through speech that we make a distinct and undistracted choice to disclose who we are and where we stand on issues of value; we make that choice in a way that can be apprehended and responded to directly, without the distraction of whatever consequences flow from a particular action that doesn't necessarily contain the element of speech.

How does this work for hate speech? The hate-speaker has his values: his loathing for members of a minority race, his convictions about their malevolence, his opinion that they are a lesser bred and need to be sent back to Africa or whatever. These values, these convictions, define, in a way, who he is. The values may be apparent in a violent attack that he launches or in some trick that he plays on a trusting minority member; but those actions have their own consequences for him and others to consider, and people's response to them may be riveted more on these consequences than on the values that inform and motivate the actions. When he spits out his hatred in speech, however, or paints it on a poster or prints it in a pamphlet, there is no doubt that what he is offering for consideration, in a world full of valuers, speakers, and considerers, are his own values. *There they are,* with no distractions: the world has an opportunity to consider who he is and respond directly to his self-presentation. If we enact laws against racist violence or arson, we deprive him of at least one mode of self-disclosure, though not the central one. If, however, we enact laws against hate speech, we deny the racist his elementary autonomy of self-disclosure (as race-hater) in its paradigmatic form.

That's how he wants to present himself to others, and these are the values of his that he wants to offer for their (autonomous) consideration. "Racist hate speech embodies the speaker's . . . view of the world," says Baker, "and, to that extent, expresses her values. . . . Law's purposeful restrictions on her racist or hate speech violate her formal autonomy."[32]

I do not dispute Baker's account of the importance of self-disclosure through speech. I think he makes the best case that can be made for respecting free speech—better than the accounts oriented to "the marketplace of ideas," and better than the arguments about political legitimacy that we will consider in Chapter 7.[33] And I have tried to put his position in the best light possible.

However, the harmful consequences of the speech that interests us in this book do not evaporate in the face of the power and elegance of Baker's account. It remains the case that hate speech damages the dignity and reputation of individuals in vulnerable groups; it remains the case that it undermines the public good of socially furnished assurance with which the dignity of ordinary people is supported; it remains the case that the hateful disclosure of racist attitudes through public speech defaces and pollutes the environment in which members of vulnerable groups, like the rest of us, have to live their lives and bring up their children. Something has to be said, then, about the relation between these harms and the importance of the autonomous presentation of people's values through their speech.

A first point is that speech is not as pure a means of self-disclosure as Baker takes it to be. He says "[t]he speaker typically views her own expression as a manifestation of autonomy; the speech presents or embodies her values."[34] And he distinguishes this from cases of assault or arson, which, though expressive in a way, are performed mostly for the sake of their material consequences. But speech acts are never purely expressive or presentational. They also can be designed to wound, terrify, discourage, and dismay. Baker acknowledges this, but maintains that these are "instrumental" uses of speech—uses which instrumentalize some of the consequences of speaking in order to achieve further consequences that the speaker desires. He is right. But I'm afraid I do not understand why the aspect of instrumentalization should make a difference here. But for what it is worth, I would like to point out that the harms emphasized in this book are often harms *constituted* by speech, rather than merely *caused* by speech.

In Chapter 4, I considered that hate speech has two aspects about which a free society needs to be particularly concerned. First, it aims to dispel the sense of assurance that we attempt to provide for one another, a sense of assurance that constitutes the social upholding of individual dignity. Hate speech aims to undermine this, to discredit it, and erode its credibility. The work that hate speech does in this aspect is largely performative[35]— indeed, the public disclosure of attitude and value that Baker thinks so important is precisely what discredits the community's assurance to its most vulnerable members. By publicly presenting attitudes that display abuse and exclusion, hate speech sets out to refute the community's generalized assurance that is supposed to underpin the ordinary dignity of its most vulnerable members. The community says, "In our eyes, you are unreservedly welcome here, same as anyone else." The hate speech says, "Hell, no! Not here—not in these eyes, you're not. Be unsure of acceptance; be afraid; be ready for hateful exclusion." Part of this can be expressed in Baker's terms. The hatemonger is disclosing himself as a dissident, putting on record his refusal to participate in and his determination to undermine this social enterprise. But precisely for this reason, Baker's emphasis on the instrumental distance between the speech act and the bad consequences of the hate speech does not hold water. The harm *is* the dispelling of assurance, and the dispelling of assurance is the speech act—it is what the speaker is doing in his self-disclosure, as far as he is capable.

Second, as I said in Chapter 4 (in the section entitled "Rival Public Goods"), the hate-speaker is trying to construct an alternative public good: solidarity among like-minded people. Isolated racists sit smoldering in their dens, lamenting the fact that their hateful views are not widely shared. "Cheer up!" says the hate-speaker in his public self-disclosure: "Here I am. Know that you are not alone in your antagonism." Again, this is not something merely consequent to Baker's value of self-disclosure. In this context, it is exactly what self-disclosure is all about.

Thus, both in their destructive aspects and in their constructive aspects, these acts of self-disclosure have a deep significance —and are intended to have a deep significance—for a well-ordered society. The goods that are imperiled by these speech acts are vital, indispensable for the collective maintenance of each person's dignity; and the evils that are constituted by them cannot be ignored. Not only that, but society's solicitude for these goods and its concern about these evils are not things which ignore or sideline the aspect of self-disclosure. They focus exactly on that aspect. Self-disclosure, in this context, is inherently dangerous. As in many moral hard cases, one and the same action, described in one and the same way, has aspects that are important—autonomous beings disclosing themselves and their values —and aspects that are destructive of important social goods.

Baker is not unaware of the harm that free speech does. How, then, does he maintain what he calls his free-speech absolutism? He points out that almost all the harm that free speech does is mediated causally by the mental processes of those to whom the speech is addressed. Harm is done, no doubt, when a speaker asserts that corn dealers are starvers of the poor, and does so before an excited crowd assembled in front of the house of a corn dealer.[36] The house is set alight and the corn dealer and his family are threatened. But the speech itself does not ignite the blaze or buffet the family. In order for these harms to accrue, the speaker's words have to reach the mind of the members of the crowd, and it is because of their autonomous decisions that the premises are set ablaze and the people inside assaulted. That, according to Baker, is the proper intervention point for the law, because the decision-making of the members of the crowd is where the chain of harmful consequences is autonomously generated.

> The speaker contributes only through "mental mediation." . . . The hearer must determine a response. Whether harm occurs depends on that response. . . . Any consequences involved in the listener's reaction or response, if the speaker's autonomy is protected and the listener's recognized, must be

attributed, in the end, to the listener. The result is a right of the speaker to present her viewpoint even if its assimilation by the listener leads to or constitutes serious harm.[37]

Now, if what I said a moment ago is right, this account does not yet disarm the primary contention about hate speech. For the concern there is not just about incitement; it is about the under- mining of a public good, the dispelling of an assurance given by society to its most vulnerable members. This need not work through the "mental mediation" of the minds of the members of an excitable audience. I have said that the speech act constitutes the dispelling of the assurance, whether other racists are influ- enced by it or not. In Baker's view, however, this is not an accu- rate description. The hateful racist speech act can be character- ized as the dispelling of an assurance essential to dignity only because it is heard in a certain way by those whose dignity is at stake.

> A speaker's racial epithet . . . harms the hearer only through her understanding of the message. The harm occurs because the speech expresses (or, at least, is understood to express) the speaker's values and visions; and it occurs only to the extent that the hearer (mentally) responds one way rather than another, for example, as a victim rather than as a critic of the speaker. Despite the predictable and understandable occurrence of serious harm, the possibility always exists for a hearer to use the available information in creating or main- taining an affirmative identity. The racist . . . is a louse, a

contemptible threat to decent people. In other words, again in [this] case, harm depends on mental mediation. The hearer must determine a response.[38]

There is something to this, but not very much. It is true that any impact speech has in the world must depend upon its being understood. The speaker discloses his intended meanings by using words conventionally associated with the intention to be understood as conveying just such-and-such a meaning. One uses words like "All blacks should be sent back to Africa" when one wants to convey to the mind of a hearer that it is the speaker's view that all blacks should be sent back to Africa. The hearer— the member of a vulnerable minority—plays her part in this connection of understandings, but it is a conventionally ordained part once the noise is understood as meaning-laden speech. If the hearer is not a speaker of English, or if, due to the malfunctioning of an amplifier, the speech sounds like nothing more than an electronic howl, then she will not get this message. But the point about conventional word- and sentence-meaning is that once the noise is recognized as speech by a speaker of English, there is little leeway in what to make of it. I suppose Baker is right that hearers could "choose" to hear it as "Blacks are welcome here," and that it is only in the exercise of their autonomy that they do not. But this is silly—a fanciful possibility that is incapable of supporting the sort of serious position Baker wants to maintain. Perhaps what he means is that, once the message is understood, it is still up to the hearer to make what she can of it. She can be demoralized by the abusive and exclusionary message that—in my view—she has no choice but to hear in the speaker's words.

Or she can respond in the defiant posture of a critic, willing to play her part as a member of society in good standing, despite the best efforts of the racist to denigrate that status. No doubt. But the point of a general and implicit assurance given by society to all of its members, sustaining their ordinary dignity, is that it should not be necessary for them to laboriously conjure up the courage to go out and try to flourish in what is now presented to them as a partially hostile environment. To the extent that the message conveyed by the racist already puts them on the defensive, and distracts them from the ordinary business of life with the grim determination to try and act like a normal citizen against all the odds— to that extent, the racist speech has already succeeded in one of its destructive aims.

I do not think, therefore, that Baker can finesse the issue of harm by drawing attention to this element of "mental mediation." The damage is done by the speech in requiring its targets to resort to the sort of mental mediation that Baker recommends, and he gives no convincing reason why society should not pay attention to the harm that is wrought at this stage, the harm of requiring them to do so.

I am not saying that such harm *obviously* calls for a social or a legislative response. It may or may not, depending on the circumstances, and I believe we should stick with the balancing model recommended in the opening section of this chapter—weighing the importance to individuals of the kind of autonomous self-disclosure that Baker talks about against the importance of the social and individual values that are compromised when the act of self-disclosure goes public, particularly in the relatively permanent and inerasable form discussed in Chapters 3 and 4. That balance might not require the suppression of every word or epithet that counts colloquially as hate speech. It may require us to attend to the most egregious forms of group libel, particularly when the threatening or abusive form in which it is presented makes the destructive intention of the self-disclosure more or less explicit. And, on the other hand, it may require us to ensure that there are legally innocuous modes and forms of expression—where similar views can be aired (similar values and attitudes disclosed) in ways that minimize the damage to social values and individual dignity. These are matters for legislators to consider as they engage in the balancing exercise. There is, in my view, no way of avoiding this need for balance. There really are rival values in play here. And in the end, what Ed Baker has done, most adeptly, is account for the importance of one of the values rather than dispelling our sense that other values are also at stake.

7 Ronald Dworkin and the Legitimacy Argument

We find in the literature a number of arguments linking the protection of free speech to the flourishing of self-government in a democracy. Some say little more than that, though they say it sonorously and at great length.[1] In a few of these arguments, however, the position is advanced beyond a general concern for the democratic process. It is sometimes said that free and unrestricted public discourse is a *sine qua non* for political legitimacy in a democracy, not just for the quality of democratic engagement.[2] This raises the stakes a little. Saying that free speech improves democracy, when it is untrammeled by restrictions such as the ones we are considering, is one thing; saying that these restrictions may undermine the legitimacy of our democracy is another. And some make the point even sharper than this. They suggest that *the legitimacy of certain specific legal provisions* may be imperiled by the enactment and enforcement of hate speech laws.

Dworkin's Argument

The most powerful argument of this kind is presented by Ronald Dworkin, in a brief foreword he contributed to a recent, large, and valuable volume entitled *Extreme Speech and Democracy,* edited by Ivan Hare and James Weinstein.[3] According to Professor Dworkin, freedom for hate speech or freedom for group defamation is the price we pay for the legitimacy of our enforcing certain laws that the hatemongers oppose (for example, laws forbidding discrimination). We want to be able to enforce laws prohibiting discrimination; Dworkin says we can do that legitimately only if we allow an open debate about such laws that includes what we would ordinarily describe as hate speech (if that is how some citizens want to express themselves). Here is how his argument goes.

Dworkin begins from premises that he shares with the proponents of restrictions on hate speech. He agrees that it is important to protect people, particularly vulnerable members of minorities, not only from violence but also from discrimination: "We must protect them against unfairness and inequality in employment or education or housing or the criminal process, for example, and we may adopt laws to achieve that protection."[4] Dworkin is as firmly committed to these anti-discrimination laws as any proponent of racial and ethnic equality. But, like them, he acknowledges that if we adopt such laws, often we will have to do so over the opposition of a few people who favor discrimination and who might welcome the opportunity for racial violence. In the face of such opposition, we usually say it is enough that a legislative proposal be supported by a majority of voters or a majority of elected representatives in a legislature, provided that the opponents are not disenfranchised from that process. But actually, says Dworkin, this is not all that is required:

> Fair democracy requires . . . that each citizen have not just a
> vote but a voice: a majority decision is not fair unless every-
> one has had a fair opportunity to express his or her attitudes
> or opinions or fears or tastes or presuppositions or preju-
> dices or ideals, not just in the hope of influencing others
> (though that hope is crucially important), but also just to
> confirm his or her standing as a responsible agent in, rather
> than a passive victim of, collective action.[5]

Free expression, in other words, is part of the price we pay for political legitimacy: "The majority has no right to impose its will on
someone who is forbidden to raise a voice in protest or argument
or objection before the decision is taken."[6] If we want *legitimate*
laws against violence or discrimination, we must let their opponents speak. And then we can legitimate the enactment and enforcement of those laws by voting.

Now, some opponents of anti-discrimination laws will not
have any desire to express their opposition hatefully. But some
may. For these opponents, defaming the groups that the laws in
question are supposed to protect and denigrating the humanity
of their members is the essence of their opposition. Dworkin's
position is that we must permit them to voice this opposition,
however hatefully they want to express it. Otherwise, no legitimacy will attach to any laws that are enacted over their opposition. For the purposes of Dworkin's legitimacy argument, it
doesn't matter how foul and vicious the hatemonger's contribution is. He must be allowed his say. It doesn't even matter that the
hatemonger's speech is not couched as a formal contribution to
political debate:

A community's legislation and policy are determined more by its moral and cultural environment, the mix of its people's opinions, prejudices, tastes, and attitudes, than by editorial columns or party political broadcasts or stump political speeches. It is as unfair to impose a collective decision on someone who has not been allowed to contribute to that moral environment, by expressing his political or social convictions or tastes or prejudices informally, as on someone whose pamphlets against the decision were destroyed by the police.[7]

Whether the expression is scrawled on the walls, smeared on a leaflet, festooned on a banner, spat out onto the Internet, or illuminated by the glare of a burning cross, it has to be allowed to make its presence felt in the maelstrom of messages that populate the marketplace of ideas. "The temptation may be near overwhelming to make exceptions to that principle, to declare that people have no right to pour the filth of pornography or race-hatred into the culture in which we all must live. But we cannot do that without forfeiting our moral title to force such people to bow to the collective judgments that do make their way into the statute books."[8] That is the gist of the legitimacy argument.

I should mention that Professor Dworkin has his doubts about some of the causal claims made by defenders of hate speech laws regarding the consequences of pouring "the filth of . . . race hatred into the culture in which we all must live." "Many of these claims are inflated," he says, "and some are absurd."[9] That is a separate line of attack, and I am not going to try to refute it here. It seems to me that these facts about consequences are something for legislators to consider (if only the courts will let them). But it is interesting to see how firmly and confidently—and perhaps even hopefully—the opponents of hate speech legislation announce that the causal claims must be wrong. Indeed, sometimes the case lurches over to become a reverse argument: that the causal claims *must* be wrong *because* something like the American constitutional position on free speech is correct. Let us leave that disreputable reverse argument aside for a moment (I will discuss a Dworkinian version of it in a moment). For present purposes, Dworkin's position is that even if the defenders of hate speech laws are right about the causes of violence and discrimination, there is only so much we can do about those causes without forfeiting legitimacy for the laws we most care about. Perhaps we can legislate against incitement; maybe we can go that far [10] "But we must not try to intervene further upstream, by forbidding any expression of the attitudes or prejudices that we think nourish . . . unfairness or inequality, because if we intervene too soon in the process through which collective opinion is formed, we spoil the democratic justification we have for insisting that everyone obey these laws, even those who hate and resent them."[11]

Why is legitimacy important? I think Dworkin believes it is a matter of fairness. We expect racists and bigots to obey the laws adopted by democratic majorities, including, for instance, laws prohibiting discrimination in education and employment. We expect this because we believe such laws issue from a fair political procedure in which each side has an opportunity to put forward its opinion and ask others for their support. But, according to Dworkin, legislation that forbids one side from expressing its opinion to the public—its opinion, for instance, that blacks are inferior creatures who should be sent back to Africa—destroys that fairness. It deprives us of our right to enforce laws against those who have been denied a fair opportunity to make a case against their enactment.

The structure of the position is interesting. Dworkin notices that arguments about hate speech often involve two sorts of laws, not one. On the one hand, there are the hate speech laws themselves—or the proposals for hate speech laws—which would restrict expressions of racial hostility, religious hatred, group defamation, and so on. On the other hand, there are laws in place protecting the people who are supposedly also protected by hate speech laws—I mean laws against violence, laws against discrimination, laws against blocking access to polling places, laws guaranteeing equal opportunity, laws against racial profiling, laws against various forms of disorderly conduct, and so on. Following Dworkin's metaphor, I am going to call these *upstream laws* and *downstream laws*. The downstream laws are the laws against violence, discrimination, and so on, and the upstream laws are laws against hate speech. Those who support hate speech laws often say that they are necessary in order to address the causes of violations of downstream laws. They say that if we leave hate speech alone, then we are leaving alone the poison that leads to violence and discrimination downstream. Dworkin turns the tables on this argument by saying that if you interfere coercively upstream, then you undermine political legitimacy downstream. And this should not be something that believers in the downstream laws try to do. They want to be able to proceed not just coercively but legitimately against downstream violence and discrimination; and they cannot do this if their campaign against violence and

Upstream laws and downstream laws

discrimination targets certain upstream causes of violence and discrimination. If you want to be tough on crime, legitimately tough on offenses like racial violence and discrimination, then you have to be tolerant of the causes of crime; that is what Dworkin's position amounts to.

Of course, attacking the causes of violence and discrimination is not the only motivation for laws against hate speech or group defamation. Sometimes what we are calling upstream laws are enacted not in order to make it easier to enforce downstream laws or to reduce the number of downstream violations, but simply to secure the dignity or reputation of members of vulnerable groups. That is the gist of the position I outlined in Chapters 3 and 4. But it makes little difference. Dworkin's argument is at its tightest when it is directed at hate speech laws that are intended to address the causes of violations of downstream laws. But even if the upstream laws are intended to do something else, they still will have the effect of weakening the legitimacy of downstream laws. At best, then, we will face a trade-off between the value we place on the upstream laws and the value we place on the legitimacy of our enforcement of the downstream laws.

In some contexts, Dworkin goes even further. In his debate with Catharine MacKinnon about the effects of pornography, he suggests that the delegitimizing effect of laws suppressing free speech should lead us simply to dismiss from consideration propositions about the harm that such speech causes.

> Some feminist groups argue . . . that pornography causes . . . a more general and endemic subordination of women. . . . But even if it could be shown, as a matter of causal connection, that pornography is in part responsible for the economic structure in which few women obtain top jobs or equal pay for the same work, that would not justify censorship under the Constitution. It would plainly be unconstitutional to ban speech directly advocating that women occupy inferior roles, or none at all, in commerce and the professions. . . . So it cannot be a reason for banning pornography that it contributes to an unequal economic or social structure, even if we think it does.[12]

This last sentence is very striking. Its upshot seems to be that the social and economic effects of pornography are simply not worth being considered as reasons for censorship. Such peremptory dismissal cannot be right, in my view, and I think many people would say that it gives the anti-regulation view a bad name. The social and economic effects of pornography—and their analogues for hate speech—are surely at least *worthy of consideration* in connection with possible justifications for what we are calling upstream laws, even if they are eventually outweighed by delegitimizing consequences downstream. It has long been part of the wisdom of Western liberalism that considerations which are outweighed in a given context do not lose their interest for us.[13] Dworkin's position gains its credibility from his reference to what "would not justify censorship *under the Constitution.*" But since the U.S. Constitution as currently interpreted by Dworkin and others is the target of MacKinnon's attack, this is just questionbegging. If the social and economic effects of pornography are as bad as MacKinnon and others suggest, then there may be a case for modifying our understanding of the Constitution or modifying the Constitution itself, if its correct interpretation requires us to turn a blind eye to these matters. (I labor this point about the consideration of argument and evidence on both sides because I have sometimes heard opponents say that even the consideration of evidence or the setting out of arguments in favor of hate speech regulation counts as a betrayal of First Amendment principles. It's as though one betrays free speech by even raising the issue.)

Can Dworkin's Argument Be Confined?

How should defenders of hate speech laws respond to Professor Dworkin's argument about the connection between hate speech and political legitimacy? As I said, his argument is not just a

vague Meiklejohn-style concern about self-government and public discourse. It has a specific bite to it. It claims that hate speech
laws undermine the legitimacy of certain other laws we all value.
This is a frightening prospect.

One preliminary response is to wonder whether Dworkin's argument can be kept under control. For if I understand its structure, Dworkin's argument does not work only as an argument
about hate speech. Its logic will apply to virtually any asserted
exception to the free speech principle—to fighting words, obscenity, individual libel of private persons, disorderly conduct, sedition, and so on. In each case, we have individuals who wish to
participate (formally or informally, in a focused or unfocused
way) in public debate about certain legislation—which, as before,
we will call "downstream legislation." The trouble is with the
form they want their participation to take: some of them are so
incensed about the proposal for downstream legislation that they
want to shout "Fuck!" in public, or challenge the legislation's proponents to a fight, or urge mutiny by the armed forces, or display
child pornography. But we have upstream laws against all of these
actions (either in general or in the circumstances in which the
individuals want to perform them). If we enforce these upstream
laws and forbid the obscenity, the fighting words, the subversion
of the state, or the child pornography despite the fact that they
impinge on free speech, do we not thereby diminish the legitimacy of the downstream laws (according to Dworkin's argument)
if those laws are adopted in a process of public deliberation from
which these various elements have been purged?

Someone might respond that the individuals in question are

permitted to express their opposition to the downstream laws in other ways. They don't need to use *fighting* words to express their opposition; they can use ordinary words. And the same latitude is permitted by the other upstream laws: the individuals can express their opposition to the downstream laws without resorting to obscenity, subversion, or the display of child pornography. And it is reasonable to ask them to do so, because everyone knows these particular forms of expression are harmful. So what we say in these cases is this: to the extent that the individuals' preferred means of expression is harmful, and to the extent that other means of expression are available for communicating their opposition to the downstream laws— to that extent, the loss of downstream legitimacy incurred as a result of the banning of speech of these particular kinds is minimal or nonexistent.

The trouble is that exactly the same points apply to the case of hate speech as well. Racist speech is harmful. (I know Dworkin might disagree with that, too, but he was offering the legitimacy point as an argument against regulation that would work even if the harm of hate speech is acknowledged.)[14] And the racist doesn't *need* to use the sort of vicious hate propaganda that the law punishes in order to express his opposition to laws about discrimination and so on. Most racial and religious hatred laws that exist in the world define a legitimate mode or a legitimate forum for roughly equivalent expression that will not incur legal sanctions. So banning hate speech probably has no greater effect on political legitimacy than banning fighting words or these other acknowledged exceptions to the free-speech principle.

So that is a preliminary difficulty with Dworkin's argument. It seems to prove too much. This impression—of an argument that has gotten out of hand—is confirmed when we scrutinize the terms of the case he is making.

What Legitimacy Means

Hate speech laws, says Dworkin, deprive other laws of their legitimacy. But there is a question about what undermining legitimacy amounts to. In social science, legitimacy often means little more than popular support. Dworkin, however, means it as a normative property. Normatively speaking, the legitimacy of a law can mean either the existence of a political obligation to obey the law in question, or it can mean the rightness of using force to uphold it, or both.[15] Thus, if a law is illegitimate, that means it is wrong or unfair to enforce it, and/or it means that those to whom the law is addressed have no obligation to obey it and may treat it with indifference if they judge it safe to do so. Whichever of these meanings Dworkin has in mind, there is a question of how literally we should take his claim that downstream legitimacy is spoiled by the enforcement of hate speech laws.

I am asking, in effect, for a reality check. Does Dworkin really believe what he says about legitimacy? Does he believe (does he really think *we* should believe) that the enforcement of hate speech laws makes the enactment and enforcement of downstream laws, such as laws forbidding discrimination, literally illegitimate? Is he serious about this, or is he just playing?

I ask because the real-world consequences of Dworkin's position are (if I understand it correctly) quite disturbing. In Britain, there are laws forbidding the expression of racial and religious hatred.[16] These are the upstream laws—the targets of Dworkin's legitimacy argument. There are also laws forbidding racial discrimination,[17] not to mention ordinary criminal laws that forbid racial and ethnic violence and intimidation, and that protect mosques and synagogues from arson and desecration. These are the downstream laws, whose legitimacy Dworkin believes is hostage to the enforcement of laws about racial and religious hatred. Does he really believe that the enactment and enforcement of all these downstream laws in Britain is illegitimate as a result of the existence of the upstream laws? Remember what illegitimacy means: it means that enactment of the laws was inappropriate in the circumstances, and that enforcement of them is morally wrong. The use of force to uphold them is just like any other illegitimate use of force.

So: a wealthy landlord systematically discriminates against English families of South Asian descent. Dworkin's position seems to be that no action should be taken against the landlord, at least so long as English law contains provisions banning him and others from publishing hateful and virulent anti-Pakistani opinions. Some skinheads beat up a Muslim minicab driver after the London bombings of July 7, 2005; Dworkin's view seems to imply that it is wrong for the police to pursue, arrest, and indict these assailants because Britain has religious hate speech laws that take away the legitimacy of downstream laws against assault. The police must stand by and not intervene, because any intervention would be wrong. That's what "deprived of legitimacy" means.

And the issue goes beyond Britain. Almost all advanced democracies have hate speech laws, which, on Dworkin's account, undermine the legitimacy of all their anti-discrimination laws and their laws forbidding racial violence and attacks on churches, synagogues, and mosques. The only advanced democracy entitled to have and enforce such laws is the United States, because the U.S. Constitution bans the sort of speech restrictions that would otherwise deprive downstream laws of their legitimacy. This is American exceptionalism with a vengeance!

That is why I ask how serious Dworkin is in his claim that hate speech laws "spoil the only democratic justification we have for insisting that everyone obey [the downstream] laws."[18] I guess it is possible he would accept the conclusions we have drawn, urging an end to the enforcement of laws against discrimination and racial violence in most democracies, on the grounds that they are, in those countries, illegitimate. Most of us would not. This means that most of us cannot accept the tight link between the enforcement of hate speech laws and the conditions of the legitimacy of other (downstream) laws that Dworkin asserts. But of course it is not to enough to respond to Dworkin's argument simply with a contrary intuition about legitimacy: we must explain why the connection is not as he says it is.

Is Legitimacy a Matter of Degree?

Maybe we should not take Dworkin's argument about legitimacy literally. After all, any argument will look silly if, as they say in England, "it is pushed to an extreme."[19] So let us consider some more moderate interpretations of the case Dworkin is making.

One possibility is that the enforcement of hate speech laws undermines the legitimacy of some downstream laws and not others. Perhaps it undermines the legitimacy of laws forbidding discrimination but not the legitimacy of laws forbidding racial violence or vandalism. After all, laws of the latter type have independent reasons in their favor, quite apart from the debate over race. (And police intervention to stop violence or rescue people from attack may not need the sort of legitimation that the political process is supposed to provide.). But this position will be hard for Dworkin to maintain in light of his more holistic observations about the importance, for legitimacy, of speech that is just part of the cultural environment, even when it is not intended as a contribution to formal discussion of any particular law.[20] And anyway, it still leaves us stuck with the unpalatable conclusion regarding the legitimacy of antidiscrimination laws.

A second possibility (compatible with the first) is that legitimacy is relative to persons. Robert Post has suggested a version of this: "If the state were to forbid the expression of a particular idea, the government would become, *with respect to individuals holding that idea,* heteronomous and nondemocratic."[21] In Dworkin's argument, one might say the downstream law becomes legitimately unenforceable against the person silenced by the upstream law, even though it may be legitimately enforceable against others. Bear in mind, though, that the upstream laws do not provide for the silencing of persons; Robert Post's formulation is careless in this regard. Hate speech laws provide only for the suppression of certain forms of intervention. The persons whose interventions are silenced in this way may say anything else, contribute anything else they like to the political process. In any case, this second possibility gets tangled up in rule-of-law issues about generality. Hate speech laws are presented as quite general: they forbid *anyone* from hateful defamation of racial, ethnic, and religious groups. Even if they need to be enforced only against a few extremists, they have a potential effect on everyone's speech. To the extent that this is so, it may be hard to identify the basis for *in personam* illegitimacy of the type that the second possibility suggests.

A third possibility (also compatible with the other two) is that the legitimacy of any given law, for any person, is itself a matter of degree; and that, on a moderate version of Dworkin's argument, the enforcement of hate speech laws *diminishes*—or, as he puts it, "spoils"—the legitimacy of downstream laws without destroying their legitimacy altogether. (And we may say the same about political obligation: it, too, is a matter of degree.) This seems the most plausible moderate version of Dworkin's position. And I think it is what Dworkin wants to say. In his book *Is Democracy Possible Here?*, Dworkin has spoken of legitimacy as "not an all-or-nothing matter."[22] This opens things up in an interesting way. For it means that the enactment and enforcement of hate speech laws may have a great impact or a slight impact (or any sort of impact in between) on the legitimacy of downstream laws against discrimination and violence. I think what he wants to say is that there is something morally to regret when we enforce nondiscrimination laws against racists who were not allowed to influence the formal and informal political culture as they wished. But the *something to regret* might be more or less considerable; the "deficit in legitimacy" might be larger or smaller. If the deficit is slight, then it may not generate a compelling case against hate speech laws when the stakes on the other side (the harms that such laws might avert) are very high. Not only that, but if we are going to talk about differences of degree, then we should correlate them with different kinds of hate speech legislation. Let me explain.

On a given issue—say, the desirability of an antidiscrimination law, L—an individual, X, may hold any of a range of views:

(1) X opposes L because he thinks L will make him worse off.

(2) X opposes L because he thinks L will generate perverse economic incentives, undermining economic efficiency in society.

(3) X opposes L because he distrusts the bureaucracy necessary to administer L.

(4) X opposes L because he denies that the intended beneficiaries of L are worthy of the protection that it offers them.

Now, focus particularly on (4). That view may be expressed in various ways:

(4a) X expresses his dissent from the broad abstract principle that governments must show equal concern and respect to all members of the community.

(4b) X expounds some racial theory which he thinks shows the inferiority, by certain measures, of certain lines of human descent.

(4c) X gives vent to the view that the citizens who are intended to be protected by the anti-discrimination law are no better than animals.

(4d) X prints in a leaflet or says on the radio that these citizens are no better than the sort of animals we would normally seek to exterminate (like rats or cockroaches).

Out of all these various views and expressions, laws against hate speech and group defamation—of the kind we are familiar with in existing democracies—are almost certain to restrict (4d), quite likely to restrict (4c), and possibly likely to restrict some versions of (4b), depending on how virulently they are expressed. On the other hand, most such laws bend over backwards to ensure that there is a lawful way of expressing something like the propositional content of views that become objectionable when expressed as vituperation. They try to define a legitimate mode of roughly equivalent expression. Though, as I said in Chapter 5, restrictions on hate speech are undoubtedly content-based restrictions, they do also require the presence of certain adverbial and intentional elements. So, for example, the United Kingdom's Public Order Act of 1986 prohibits the display of "any written material which is *threatening, abusive* or *insulting*" (my emphasis) if its display is associated with an intention "to stir up racial hatred."[23] No offense is committed if the same material is not presented in a threatening, abusive, or insulting manner, or if the person concerned "did not intend . . . the written material, to be, and was not aware that it might be, threatening, abusive or insulting."[24]

Some laws of this type also try affirmatively to define a sort of "safe haven" for the moderate expression of the gist of the view whose hateful or hate-inciting expression is prohibited. The most generous such provision I have seen is in Australia's Racial Discrimination Act, which says that its basic ban on actions that insult, humiliate, or intimidate a group of people because of their race, color, or national or ethnic origin "does not render unlawful anything said or done reasonably and in good faith: . . . in the course of any statement, publication, discussion or debate made or held for any genuine academic, artistic or scientific purpose or any other genuine purpose in the public interest."[25] The purpose of all these qualifications is precisely to limit the application of the restriction to the bottom end of something like a (4a)–(4d) type of spectrum.

Now, if we accept the basic framework of Dworkin's position, we may want to say that a law which prohibited the expression of (4a) and (4b) as well as (4c) and (4d) would have a worse effect on downstream legitimacy than a law which merely forbade something like (4d). It would—as suggested by the third of the moderate responses which we are attributing to Dworkin—be a matter of degree. And if we had a law that was specifically tailored to prohibit only expression at the viciously vituperative end of this spectrum, it might be an open question whether it would have anything more than a minimal effect on the legitimacy of the downstream law.

Part of our estimation of the effect on legitimacy would surely also revolve around the reasonableness and importance of the objectives being sought by the restrictive upstream laws. We see this all the time with regard to other non-content-based restrictions on speech (laws restricting time, place, and manner of political demonstrations, for example). If they are arbitrary, or motivated by only very minor considerations of public order, we might say that they gravely impair the legitimacy of collective decisions on the matters that the protesters wanted to demonstrate about. But if the motivation is based on serious considerations of security, we might be more understanding and less willing to say that legitimacy was utterly compromised. So, similarly, in the case of hate speech laws. A motivation oriented purely to protect people's feelings against offense is one thing; I argued in Chapter 5 that this is not a good reason for restricting speech. But a restriction on hate speech oriented toward protecting the basic social standing—the elementary dignity, as I have put it—of members of vulnerable groups, and to maintaining the assurance they need in order to go about their lives in a secure and dignified manner, may seem like a much more important objective. And the complaint that attempting to secure it greatly undermines the legitimacy of the enforcement of other laws may be much less credible as a result.

The Cessation of Serious Controversy

There is one other consideration I would like to introduce at this stage. In Chapter 2 of his essay *On Liberty,* John Stuart Mill pondered how the gradual increase in human knowledge might affect free expression:

> As mankind improve, the number of doctrines which are no longer disputed or doubted will be constantly on the increase: and the well-being of mankind may almost be measured by the number and gravity of the truths which have reached the point of being uncontested. The cessation, on one question after another, of serious controversy, is one of the necessary incidents of the consolidation of opinion; a consolidation as salutary in the case of true opinions, as it is dangerous and noxious when the opinions are erroneous.[26]

I don't think Mill envisioned the emergence of absolute unanimity on any point. There would always be a few crazies who insisted on the flatness of the earth or the Ptolemaic structure of the universe. But by and large, intelligent opinion would be united on numerous well-established truths. And this would not be a matter of scientific truth alone. On certain moral issues or mixed issues of fact and value, we should likewise expect this sort of salutary consolidation of opinion. People once believed, for example, that the different races of mankind represented different species, some superior and some inferior. But this is now very widely rejected, and serious controversy has more or less ceased on this point. Again, there are one or two outliers who believe, or pretend to believe, that the members of certain racial minorities are of a different species of primate from the species that they (the racists) say they belong to. But again, we can assert that, by and large, the truth which they pretend to deny is no longer seriously contested in our civilization. There is no longer any intelligent contestation on this issue, and contestation on this issue is no longer necessary in order to ascertain the truth.

However, Mill's position in *On Liberty* was that truth-seeking was not the only point of controversy. Controversy was also important, he said, to sustain among the public a "lively apprehension" of established truths, so that they "penetrate the feelings, and acquire a real mastery over the conduct"—in other words, so that they don't just become empty husks of doctrine. From this point of view, the emergence of consensus might seem like a drawback: "The loss of so important an aid to the intelligent and living apprehension of a truth, as is afforded by the necessity of

... defending it against opponents, though not sufficient to out-weigh, is no trifling drawback from, the benefit of its universal recognition."[27] And Mill toyed with the idea that, in the interest of public education, we might sometimes have to artificially cre-ate devil's advocates, opponents of established truths—or "some contrivance for making the difficulties of the question as present to the learner's consciousness, as if they were pressed upon him by a dissentient champion, eager for his conversion"—just in or-der to keep the spirit of debate alive.[28]

I think most of us part company with Mill at that point—at least in the context of our discussion, where the implication would be that racism and religious bigotry need to be artificially cultivated in order to enliven our egalitarian convictions. Even a more moderate version of his view seems problematic: "If there are any persons who contest a received opinion, or who will do so if law or opinion will let them, let us thank them for it, open our minds to listen to them, and rejoice that there is someone to do for us what we otherwise ought, if we have any regard for . . . the vitality of our convictions, to do with much greater labor for our-selves."[29] This is not the attitude—appreciation—that we would normally think of taking towards racists and bigots, not least be-cause the expression of their views would have not only an "enliv-ening" effect on public debate, but an injurious effect on the dig-nity, security, and assurance of vulnerable members of society.

But Mill's willingness to address this issue does raise a number of questions for us. First, what significance should we accord to the emergence of consensus around certain truths? Does it make any difference to the Dworkinian argument about legitimacy?

Suppose someone puts up posters conveying the opinion that

people from Africa are nonhuman primates. No doubt, if this opinion were scientifically true, it might have implications for public policy. And maybe there was a time when we needed to have a great national debate about *race*—about whether there were different kinds of human beings, inferior and superior lines of human descent, ranked in hierarchies of capability, responsibility, and authority, and, if there were, what the implications would be for justice, morality, and public policy.[30] Maybe there was a time when social policy generally—and perhaps immigration policy and cultural policy, in particular—could not adequately be debated without raising the whole issue of race in this sense. But that is not our situation today. It would be fatuous to suggest that our political community is in the throes of such a debate right now—a vital and ongoing debate crucial to the legitimacy of public policy. It would be fatuous to suggest that it is the importance of our continuing engagement in a debate of this kind that requires us to endure the ugly invective of racial defamation in the marketplace of ideas. In fact, the fundamental debate about race is over— won; finished.[31] There are outlying dissenters, a few crazies who say they believe that people of African descent are an inferior form of animal; but for half a century or more, we have moved forward as a society on the premise that this is no longer a matter of serious contestation.[32]

In my Holmes lectures, I suggested that all this might lessen the impact of the suppression of the virulent expression of racist views on political legitimacy.[33] Once we acknowledge that legitimacy is not an all-or-nothing matter (i.e., once we acknowledge that it is a matter of degree), our concern about it might well be affected by a sense of whether the hateful views being regulated are views whose truth is a live issue—an open question in our politics—or views whose falsity the politically community is entitled to regard as more or less settled.[34] I said that when something is no longer a live issue in the sense we have just been discussing, perhaps we should be less solicitous of political legitimacy when we decide how to deal legislatively with the harm inflicted on the dignity of minority members by the public expression of these outlier views. I am no longer sure that I want to commit myself to that position. But I do believe it is important to confront the issues raised by Mill's discussion, particularly in light of what I think is a rather misleading presupposition informing Dworkin's view—namely, that the discourse to which racist hatemongers offer their "contributions" is a living element of public debate, on which we have divided temporarily into majorities and minorities, but with respect to which no majoritarian laws can be legitimate unless there is some provision for this important debate to continue, so that the losers (the racists and the bigots) have a chance to persuade the majority of the truth of their position the next time around.

Of course, one can see what Dworkin means; but I wonder if readers share my sense of how *weird* his position is. It seems to assume that debates are timeless and that considerations of political legitimacy relative to public debate must be understood as necessarily impervious to progress. I think we do need to ask whether we are past the stage where society is in such need of a robust debate about fundamental matters of race that we ought to bear the costs of what amount to attacks on the dignity of minority groups. Think of what those costs may involve. Are we really in need of such robust debate on racial ontology that we have no choice but to require individuals and families within minority groups to bear the costs of such humiliating attacks on their social standing?

Robert Post on Community and Democracy

I said that Dworkin's is the sharpest argument connecting democratic legitimacy to the rejection of hate speech laws. But there are others. Robert Post has developed an intriguing contrast between the norms that regulate a community—norms of civility— and the norms that regulate democracy, which is the forum in which we settle on some of the rules for our community.[35] As I understand Post's position, the whole point of democratic discourse is to put up for grabs the very things that might have to be taken for granted in community life. Our community will be structured by rules of civility, and such rules may well designate and punish forms of racist or religious hate speech as inappropriate. On the other hand, we want our community to be, in some Rousseauian sense, self-determined; and it is the task of debate and voting in the democratic realm to associate our communal norms with genuine processes of self-determination. This means, according to Post, that we must allow even the most cherished norms of our community to be challenged democratically in a contest in which it is possible that they might be denigrated and even rejected. If we do not allow them to be challenged in this way, we dissociate our communal life from our sense of collective and individual autonomy, and that is a serious loss.

It is Post's view that this challenge must in principle extend to the rules of civility that prohibit hate speech. We want a civil community—and he concedes that hate speech is at odds with that—but above all, we want to be a self-determining civil community, and that means we must allow even the norms of civility to be challenged. Of course, if I am right in what I said in the previous section, such challenges may well be forlorn. Racists may attack what they call norms of "political correctness." But few others will stand with them in this challenge, and they will probably lose. Nonetheless, the fact that they had an opportunity to mount the challenge is what marks our community as self-determining. And for this reason, such challenges must not be ruled out, no matter how uncivil they seem.

So far, this is an argument for not excluding hatemongers from political life, and as such I accept it. It is also an argument for not excluding any challenge to any of our laws on matters of race and religion, whether they are downstream laws forbidding discrimination and violence, or upstream laws forbidding hate speech (because that is judged a possible cause of discrimination and violence). Everything must be up for grabs—or, more soberly,[36] everything must be open to debate and challenge in a free and democratic society, no matter how important the objects of challenge seem to be to the culture and identity of our community. I accept that, too.

The question is whether hate speech laws do actually exclude people from the political process, whether they do actually insulate certain norms of civility from challenge. I think they don't, and I believe that Post recognizes this. After all, one can challenge a law against discrimination without engaging in hate speech; and, indeed, one can challenge a hate speech law without engaging in hate speech. (Many of my best friends challenge hate speech laws, civilly, in just this way.) Even though civility rules may be the target of democratic challenge, they can still work— up until the point at which they are overturned as a result of that challenge—to structure and regulate the terms in which the challenge is mounted. In a more recent essay, Post acknowledges a point we have emphasized several times: "Much hate speech regulation . . . permits statements about race, nationality, and religion, so long as such speech maintains a 'decent and moderate' manner."[37] Generously interpreted, this permits the racist and the Islamophobe to speak, to mount the challenges that they want to mount; they just have to take care with the mode and manner in which their challenge is expressed.

So a further step needs to be added to Post's argument if it is supposed to be an argument against rules restricting speech and the dissemination of material which is "threatening, abusive or insulting." So far as I can tell, the further step that Post wants to take involves an assertion that there is something self-contradictory or question-begging, or at any rate paradoxical about patrolling the process of democratic self-determination with norms that may themselves be the target of challenge in the framework of democratic self-determination.

But I find it hard to understand Post's concern. Maybe there is a whiff of paradox in insisting on civil challenges to norms of civility until such time as those norms are altered. But it is not clear that the paradox is vicious, or that enforcing a civility norm blunts the self-determining character of a process in which that very norm is under challenge. In fairness, I should say that Post is less interested in constructing a knock-down argument than he is in exploring (in a generous and open-minded way) the various sources of unease in this area. That I applaud. Nevertheless, it is important to see how the air of paradox can be dispelled.

Consider an analogy. In recent years, the United Kingdom has amended its constitution in various ways. For example, in 1999 Parliament enacted the House of Lords Act, section 1 of which states that "No-one shall be a member of the House of Lords by virtue of a hereditary peerage."[38] The act was passed by Parliament, and it was voted on by all hereditary peers who chose to participate. It was approved in the House of Lords by a strong majority. My point is that the very voting rule that was used was the voting rule that was "up for grabs" in the vote. And there was nothing contradictory about this. Analogously, there is nothing self-contradictory about regulating a debate concerning norms of civility with norms of civility. That is the normal way in which we change, modify, or endorse the procedural rules of our political life.

The only remaining sense I can make of Post's concern is that he thinks it is somehow inherently inappropriate to enforce civility norms with legislation. Perhaps he thinks it is like trying to enforce etiquette with legislation. Or rules of good sportsmanship or personal ethics. In some of these areas, Post's concerns may be justified. But everything depends on what is stake in upholding the norms in question. If they are just designed to make us "nice" to each other and to protect people against hurt feelings, then Post is probably right. These are not good aims for a legislator to adopt; and to this extent, much popular resentment against the legislative enforcement of "political correctness"—in vocabulary, pronoun use, and so on—is intelligible and justified. But that is not the sort of case I have made in this book. I have argued that some of what Post calls "civility norms" are essential for a society's ability to guarantee basic dignity and provide implicit assurance to vulnerable people that their status as ordinary members of society in good standing is respected. I know that Robert Post does not think this is inherently an objectionable enterprise, and I don't see how that changes simply because "civility norms" might need to be enforced in order to secure it.

Distrust of Government

I am aware that I have not even come close in these chapters to addressing all the arguments against hate speech legislation. For example, I haven't said anything to address the mistrust of government which, if Geoffrey Stone is right, underlies all First Amendment concerns and explains why many American legal scholars are so opposed to hate speech laws.[39] Let me say something about that now.

As I understand it, the idea is that government interference is always likely to be motivated by officials' lust for power, or their vanity, or their misguided insecurity, or their undue responsiveness to majoritarian prejudice, anger, or panic. They may not always get it wrong, but there is a standing danger that they will.

Why this is felt particularly in the area of speech (as opposed to government actions generally), and in the even more particularized area of content-based restriction on speech, I am not quite sure. There is something to it, I guess, when the best explanation of some of the prosecutions under the 1798 Sedition Act is the wounded vanity of high officials, or when the best explanation of some of the twentieth-century prosecutions—beginning with the World War I examples and culminating with the 1950 decision about the application of the Smith Act in *Dennis v. United*

States—has more to do with the unpopularity of a view held by a minority (members of the Communist Party, for example) than with any real-world danger that that view poses to the state.[40] But why would anyone think this was true of hate speech legislation, or laws prohibiting group defamation? Why is this an area where we should be particularly mistrustful of our lawmakers?

The worry about majoritarianism seems particularly strange. No doubt there are cases where majorities legislate for their own interests, to the disadvantage of vulnerable minorities: the legacy of segregation laws and anti-immigration laws reminds us of that. But hate speech laws represent almost exactly the opposite: a legislative majority bending over backwards to ensure that vulnerable minorities are protected against hatred and discrimination that might otherwise be endemic in society.

I have heard it said by colleagues that my opposition to constitutional restrictions on hate speech laws is best explained by my well-known opposition to judicial review of legislative decisions in general.[41] It is not quite as simple as that. Many countries that regulate hate speech also have strong judicial review: Germany and Canada are examples. But in a broader sense, these colleagues are right. I have long believed that American constitutional jurisprudence exaggerates the likelihood that majoritarian legislation will simply promote the interests of the majority at the expense of vulnerable minorities, who therefore need protection by the courts. And I have written about this incessantly, some would say incorrigibly.

But hate speech is an area where, against all the odds, majorities prove us wrong. In every advanced democracy where they are given the opportunity, majorities legislate to put this sort of protection in place because they care about the plight of minority communities. And by and large, this legislation is administered responsibly. Certainly, hate speech laws do not seem to have been transformed into vehicles for the promotion of majority interest in the way that Stone's general distrust of government interference would suggest.

You may say, "Well that's because you're focusing on the wrong minority. The relevant minority here is not the community of African Americans or Muslims or gays. The real minority disadvantaged by hate speech prohibitions are the unpopular racists and bigots and virulent Islamophobes whose beliefs are detested by those who make these laws. Attacking *those* unpopular groups is just as much an instance of the tyranny of the majority as an attack on Communists or atheists." I am afraid I have no patience for that recharacterization. It certainly doesn't affect the point that hate speech laws really are enacted for the benefit of vulnerable racial, ethnic, and religious minorities, to uphold their reputation and their dignity. It just introduces an additional minority into the picture. And it is a desperate maneuver: one might as well say that laws against drinking-and-driving represent an attack on the discrete minority of drunk drivers. In both cases, we have an account of a serious social harm that certain activities, if they are left unregulated, are likely to cause. In both cases we have a minority of potential victims of that harm to consider, as well as a minority of potential offenders. We can play word games with "majority" and "minority" until the end of time, but the fact remains: hate speech laws do not involve putting the interests of the majority above those of vulnerable groups.

8 Toleration and Calumny

This final chapter takes a different turn. In the past, I have written about toleration, particularly the seventeenth-century debate about toleration conducted by philosophers like Pierre Bayle, Thomas Hobbes, and John Locke.[1] Until recently, I never thought to make a connection between that debate and the debate about hate speech. But I believe now that there is a connection to be made, and this chapter attempts to set it out. If nothing else, it may help to add a dimension of historical richness to our often flat and colorless constitutional debates about these issues.

Osborne's Case

In 1732, somebody called Osborne (spelled with an "e" or without an "e"—"Osborn"—depending on which law report you read)[2] published and distributed a broadsheet in London. Its title was *A true and surprizing Relation of a Murder and Cruelty that was committed by the Jews lately arrived from Portugal; shewing how they burnt a Woman and a new born Infant the latter End of February, because the Infant was begotten by a Christian*. In the body of the paper, Osborne set forth "a particular Account of the whole Transaction," and maintained "that the like Cruelty had often been committed by the Jews." The pamphlet inflamed anti-Semitic sentiment in London. We are told that "Jews were attacked by multitudes in several parts of the city, barbarously treated and threatened with death, in case they were found abroad any more."[3] One of those who was attacked was an attorney called Fazakerly, and Mr. Fazakerly laid an information for libel against Osborne, the author of the broadsheet, supported by affidavits to the effect that "this Paper had so much incensed the Mob against the Jews, that they had assaulted and beat in a most outrageous Manner the Prosecutor, who was a Jew."[4]

The court's initial response was to strike out the action, on the ground that the allegation contained in the paper "was so general that no particular Persons could pretend to be injured by it."[5] The chief justice, Lord Raymond, said that he believed the Court could do nothing in the case, because no particular Jews were able to show to the Court that they were pointed at in the paper more than any others.[6] But eventually the Court was persuaded to entertain the action, if not as a criminal libel, then on public-order grounds. According to one report, the Court was moved precisely by the generality of the charge. The story in Osborne's paper was that this was something "which the Jews have frequently done; and therefore the whole community of the Jews are struck at."[7] Another report says that the Court emphasized the public-order aspect: "This is not by way of Information for a Libel that is the Foundation of this Complaint, but for a Breach of the Peace, in inciting a Mob to the Distruction of a whole Set of People; and tho' it is too general to make it fall within the Description of a Libel, yet it will be pernicious to suffer such scandalous Reflections to go unpunished."[8] A third report has the Court taking a similar line, but even more forcefully: "Admitting an information for a libel may be improper, yet the publication of this paper is deservedly punishable in an information for a misdemeanour, and that of the highest kind; such sort of advertisements necessarily tending to raise tumults and disorders among the people, and inflame them with an universal spirit of barbarity against a whole body of men, as if guilty of crimes scarce practicable, and totally incredible."[9]

It is a remarkable case, because England was not known for its acceptance of Jews as a proper subject of public solicitude in the early eighteenth century. One of the reports we have of Osborne's case is an indirect report from an 1819 decision in which the Lord Chancellor had held that Jewish children were not entitled to seek places in a free school established in Bedford.[10] In that case, the Lord Chancellor mentioned (without comment) a notorious dictum of the great jurist Sir Edward Coke, cited against the Jewish petitioners, to the effect that "[a]ll infidels are in law *perpetui inimici,* perpetual enemies (for the law presumes not that they will be converted, that being *potentia remota,* a remote possibility), for between them, as with the devils, whose subjects they be, and the Christian, there is perpetual hostility, and can be no peace."[11] (But Coke's dictum was contested by counsel for the petitioners and powerful dicta were cited against it.)[12] The Lord Chancellor did say that that "it is the duty of every judge presiding in an *English* Court of Justice, when he is told that there is no difference between worshipping the Supreme Being in chapel, church, or synagogue, to recollect that Christianity is part of the law of *England*."

That's the background. So the decision in Osborne's case—convicting someone for anti-Semitic libel or for fomenting anti-Semitic disorder—almost ninety years earlier is all the more remarkable.

In this chapter, I want to begin with Osborne's case and go backwards—back to the idea of a tolerant society that emerged in the late-seventeenth and eighteenth centuries. I want to consider the role that anti-defamation, the sort of public-order-based prohibition on group libel that we see at work in 1732 in Osborne's case, played in contemporary conceptions of toleration.

Conceptions of Toleration

My questions are: How large did the issue of hateful defamation loom in Enlightenment theories of toleration? Were seventeenth- and eighteenth-century *philosophes* committed to the idea that people should refrain not only from violence against one another on religious grounds, but also from expressions of hatred and vituperation? I want to ask about the imagery of a tolerant society that we find in Enlightenment philosophy ranging from Locke and Bayle to Montesquieu, Diderot, and Voltaire: Is a tolerant society just a society free from religious persecution, or is it a society in which people cohabit and deal with one another in spite of their religious differences in an atmosphere of civility and respect, an atmosphere that is not disfigured by grotesque defamations of the sort that we saw in the case of *R. v. Osborne?*

Toleration, we know, is a principle that can be more or less expansive, more or less grudging. Everyone agrees that at its core is a requirement that force or legal sanctions should not be used against people to coerce them to abandon their religious beliefs and practices or adopt those approved by the state. Almost everyone agrees that toleration imposes duties on ordinary members of society as well; they must not press their government to impose penalties or coercion on members of unpopular religions or religious minorities, and they themselves must refrain from acts of violence against people who do not share their faith or worship as they do. That's the core of toleration. But our conception of the state's duty of toleration can be expanded to include not just nonpersecution, but disestablishment or even comprehensive dissociation of state and law from religion—what Richard Hooker called "a wall of separation between church and state."[13] And equally our conception of the citizen's duty of toleration can also be expanded to include not just refraining from religiously motivated violence, but refraining also from religious insult, libel, and vituperation; the citizen might also be conceived to have a duty of nondiscrimination on religious grounds; he might even have, as John Locke argued, a duty of "charity, bounty, and liberality" toward those of other religions, a duty required of us by what Locke called "that natural fellowship" that exists between all men, regardless of their faith.[14] On each of these issues—each of these possible expansions or elaborations of the duty of toleration—there is debate in modern times, and perhaps there was also debate in Enlightenment times, when our modern conceptions of toleration were formed. That's what I want to investigate. What was there in the way of consideration of what we nowadays would call religious hate speech in Enlightenment theories of toleration?

Religious hate speech, too, is something that can be understood in a more or less expansive way. It can range from the sort of horrendous blood libel that we see in Osborne's case, through more straightforward but still vicious insults and vituperations, such as the claim that followers of a certain dissident faith are dishonest or promiscuous, all the way to what might possibly be regarded as simple inferences from the speaker's own theology, such as that the followers of a certain faith are God-forsaken or idolaters or damned. In our day, it can include proclamations that followers of Islam are inclined by their faith to be supporters of terrorism.

We can understand the range of religious hate speech along a number of spectrums. (1) The simplest is the one I just mentioned: a spectrum of viciousness or intensity, where the hate speech varies, for example, according to the monstrosity of the content conveyed. (2) Or we can imagine a spectrum strung between two poles— the pole of public order at one end (where religious hate speech may be assimilated to incitement to disorder), and, at the other end, the pole of simple disagreement, where hate speech merges into what is merely the forceful expression of disagreement with another's position. (3) Or we can imagine a different sort of spectrum where an attack on the precepts and practices of a given church is distinguished from an attack on the personality and dignity of the members of the church: one might say "Transubstantiation is nonsense" or one might say "All Catholics are drunkards." We are conscious of some such range in the laws currently administered in the United Kingdom—laws that, on the one hand, prohibit public expressions of religious hatred when they take an abusive and threatening form, and, on the other hand, privilege (in the words of section 29J) "discussion, criticism or expressions of antipathy, dislike, ridicule, insult or abuse of particular religions."[15]

One might imagine that the case for banning hate speech is strongest when the speech in question is at the extreme end of each of these spectrums: it conveys a terrible defamation; it threatens public order; and it attacks the dignity of the person, not just the reputation of his church. Osborne's case illustrates all three extremities. Our hypothesis might be that calumnies and libels of this extreme kind come close to being prohibitable by the principles of mutual toleration, just as laws prohibit physical attacks against people and their property.

The *Philosophes* on Hate Speech

With all this in mind, what does an investigation of the historical texts reveal about Enlightenment models of toleration? What do the *philosophes* say about libels, hate speech, and religious calumnies?

The first thing to notice is that a reading of the Enlightenment literature on toleration reveals nothing on this matter comparable in explicitness or extent to the *philosophes'* discussion of the use of force and legal sanctions by the state against religious minorities. John Locke's *Letter Concerning Toleration* is the most sustained piece of writing on all this in the early modern period —sustained not so much in length (Pierre Bayle's *Philosophical Commentary on . . . Luke 14:23* is much longer) as in the analytic density of argumentation. The *Letter* devotes a tremendous amount of discussion to the relation between coercion and belief, and a considerable amount of discussion to the philosophical difference between the idea of a church and the idea of civil society; but Locke devotes nothing comparable in the way of space or argument to the question of how we should regard vituperation in the context of religious diversity.

Nothing comparable—but the theme is there if you read the *Letter* carefully. Locke's view of an intolerant society is in part a conception of anger and uproar: "No man is angry with another for an error committed in sowing his land or in marrying his daughter. . . . But if any man do not frequent the church, . . . or if he brings not his children to be initiated in the sacred mysteries of this or the other congregation, this immediately causes an uproar. The neighbourhood is filled with noise and clamour."[16] In characterizing the horrors of an intolerant civil society, Locke talks about the "endless hatreds" between religious groups. He lambastes ministers for what they preach from the pulpit: "[A]ll men, whether private persons or magistrates (if any such there be in his church), [should] diligently endeavour to allay and temper all that heat and unreasonable averseness of mind which either any man's fiery zeal for his own sect or the craft of others has kindled against dissenters."[17] What we need to do is calm the furious vituperations. And Locke intimates "how happy and how great would be the fruit, both in Church and State, if the pulpits everywhere sounded with this doctrine of peace and toleration."

Speaking more specifically of the duties that the principle of toleration imposes upon churches, Locke says: "[N]o church is bound, by the duty of toleration, to retain any such person in her bosom as, after admonition, continues obstinately to offend against the laws of the society [by which Locke means the church's own laws of faith and worship]. . . . [N]evertheless, in all such cases care is to be taken that the sentence of excommunication, and the execution thereof, carry with it *no rough usage of word or action* whereby the ejected person may any wise be damnified in body or estate."[18] "No rough usage of word or action": this strongly suggests that Locke favors limits on what may be said about excommunicates, as well as on what may be done to them.

Even when Locke is conceding to Jonas Proast, in the later *Letters on Toleration,* that coercion may perhaps work indirectly to promote religion, he still opposes it; and it is interesting that the doubts he expresses include doubts about the use of attacks on people's honor, as well as about attacks on their person and property:

> Loss of estate and dignities may make a proud man humble: sufferings and imprisonment may make a wild and debauched man sober: and so these things may "indirectly, and at a distance, be serviceable towards the salvation of men's souls." I doubt not but God has made some, or all of these, the occasions of good to many men. But will you therefore infer, that the magistrate may take away a man's honour, or estate, or liberty for the salvation of his soul; or torment him in this, that he may be happy in the other world?[19]

That it occurred to Locke that this duty might be a duty upheld by law is evident from the terms of the *Fundamental Consti-*

tutions of Carolina, in whose drafting he had a hand. Article 97 of
the 1669 version reads: "No person shall use any reproachful, reviling, or abusive language against the religion of any church or
profession, that being a certain way of disturbing public peace,
and of hindering the conversion of any to the truth, by engaging
them in quarrels and animosities, to the hatred of the professors
and that profession, which otherwise they might be brought to
assent to."[20] We can't quite infer that this was Locke's view, any
more than we can infer Locke's views about slavery from other
provisions in the *Constitutions*.[21] Locke was a secretary for the
colonial enterprise in the Carolinas, not its lawgiver. But his evident familiarity with a legal prohibition on religious calumny
shows that it is not out of the question to attribute this position
to him.

So we have two themes from Locke. One is a belief that public
expressions of hatred and vilification are typical of an intolerant
rather than a tolerant society. And the second is the claim that
there is a specific duty—perhaps even a legal duty—to refrain
from rough usage of word, as well as rough usage of action, if that
is calculated to have a detrimental impact on an individual's person or honor or estate.

A third theme from Locke is one that we have already noticed.
For Locke, the duty of toleration is bound up with a general duty
of charity, civility, and good fellowship:

[N]o private person has any right in any manner to prejudice another person in his civil enjoyments because he is of
another church or religion. All the rights and franchises that
belong to him as a man, or as a denizen, are inviolably to be

preserved to him. These are not the business of religion. No violence nor injury is to be offered him, whether he be Christian or Pagan. Nay, we must not content ourselves with the narrow measures of bare justice; charity, bounty, and liberality must be added to it. This the Gospel enjoins, this reason directs, and this that natural fellowship we are born into requires of us.[22]

But isn't "charity, bounty, and liberality" just happy talk, not a serious requirement of toleration? Who ever heard of anyone having a *right* to another's "charity, bounty, and liberality"? Well, actually John Locke did believe that, as is evident from the famous doctrine of charity set out in Chapter IV of the *First Treatise*.[23] And I am with historian John Marshall in insisting we should not underestimate either the force or the importance of this strand in Locke's theory.[24] Locke talks of our duty to maintain "love and charity in the diversity of contrary opinions," and adds that by this he means not just "an empty sound, but an effectual forbearance and good will."[25] We may be nervous about this because we worry that a doctrine of charity is to be understood as a specifically Christian doctrine—in the passage just quoted, Locke calls it "an indispensable duty for all Christians"[26]—and we want, if possible, to recover from Locke's work a theory of toleration with a broader foundation than that. But it is far from clear that Locke would endorse such a project.

The three points I have drawn from Locke—(1) public execration as typical of an intolerant society, (2) the claim that there is a specific obligation to refrain from using words to harm people you disagree with, and (3) an affirmative image of peace and charity amid diversity—these themes are developed also in a much longer work, Pierre Bayle's *Philosophical Commentary on These Words of the Gospel, Luke 14.23, "Compel Them To Come In, That My House May Be Full,"* published in 1686, a few years before Locke's *Letter.*

Of the second point, that it is possible to harm people by execration as well as by physical violence, Bayle has no doubt. He knows that religious authorities use this method; on their view, "smiting and slaying Men, blackning 'em by all kind of Calumny, betraying 'em by false Oaths, are all good Actions in a Member of the true, against a Member of a false Church."[27] Bayle talks of slander as "that Pest of Civil Society,"[28] and insists that its use is never justified, any more than murder, theft, or perjury, for the sake of bringing a heretic to salvation: "[R]efraining from the Goods or Good Name of our Neighbor, not swearing a false Oath, not debauching our Neighbor's Wife or his Daughter, not smiting, reviling, or insulting him, are all matters of Obligation; and therefore whatever Benefit he may be suppos'd to reap from our calumniating . . . with regard to Salvation, it's by no means allowable to treat him after this manner."[29] Bayle, like Locke, is in no doubt that execration as well as violence is typical of the horrors of an intolerant society: "Must not this exasperate the Spirits of both sides, kindle a deadly *Hatred* to one another, force 'em to traduce and slander each other, and become mutually wickeder and worse Christians than they were before?"[30]

And when Bayle concocts his affirmative vision of a tolerant society characterized unavoidably by religious diversity, it is a society free of reviling—free of "the furious and tumultuous Outcrys of a Rabble of Monks and Clergymen"—as well as of the more tangible forms of persecution. The imagery Bayle uses is that of the marketplace or bazaar: "the Diversity of . . . Churches, and Worship, wou'd breed no more Disorder in Citys or Societys, than the Diversitys of Shops in a Fair."[31]

> Did each Party industriously cultivate that Toleration which I contend for, there might be the same Harmony in a State compos'd of ten different Sects, as there is in a Town where the several kinds of Tradesmen contribute to each others mutual Support. All that cou'd naturally proceed from it wou'd be an honest Emulation between 'em which shou'd exceed in Piety, in good Works, and in spiritual Knowledge. . . . Now it's manifest, such an Emulation as this must be the Source of infinite publick Blessings; and consequently, that Toleration is the thing in the world best fitted for retrieving the Golden Age, and producing a harmonious Consort of different Voices, and Instruments of different Tones, as agreeable at least as that of a single Voice.[32]

The marketplace image—not Oliver Wendell Holmes's "marketplace of ideas," but the economic market as an image of tolerant and amicable interchange—is well known from the later Enlightenment as well, in Voltaire's portrayal of the Royal Exchange in London in his *Letters on the English* (1734). Voltaire speaks of the Royal Exchange in London "where the representatives of all nations meet for the benefit of mankind."

> There the Jew, the Mahometan, and the Christian transact together, as though they all professed the same religion, and give the name of infidel to none but bankrupts. There the

Presbyterian confides in the Anabaptist, and the Church-
man depends on the Quaker's word. At the breaking up of
this pacific and free assembly, some withdraw to the synagogue, and others to take a glass. This man goes and is bap-
tized in a great tub, in the name of the Father, Son, and Holy
Ghost: that man has his son's foreskin cut off, whilst a set of
Hebrew words (quite unintelligible to him) are mumbled
over his child. Others retire to their churches, and there wait
for the inspiration of heaven with their hats on, and all are
satisfied.[33]

But all can gather together civilly and do business in the Royal
Exchange without hatred, without vituperation.

For his own part, Voltaire added this about spoken expressions
of hatred: even though he condemned certain aspects of the religious practice of Muslims, "destest[ing] them as tyrants over
women and enemies of the arts," he said "I hate calumny" even
more, and added that for this reason he would refrain from defaming "the Turks," as he called them.[34] (I will come back in a
moment to this question of whether a prohibition on expressions
of hatred can interfere with the vehement expression of disagreement.) The hatred of calumny seems to be a matter of personal
ethics, rather than political morality. But Voltaire saw a clear connection between private and public intolerance: "Who is a perse-
cutor? It is he whose wounded pride and furious fanaticism irri-
tate the prince or magistrate against innocent men guilty only of
the crime of holding different opinions."[35] Persecution is not just
what the state does. Voltaire makes it clear that it includes individuals' use of public denunciations in order to goad the state into
the wrongful use of law.

Let us round off our little survey of Enlightenment views on these matters with some material from Denis Diderot's *Encyclopédie*. My reference is to the entry titled *Intolérance*. The striking thing about Diderot's conception of intolerance is that he associates it with hatred and expressions of hatred: "The word 'intolerance' is commonly understood as this ferocious passion that stirs one to hate people that are in the wrong. . . . Instruction, persuasion, and prayer, here are the only legitimate ways to spread religion. Any means that would excite hatred, indignation, and scorn, is impious."[36] Like Voltaire, Locke, and Bayle, Diderot also associates intolerance with the breaking of the ordinary bounds of sociability—the use of ostracism, for example—as well as with more violent means of persecution. "Civil *intolerance* consists in breaking all relations with other men and in pursuing, by violent means of every sort, those whose way of thinking about God and His worship is different from our own. . . . It is impious to expose religion to the odious imputations of tyranny, of callousness, of injustice, of unsociability, even with the aim of drawing back to the fold those who would unfortunately have strayed away from it."[37]

So these are the points I want to stress: on the one hand, the natural association, in the minds of these Enlightenment thinkers, of intolerance with hatred and abuse, as well as with physical persecution; and, on the other hand, the natural association of tolerance with the ordinary bonds of charity and sociability.

Sociability

The latter point, about sociability—the suggestion that public calumnies should be banned because they disrupt ordinary sociable relations among members of the same society—I think is quite important.

The idea is that not only do religious minorities have the right to be secure from attack and from being physically sanctioned for their faith or religious practice; they also have the right to be treated as members of society in good standing, with a status and acceptance that enables them to participate confidently in the ordinary routines and transactions of everyday social life. They don't have to be loved or befriended by those who differ from them on matters of religion. But they must be able to engage in ordinary dealings among people who are, in the circumstances of mass society, strangers to one another—I am thinking of Adam Smith's observation at the beginning of *The Wealth of Nations:* "In civilized society [man] stands at all times in need of the co-operation and assistance of great multitudes, while his whole life is scarce sufficient to gain the friendship of a few persons."[38] And dealings among people on this basis are the currency of ordinary dignity and respect. That's why the Voltaire passage about the Royal Exchange in London is so important.

I think it is a requirement of human dignity that we should deal with one another in this relaxed and civilized way. It may seem strange to associate dignity with dealings so mundane and materialistic; we think of dignity as carrying a sort of shimmering Kantian aura, fitting it for a much more transcendent role in political morality than this. But that's a mistake. The primary habitat of human dignity is the mundane. Philosophically, dignity may be a Kantian conception of immeasurable worth *(Würde)*, personality as something noumenal, an end in itself, and so on.[39] But in law, it is a matter of status—one's status as an ordinary member of society in good standing, entitled to the same liberties, protections, and powers that everyone else has—and it generates demands for recognition and treatment which accord with that status. The guarantee of dignity is what enables a person to walk down the street without fear of insult or humiliation, to find the shops and exchanges open to him, and to proceed with an implicit assurance of being able to interact with others without being treated as a pariah.

I believe that this conception of dignity as a matter of ordinary presence—the status of being respected in myriad anonymous interactions as a member of society in good standing—is actually a large part of what is at stake with toleration. The virtue of the passages I have quoted to you from Bayle and Locke, Diderot and Voltaire, is that they emphasize how incomplete a régime of toleration is when it merely restrains coercion and violence, leaving hatred, insult, and ostracism untouched.

It may be worth adding one other point. Peter Gay, in his work on Enlightenment, has emphasized the continuity between Enlightenment thinking about toleration and Enlightenment thinking about peace in international affairs.[40] In international affairs, the analogue of a narrow conception of toleration limited only to nonpersecution and a prohibition on the use of violence or coercion for religious ends would be a conception of peace that was simply an absence of war. I think it is interesting that, by and large, Enlightenment theorists were not satisfied with that image of peace. They looked forward to a more affirmative harmony among nations. The idea that peace could coexist with mutual denunciation among nations, so long as disagreements didn't issue in actual fighting—this possibility, analogous to the idea of those who argue both for religious toleration and for the protection of religious hate speech—would have struck them as absurd.

Exegesis and Excavation

I acknowledge that I have had to dig a little to find these Enlightenment materials. They are not front and center in seventeenth- and eighteenth-century writings on toleration; and, as I said at the beginning of the previous section, they are not discussed in anything like the detail or with anything like the analytic power that Locke and Bayle, for example, devote to the issue of physical coercion.

The fact that one has to excavate in order to find something to support the conclusion that religious hate speech might be as much at odds with toleration as more physical forms of persecution might persuade some people that the *philosophes* didn't really regard public expressions of religious hatred as a matter of concern at all, and that they did not really regard the suppression of religious insult as part of their tolerationist agenda. Their relative silence on the matter might be thought to support the modern "First Amendment position" that suppression of religious insult is not required —indeed, that it is prohibited—by liberal principles.

I think that would be premature. For one thing, there are the hints we have just been talking about and the quite substantial passages that have been unearthed. Something has to be said about them, before we saddle Locke, Bayle, Diderot, and Voltaire with the view that there is nothing intolerant about screaming vile insults or publishing blood libels.

There is also a question about burden of proof. There may be little that is explicit in the work of these authors, so far as a legitimate prohibition on religious hate speech is concerned. Equally, however, there is nothing that appears explicitly to support the opposite view: that toleration requires religious hate speech to be left unmolested. And fitting that second position—the modern "First Amendment position"—into the rest of what the Enlightenment philosophers say about toleration seems (for my money, at least) to be actually quite difficult. If they are to be saddled with the view that religious hate speech is not to be prohibited, then considerable doubt is cast on their overall claim that toleration augurs in a new area of peace and cooperation in civil society.

Third, whatever is said or not said explicitly, or whatever the default position is taken to be, there is the direction or tendency of their overall arguments to consider. Let me concentrate for a moment on John Locke, because I know his arguments best.

Apart from a specifically Christian argument for toleration at the beginning of the *Letter,* Locke's general position is that power used coercively is quite inappropriate in religious matters. Religion is a matter of belief. Indeed, there is a premium on sincere belief; God is not interested in the insincere variety. Now, sincere belief is not subject to the will; we can't decide what to believe. But coercion works only on the will, the association of sanctions with one course of action making us decide to choose another. Since we cannot decide what to believe, coercion is not an appropriate means to use for religious ends. That's the essence of Locke's case.[41]

How does this apply to insults or libels? Well, considered as strategies to bring about religious change or conversion, they seem to fall before the same Lockean argument. It may be thought that people will give up their deviant beliefs under the lash of public calumny. The cost of maintaining a minority faith will be simply too high: that may be the thought. But Locke's main argument refutes the proposition that the coercive power of opinion can be effective in this way. It may lead people to conceal their beliefs—to cower in hiding to avoid public expressions of hatred, and the boycotts and exclusions (not to mention the violence) that they intimate. But that won't get them to change their beliefs, because their beliefs are not subject to the will and therefore not vulnerable to this pressure. The best that a torrent of hatred and calumny can do is get them to change their religious behavior. But to aim just at that would be a mockery, Locke says.

In the second, third, and mercifully uncompleted fourth of his *Letters on Toleration,* Locke had to come to terms with an opponent (Jonas Proast) who conceded Locke's main line of argument, but suggested that coercive means applied carefully might lead to a situation in which people's beliefs changed even if they couldn't bring about that change directly. Forcing a change in behavior might result indirectly, and in the long run, in a change in belief. And I suppose the same might be true of calumny. Locke had a lot to say about the details of this argument; but he also indicated a readiness to retreat to a backup position. No doubt anything at all might bring about a given result—our Savior, Locke said, used clay and spittle to cure blindness—but we have to ask whether this particular means was ordained by God for religious conversion. Locke makes a pretty clear case that, in the preaching of Jesus Christ, there was certainly no ordaining of violent means, and it would not be hard to establish that there was no ordaining of abuse or vilification, either.

Now, as it stands, this Lockean argument that I have cobbled together is perhaps a little too quick. It ignores the fact that calumny may be used defensively rather than offensively—to warn vulnerable people who hold the orthodox faith against hob-nobbing with infidels and heretics. Maybe the point of publicly damning Jews as baby-killers, or, I don't know, denouncing Ana-baptists as sodomites, is to ensure that vulnerable Anglicans steer well clear of them. Locke doesn't address this possibility explic-itly. But the whole dynamic of religious argumentation that he imagines eschews virulent expressions of hatred, even as a defen-sive strategy. The *Letter Concerning Toleration* is dominated by a conviction that such means are vicious and ineffective, cer-tainly compared to less virulent alternatives: "[H]ow many, do you think, by friendly and christian debates with them at their houses, and by the gentle methods of the gospel made use of in private conversation, might have been brought into the church; who, by railing from the pulpit, ill and unfriendly treatment out of it, and other neglects and miscarriages of those who claimed to be their teachers, have been driven from hearing them?"[42] The methods by which the members of a congregation are to be kept in check by their religious leaders are "exhortations, admonitions, and advices,"[43] not raillery and abuse.

In addition, Locke talks specifically about denunciations and rumors of misconduct by various religious sects. Having said that the magistrate may not regulate religious worship, he imagines a response:

> You will say, by this rule, if some congregations should have a mind to sacrifice infants, or (as the primitive Christians were falsely accused) lustfully pollute themselves in promis-cuous uncleanness, or practise any other such heinous enor-

mities, is the magistrate obliged to tolerate them, because they are committed in a religious assembly? I answer: No. These things are not lawful in the ordinary course of life, nor in any private house; and therefore neither are they so in the worship of God, or in any religious meeting.[44]

His view seems to be that either the denunciations are true, in which case what is appropriate is a complaint to the authorities about unlawful conduct, or they are false, in which case they should not be voiced at all.[45] Even when he himself is voicing doubts about the toleration of Roman Catholics, what is remarkable is how careful he is to try to separate denunciations which might genuinely be matters of public concern from those used simply as a form of abuse or as a way of bolstering one's own religious position.[46]

Perhaps the most common use of calumny is not as a means to an end (either the end of drawing people to one's own faith or the end of protecting one's co-religionists from apostasy), but simply as a form of religious self-expression. Almost a century after the end of the period of Enlightenment that we are studying, John Stuart Mill confronted a similar difficulty in his essay *On Liberty*. What is to be done about social sanctions visited by some people upon others whose religion or ethics they despise? Boycotts and ostracism may be frowned upon, but they may also have an important expressive function: "We have a right . . . to act upon our unfavorable opinion of any one, not to the oppression of his individuality, *but in the exercise of ours*. We are not bound, for example, to seek his society; we have a right to avoid it (though not to parade the avoidance), for we have a right to choose the society most acceptable to us."[47] Maybe something analogous can be said about religious vituperation: we use it not for the oppression of anyone else's individuality, but in the exercise of our own.

Well, if it is just a matter of letting off steam, then I think Locke's arguments for social peace and civility require people to find other outlets. The difficulty arises when what seems like hate speech to the audience seems to the speaker to be just a natural mode of forcefully expressing his own view. It is to this knotty problem that we now turn.

Voltaire on Calumny

Earlier I quoted an observation by Voltaire, from his *Dictionary*, under the heading "Mohammedans." Voltaire said: "I hate calumny so much that I do not want even to impute foolishness to the Turks, although I detest them as tyrants over women and enemies of the arts."[48]

Now, in modern debates about hate speech—about Nazis in Skokie and so on—Voltaire is often quoted to the following effect: "I hate what you say, but I will defend to the death your right to say it." I guess everyone knows by now that Voltaire probably never said or wrote any such thing. Apparently, an English writer named Beatrice Hall, writing under a male pseudonym at the beginning of the twentieth century,[49] used this language in summing up Voltaire's attitude to the burning of a book written by Claude Adrien Helvétius. It was her readers—and, after that, countless opportunists from the American Civil Liberties Union —who made the mistake of attributing the saying to Voltaire himself.[50] And even if the words were Voltaire's, there is no evidence they were directed particularly to the protection of hate speech. But the passage I have quoted from Voltaire's dictionary has him saying specifically that he detests religious hate speech. He hates "calumny so much" that he intends himself to refrain from casting aspersions on Muslim customs. You can imagine the dictum being applied to the Danish cartoons. (The position here is not quite diametrically opposed to the quotation normally attributed to Voltaire: I suppose he could defend to the death calumnies issued against Muslims by others, even though he hates them and will not issue them himself.)

Still, the passage about Muslims raises a point that we have to confront. Isn't there a danger that, if the principle of toleration extends so far as to ban calumnies, blood libels, insults, religious defamation, and other attacks on people's dignity and honor, such a ban will also inhibit vehement discussion of others' failings, errors, absurdities, or wickedness? People might no longer be able to say what they think—to say, for example, with Voltaire, that they despise the way Muslims treat women—for fear of running afoul of the ban on expressions of racial and religious hatred. And isn't that—you may say—the real reason for confining toleration to a ban on legal sanctions and not extending it generally to prohibit speech acts that diminish the dignity of those whose beliefs and practices one despises? This may be the real reason you don't find a whole lot in Locke and in the other thinkers about banning expressions of hatred: maybe Locke and others do not want the rigors of a tolerationist regime to diminish the amount or intensity of debate and mutual criticism among different religious groups in society.

After all, Locke wants to be able to say, of many of the beliefs for which he urges toleration, "I readily grant that these opinions are false and absurd,"[51] and presumably this is not just a privilege for the philosopher: he wants others to be able to say that, too. But how can he say that if the targeted group takes it as an affront, and if the tolerationist regime cultivates a far-reaching norm of civility designed to protect people against all such affronts? "Every man," says Locke, "has commission to admonish, exhort, convince another of error, and, by reasoning, to draw him into truth."[52] Toleration is not supposed to silence us.

We might take this point even further. Some have said that toleration makes no sense except against a background of strong disagreement. We do not tolerate those of whom we approve or those to whom we are indifferent. We don't tolerate those whom we suspect might have the truth or part of the truth in a pluralistic world. We tolerate those whom we judge wrong, mistaken, or benighted.[53] And surely toleration must permit us to give voice to those judgments. Otherwise it demands too much.

Moral philosophers may be particularly sensitive on this point. I mean the kind who take their own vehemence as a mark of the objective truth of what they say, or who regard the offensiveness to others (especially people in other disciplines) of what they say as an honorable badge of their refusal to accept any scruples based on relativism. My own view (for what it is worth) is that it would be no bad thing if this vehemence and offensiveness were curbed, and if philosophers were required to secure their High Table credibility in other ways.

Even so: apart from philosophical vanity, many people do feel that they are morally and legally required to tolerate practices and opinions they believe (perhaps rightly) to be wrong. And the question is: Is it not unreasonable to impose limits on what they may say or publish in expression of that belief?

Well, the beginning of wisdom is surely to distinguish between some of the things that may be said or published in pursuance of the tolerator's beliefs and other things that maybe said or published in pursuance of them. John Locke's saying that it is absurd for Jews to deny the divine inspiration of the New Testament is one thing; presumably, Mr. Osborne's saying that Jews kill Christian babies is another. To punish those who spread a blood libel is one thing; to shut down what Locke called "affectionate endeavours to reduce men from errors" is another.[54]

But how to draw the line? Locke summed up his position by saying, "Nothing is to be done imperiously," meaning nothing is to be done by way of sanction. We may express our disagreement with a religious dissenter; but we are not to vituperate him in order to hurt him or in order to punish him. This position anticipates that of John Stuart Mill, who—in response to the problem I mentioned at the end of the previous section—permitted unpleasant reactions to others' depravity "only in so far as they are the natural, and, as it were, the spontaneous consequences of the faults themselves."[55] We may avoid someone's company because the teachings of our own faith tell us to mind the company we keep; but we are not to set out deliberately to organize boycotts or ostracism to punish him or bring him to his senses. Likewise, one can imagine Locke saying that punitive vituperation against others is not necessary for the integrity or reasonable self-expression of a person's own religious faith: Locke's insistence on the Protestant character of individual salvation establishes this.[56]

And forceful disagreement, when it is expressed, should be expressed in terms that can be engaged with intellectually, which is the only means by which belief might possibly be affected. Such interactions may of course involve vigorous debate and contestation. But this will be, in Shaftesbury's words, "a sort of amicable collision": as he put it, "We polish one another, and rub off our corners and rough sides by a sort of amicable collision. To restrain this is inevitably to bring a rust upon men's understandings."[57] It is forceful and effective, but amicable in the sense that it proceeds "without persecution or defamation."[58]

And all this is against the background of a commitment—which Locke shared with Bayle, Voltaire, and Diderot—to the common presence and respectful dignity in civil society of all those engaged in mutual toleration.

Toleration Literature and Hate Speech Literature

The issue I have been examining—the relation between religious toleration as an Enlightenment ideal and religious hate speech, epitomized by the eighteenth-century blood libel that we began with—is not one that features in the modern literature on toleration. There is a very considerable literature on hate speech (and, in England after the 2006 amendments to the Public Order Act, on religious hate speech), but most of it lacks a historical dimension going very far back beyond the passage of the Race Relations Act in the United Kingdom in the mid-1960s and the beginnings of modern First Amendment jurisprudence in the United States after 1919. And there is a very considerable philosophical and historical literature on toleration; but it hardly connects with the hate speech debate at all. Hate speech is discussed without reference to Enlightenment toleration; and the tolerationist theories of Locke and Bayle are discussed without reference to hate speech. I have tried to bridge that gap.

I have shifted the emphasis slightly, from physical sanctions to violent speech; in doing so, I may have taken the discussion of toleration out of the zone with which both the Enlightenment *philosophes* and modern philosophers have been preoccupied. And of course I don't want to minimize the importance of the concerns about legal sanctions and physical coercion—all those "horrid cruelties . . . that have been committed under the name and upon the account of religion"[59]—that, in most people's minds, particularly in the seventeenth century, were the core of what toleration had to address. Of course, the concern about physical sanctions is of paramount importance, and liberating people from the threat of them would be important even if those who were freed from the threat of violence, coercion, and punishment were left hated and despised, ostracized and boycotted, publicly libeled and dishonored. The violent stuff matters. But it is not all that matters under the heading of "toleration."

I also don't want to minimize the possibility of addressing the blood libels and other religious calumnies under the auspices of the threat they pose to public order. That was the key in Osborne's case: what we saw there was that a license to defame was likely to feed passions that would lead to pogrom. The violent potential of insult was well known in the early modern world, so much so that Thomas Hobbes identified a prohibition on offensive declarations as a leading principle of the law of nature, "because all signs of hatred, or contempt, provoke to fight,"[60] and

Machiavelli insisted that "detestable calumnies"—wild accusations put about in a legally unstructured and irresponsible way—were to be repressed by any means necessary, to prevent tumult and preserve order in a republic.[61]

Modern defenders of free speech think that they have defused the problem of hate speech by making concessions under the headings of "public disorder," "incitement," "or fighting words."[62] But what we have seen from the Enlightenment *philosophes* is that public order means more than just the absence of fighting: it includes the peaceful order of civil society and the dignitary order of ordinary people interacting with one another in ordinary ways, in the exchanges and the marketplace, on the basis of arm's-length respect. Above all, it conveys a principle of inclusion and a rejection of the calumnies that tend to isolate and exclude vulnerable religious minorities. "[I]f we may openly speak the truth," said John Locke, "as becomes one man to another, neither Pagan nor Mahometan, nor Jew, ought to be excluded from the civil rights of the commonwealth because of his religion."[63]

We began with one anti-Semitic libel; let us end with another. Montesquieu tells us, in *The Spirit of the Laws* (1748), that "[u]nder the reign of Philip the Tall, the Jews were run out of France, having been accused of allowing lepers to pollute the wells. This absurd accusation certainly should cast doubt on all accusations founded on public hatred."[64] Our temptation is to take hate speech too lightly, to forget what it contains and what its effect can be. In Osborne's case, the effect was rioting and beatings; in the case cited by Montesquieu, the effect was exclusion and banishment. Both involved fundamental assaults on the ordinary dignity of the members of vulnerable religious minorities—their dignity, equal to that of all other citizens, as members of the society in good standing. Neither type of effect, nor the calumnies that gave rise to them, should be neglected by those who care about the integrity of a well-ordered society. They should certainly not be neglected just because they involve the power of speech.

Notes

1. Approaching Hate Speech

1. Jeremy Waldron, "Free Speech and the Menace of Hysteria," *New York Review of Books* 55 (May 29, 2008). My review is reproduced in this book as Chapter 2.

2. Anthony Lewis, *Gideon's Trumpet: The Story behind Gideon v. Wainwright* (Random House, 1964); and Anthony Lewis, *Make No Law: The Sullivan Case and the First Amendment* (Random House, 1991).

3. Anthony Lewis, *Freedom for the Thought That We Hate* (Basic Books, 2007), 162.

4. Ibid. But I am not an Englishman. I am a New Zealander who emigrated first to the United Kingdom (to Oxford and then to Edinburgh), and then from Scotland to the United States, to teach law first in California, then in New York. I also now teach at Oxford, but on a visa. I am a permanent resident of the United States, but I am still a New Zealander so far as citizenship is concerned.

5. John Durham Peters, *Courting the Abyss: Free Speech and the Liberal Tradition* (University of Chicago Press, 2005).

6. Jeremy Waldron, "Boutique Faith," *London Review of Books* 20 (July 2006), available at www.lrb.co.uk/v28/n14/waldo1_.html.

7. Lewis, *Freedom for the Thought That We Hate,* 163.

8. Canada—Criminal Code 1985, Section 319(1): "Everyone who, by communicating statements in any public place, incites hatred against any identifiable group where such incitement is likely to lead to a breach of the peace is guilty of . . . an indictable offence and is liable to imprisonment for a term not exceeding two years."

9. Denmark—Penal Code, Article 266b: "Whoever publicly, or with intention to disseminating in a larger circle, makes statements or other pronouncements, by which a group of persons is threatened, derided or degraded because of their race, colour of skin, national or ethnic background, faith or sexual orientation, will be punished by fine or imprisonment for up to two years."

10. Germany—Penal Code, section 130(1): "Whoever, in a manner that is capable of disturbing the public peace: 1. incites hatred against segments of the population or calls for violent or arbitrary measures against them; or 2. assaults the human dignity of others by insulting, maliciously maligning, or defaming segments of the population, shall be punished with imprisonment from three months to five years."

11. New Zealand—Human Rights Act 1993, section 61(1): "It shall be unlawful for any person—(a) To publish or distribute written matter which is threatening, abusive, or insulting, or to broadcast by means of radio or television words which are threatening, abusive, or insulting; or (b) To use in any public place as defined in section 2(1) of the Summary Offences Act 1981, or within the hearing of persons in any such public place, or at any meeting to which the public are invited or have access, words which are threatening, abusive, or insulting; or (c) To use in any place words which are threatening, abusive, or insulting if the person using the words knew or ought to have known that the words were reasonably likely to be published in a newspaper, magazine, or periodical or broadcast by means of radio or television,—being matter or words likely

to excite hostility against or bring into contempt any group of persons in or who may be coming to New Zealand on the ground of the colour, race, or ethnic or national origins of that group of persons."

12. United Kingdom—Public Order Act 1986 section 18(1): "A person who uses threatening, abusive or insulting words or behaviour, or displays any written material which is threatening, abusive or insulting, is guilty of an offence if—(a) he intends thereby to stir up racial hatred, or (b) having regard to all the circumstances racial hatred is likely to be stirred up thereby."

13. Allegations of anti-white hate speech have excited concern, for example, in South Africa, New Zealand, and Australia.

14. For example, in the United Kingdom, in 2006, amendments to the Public Order Act prohibited hate speech against religious groups.

15. See Lewis, *Freedom for the Thought That We Hate*, p. 166. See also Chapter 2, below.

16. Jeremy Waldron, "Free Speech and the Menace of Hysteria," *New York Review of Books* (May 29, 2008), available at www.nybooks.com/articles/21452.

17. The lectures can be viewed at this website: www.law.harvard.edu/news/spotlight/constitutional-law/28_waldron.holmes.html.

18. Jeremy Waldron, "Dignity and Defamation: The Visibility of Hate," 123 Harvard Law Review 1596 (2010).

19. *Virginia v. Black*, 538 U.S. 343 (2003).

20. *R.A.V. v. City of St. Paul*, 505 U.S. 377 (1992).

21. *Collin v. Smith*, 578 F.2d 1197 (1978).

22. *Beauharnais v. Illinois*, 343 U.S. 250 (1952).

23. See Canadian Charter of Rights and Freedoms, Article 1, and the Constitution of South Africa, section 36(1).

24. ICCPR Article 20 reads: "1. Any propaganda for war shall be prohibited by law. 2. Any advocacy of national, racial or religious hatred that

constitutes incitement to discrimination, hostility or violence shall be prohibited by law."

25. ICERD, Article 4(a): "States Parties [to the Convention] . . . [s] hall declare an offence punishable by law all dissemination of ideas based on racial superiority or hatred, incitement to racial discrimination."

26. It is interesting to contrast the response of two signatory states to their obligations under ICERD. In 1994, at the time of the Convention's ratification, the United States entered a reservation: "[T]he Constitution and laws of the United States contain extensive protections of individual freedom of speech. . . . Accordingly, the United States does not accept any obligation under this Convention . . . to restrict those rights, through the adoption of legislation or any other measures, to the extent that they are protected by the Constitution and laws of the United States."

Contrast with this the reservation entered by the government of Australia at the time it ratified the ICERD in 1975: "The Government of Australia . . . declares that Australia is not at present in a position specifically to treat as offences all the matters covered by article 4(a) of the Convention. . . . It is the intention of the Australian Government, at the first suitable moment, to seek from Parliament legislation specifically implementing the terms of article 4(a)."

We see here a difference in mentality with regard to the wisdom (or otherwise) of the international community on these matters. For an excellent framework for understanding the tensions between international and national human-rights (and constitutional-rights) provisions, see Gerald Neuman, "Human Rights and Constitutional Rights: Harmony and Dissonance," *Stanford Law Review* 55 (2003), 1863.

27. See Ronald Dworkin, Foreword, in *Extreme Speech and Democracy,* ed. Ivan Hare and James Weinstein (Oxford University Press, 2009), v.

28. See Salman Rushdie, *The Satanic Verses* (Viking Press, 1988). See also Jeremy Waldron, "Religion and the Imagination in a Global Com-

munity: A Discussion of the Salman Rushdie Affair," *Times Literary Supplement* (March 10–16, 1989), 248 and 260; reprinted in Jeremy Waldron, *Liberal Rights: Collected Papers, 1981–91* (Cambridge University Press, 1993), 134, under the title "Rushdie and Religion."

2. Anthony Lewis's *Freedom for the Thought That We Hate*

1. This chapter is an expanded version of my review of Anthony Lewis's book *Freedom for the Thought That We Hate*. The review was published as Jeremy Waldron, "Free Speech and the Menace of Hysteria," in the *New York Review of Books* 55 (May 29, 2008). Page numbers in the text refer to Lewis, *Freedom for the Thought That We Hate: A Biography of the First Amendment* (Basic Books, 2007).

2. This letter is cited by Lewis at p. 11.

3. *Case of Lyon*, Whart. St. Tr. 333, 15 F. Cas. 1183 (C.C.Vt. 1798).

4. *U.S. v. Haswell*, Whart. St. Tr. 684, 26 F. Cas. 218 (C.C.Vt. 1800).

5. See John R. Howe, Jr., "Republican Thought and the Political Violence of the 1790s," *American Quarterly* 19 (1967), 147.

6. *Commonwealth v. Kneeland* 20 Pick. 206 (Mass. 1838).

7. Sir William Blackstone, *Commentaries on the Laws of England*, vol. 4, ch. 4 (Cavendish Publishing, 2001), 46.

8. *Updegraph v. Commonwealth*, 1824 WL 2393 Pa. (1824).

9. *Schenck v. United States*, 249 U.S. 47 (1919).

10. *Stromberg v. California*, 283 U.S. 359 (1931).

11. *Abrams v. United States*, 250 U.S. 616 (1919).

12. Judge George M. Bourquin in the Montana sedition cases. See also Arnon Gutfeld, "The Ves Hall Case, Judge Bourquin, and the Sedition Act of 1918," *Pacific Historical Review* 37 (1968), 163.

13. Justice Breyer in a concurring opinion in *Bartnicki v. Vopper* 532 U.S. 514 (2000).

14. *Beauharnais v. Illinois*, 343 U.S. 250 (1952).

15. *New York Times Co. v. Sullivan* 376 U.S. 254, at 270 (1964).

16. Justice Robert H. Jackson's term in his dissenting opinion in *Beauharnais v. Illinois,* at 287.

17. *Brandenburg v. Ohio,* 395 U.S. 444 (1969).

3. Why Call Hate Speech Group Libel?

1. See, e.g., Heidi M. Hurd and Michael S. Moore, "Punishing Hatred and Prejudice," *Stanford Law Review* 56 (2004).

2. My emphasis. The phrasing is from Canada's Criminal Code 1985, Section 319(1). Consider also the reference to "advocacy of national, racial or religious hatred" in article 20(1) of the International Covenant on Civil and Political Rights.

3. My emphasis. The phrasing is from section 18(1) of the United Kingdom's Public Order Act 1986 (as amended).

4. Robert Post, "Hate Speech," in *Extreme Speech and Democracy,* ed. Ivan Hare and James Weinstein (Oxford University Press, 2009), 123 and 125.

5. Post (ibid., 124n) cites Burke's aphorism, "They will never love where they ought to love who do not hate where they ought to hate," and Stephen's statement, "I think it highly desirable that criminals should be hated [and] that the punishments inflicted on them should be so contrived as to give expression to that hatred" (ibid.). Post also alludes (at 130) to Lord Devlin's infamous claim that "[n]o society can do without intolerance, indignation and disgust."

6. Opponents of hate speech regulation sometimes say that these laws are targeted at what people can say in bars or at the dinner table, and occasionally they cite examples of people being prosecuted for what they thought they were saying just among friends. See, e.g., Carly Weeks, "Conversation Cops Step in to School Students," *Globe and Mail* (Canada), November 19, 2008. Whatever the case with high school and campus codes, it is worth noting that many of the best-drafted hate

speech laws make an exception for conversations conducted in private. Section 18(2) of Britain's Public Order Act 1986 says that while "[a]n offence under this section may be committed in a public or a private place," nevertheless "no offence is committed where the words or behaviour are used by a person inside a dwelling and are not heard or seen except by other persons in that or another dwelling."

7. *Kunz v. New York,* 340 U.S. 290, 299 (1951) (Jackson, J., dissenting).

8. See, e.g., Charles R. Lawrence III, "If He Hollers Let Him Go: Regulating Racist Speech on Campus," *Duke Law Journal* (1990), 431, at 455.

9. Catharine A. MacKinnon, *Only Words* (Harvard University Press, 1993), 30.

10. See also Pascal Mbongo, "Hate Speech, Extreme Speech, and Collective Defamation in French Law," in Hare and Weinstein, eds., *Extreme Speech and Democracy,* 221, at 227, for the terms of the article prohibiting defamation of a group. Professor Mbongo classifies much French legislation of this kind as "penal suppression of abuse and defamation on grounds of race and religious belief" (ibid., 229–230).

11. Section 19(1) of Manitoba's Defamation Act prohibits "[t]he publication of a libel against a race, religious creed or sexual orientation, likely to expose persons belonging to the race, professing the religious creed, or having the sexual orientation to hatred, contempt or ridicule, and tending to raise unrest or disorder among the people."

12. See, e.g., Joseph Tanenhaus, "Group Libel," *Cornell Law Quarterly* 35 (1950), 261.

13. Harry Kalven, *The Negro and the First Amendment* (Ohio State University Press, 1965), 7.

14. *Beauharnais v. Illinois,* 343 U.S. 250, 253–254 (1952).

15. See "Note, Statutory Prohibition of Group Defamation," *Columbia Law Review* 47 (1947), 595.

16. My emphasis. This statement of aim is quoted in *Striking a Bal-*

ance: Hate Speech, Freedom of Expression and Non-Discrimination, ed. Sandra Colliver (Human Rights Centre, University of Essex, 1992), at 326.

17. Nadine Strossen, "Balancing the Rights to Freedom of Expression and Equality," in Colliver, ed., *Striking a Balance,* at 302.

18. In Chapter 1 of *Only Words* (a chapter whose title is "Defamation and Discrimination"), Catharine MacKinnon offers a different critique of the use of "defamation" in free-speech issues. In the United States, she says, calling harmful expression "defamation" confirms its protected status as speech; this makes it much more difficult to articulate objections based on direct harm and discrimination (ibid., 11 and 38). This, for MacKinnon, is particularly true of pornography, her main topic in *Only Words.* On the other hand, characterizing her own role in the *Keegstra* case in Canada (*R. v. Keegstra* [1990] 3 S.C.R. 697—a case of anti-Semitic speech by a schoolteacher that I shall discuss in more detail below), MacKinnon made use of the idea of group defamation and connected it affirmatively to discrimination and inequality: "We argued that group defamation is a verbal form inequality takes" (ibid., 99).

19. James Weinstein, "Extreme Speech, Public Order and Democracy," in Hare and Weinstein, eds., *Extreme Speech and Democracy,* 23, at 59.

20. Section 2 of the Alien and Sedition Acts, dated July 14, 1798 (Ch. 74, 1 Stat. 596), states: "[I]f any person shall write, print, utter or publish, or shall cause or procure to be written, printed, uttered or published . . . any false, scandalous and malicious writing or writings against the government of the United States, or either house of the Congress of the United States, or the President of the United States, with intent to defame the said government, or either house of the said Congress, or the said President, or to bring them, or either of them, into contempt or disrepute; or to excite against them, or either or any of them, the hatred of the good people of the United States, or to stir up sedition within the United States, or to excite any unlawful combinations therein, for op-

posing or resisting any law of the United States, or any act of the President of the United States, done in pursuance of any such law, or of the powers in him vested by the constitution of the United States, or to resist, oppose, or defeat any such law or act, or to aid, encourage or abet any hostile designs of any foreign nation against the United States, their people or government, then such person, being thereof convicted before any court of the United States having jurisdiction thereof, shall be punished by a fine not exceeding two thousand dollars, and by imprisonment not exceeding two years." (This statute expired in 1801.)

21. But for a useful and reasonably sympathetic account, see John C. Miller, *Crisis in Freedom: The Alien and Sedition Acts* (Little, Brown, 1951).

22. On attempts to have the Alien and Sedition Acts "nullified" at the state level, see Gordon S. Wood, *Empire of Liberty: A History of the Early Republic* (Oxford University Press, 2009), 269–270 (concerning the period 1789–1815).

23. William Blackstone, *Commentaries on the Laws of England*, vol. 4, ch. 4 (Cavendish Publishing, 2001), 46.

24. *Commonwealth v. Kneeland* 20 Pick. 206 (Mass. 1838).

25. *Updegraph v. Commonwealth* 1824 WL 2393 Pa. 1824.

26. *R. v. Curl* (1727) 2 Strange 788, 93 Eng. Rep. 849. See Colin Manchester, "A History of the Crime of Obscene Libel," *Journal of Legal History* 12 (1991), 36, at 38–40. There is a helpful discussion also in Leonard Williams Levy, *Blasphemy: Verbal Offense against the Sacred, from Moses to Salman Rushdie* (University of North Carolina Press, 1995), 306–308.

27. 1826 C & P 414. See also Manchester, "A History of the Crime of Obscene Libel," 44.

28. See the discussion in Chapter 2 of *Lyon's Case*, Whart. St. Tr. 333, 15 F. Cas. 1183 (C.C.Vt. 1798).

29. 4 Cranch C.C. 683, 25 F.Cas. 684 C.C.D.C. 1836. March Term 1836.

30. The book is dated 1596, and its listed title is *A Libell of Spanish*

Lies: Found at the sacke of Cales, discoursing the fight in the West Indies, twixt the English nauie being fourteene ships and pinasses, and a fleete of twentie saile of the king of Spaines, and of the death of Sir Francis Drake. With an answere briefely confuting the Spanish lies, and a short relation of the fight according to truth, written by Henrie Sauile Esquire, employed captaine in one of her Maiesties shippes, in the same seruice against the Spaniard. And also an approbation of this discourse, by Sir Thomas Baskeruile, then generall of the English fleete in that seruice: auowing the maintenance thereof, personally in armes against Don Bernaldino."

31. Civil Code, §45, quoted by Philip Wittenberg, *Dangerous Words: A Guide to the Law of Libel* (Columbia University Press, 1947), 7. The phrase seems to come originally from W. Blake Odgers, *A Digest of the Law of Libel and Slander:* see *Staub v. Van Benthuysen,* 36 La.Ann. 467, 1884 WL 7852, La., 1884: "A libel is any publication whether in writing, printing, picture, effigy, or other fixed representation to the eye which exposes any person to hatred, contempt, ridicule, or obloquy, or which causes him to be shunned or avoided, or which has a tendency to injure him in his occupation. *Odgers on Libel and Slander,* 7, 20."

32. *Ostrowe v. Lee,* 256 N.Y. 36, 39, 175 N.E. 505, 506 (1931), quoting from *Harman v. Delany,* Fitzg. 253, 94 Eng. Rep. 743 (1729): "words published in writing are actionable, which would not be so from a bare speaking of the same words, because a libel disperses and perpetuates the scandal."

33. In the case of *Curl* (the 1727 case concerning the libel *Venus in the Cloisters*), this was crucial to an understanding of why Curl's obscenity was a matter for the temporal courts, rather than for a spiritual tribunal set up by a bishop. "The Spiritual Courts punish only personal spiritual defamation by words; if it is reduced to writing, it is a temporal offence. . . . This is surely worse," said Reynolds, J., "than *Sir Charles Sedley's case,* who only exposed himself to the people then present, who might choose

whether they would look upon him or not; whereas this book goes all over the kingdom." (*R. v. Curl,* 2 Strange 788, 93 Eng. Rep. 849, at 850–851.)

34. Crimes Act 1961, section 211, repealed by Defamation Act 1992, section 56(2).

35. For a discussion of *scandalum magnatum,* see John C. Lassiter, "Defamation of Peers: The Rise and Decline of the Action for *Scandalum Magnatum,* 1497–1773," *American Journal of Legal History* 22 (1978), 216.

36. Immanuel Kant, *The Metaphysics of Morals,* trans. Mary Gregor (Cambridge University Press, 1991), 139 (6: 329–330 in the Prussian Academy edition of Kant's works).

37. Section 224a of Division 1 of the Illinois Criminal Code, Ill. Rev. Stat. 1949: "It shall be unlawful for any person, firm or corporation to manufacture, sell, or offer for sale, advertise or publish, present or exhibit in any public place in this state any lithograph, moving picture, play, drama or sketch, which publication or exhibition portrays depravity, criminality, unchastity, or lack of virtue of a class of citizens of any race, color, creed or religion which said publication or exhibition exposes the citizens of any race, color, creed or religion to contempt, derision, or obloquy or which is productive of breach of the peace or riots."

38. *Beauharnais v. Illinois,* 343 U.S. 250 (1952).

39. All emphasis, uppercase, and ellipses are in the original.

40. See *People v. Beauharnais* 408 Ill. 512, 97 N.E.2d 343 Ill. (1951).

41. For discussion at the time, see Joseph Tanenhaus, "Group Libel and Free Speech," *Phylon* 13 (1952), 215.

42. *Beauharnais v. Illinois* 343 U.S. 250 (1952), at 274 (Black, J., dissenting).

43. *Beauharnais v. Illinois* 343 U.S. 250 (1952), at 284 (Douglas, J., dissenting).

44. However, for the objection that the court in *Beauharnais* failed to confront the issues in the case using the idea of equality, see MacKinnon, *Only Words,* 81–84.

45. Nadine Strossen, "Balancing the Rights to Freedom of Expression and Equality," in Colliver, ed., *Striking a Balance,* at 303.

46. See *Bevins v. Prindable,* 39 F.Supp. 708, at 710, E.D.Ill., June 17, 1941.

47. *People v. Beauharnais* 408 Ill. 512 (1951), at 517–518. "The libelous and inflammatory language used in said exhibit A was designed to breed hatred against the Negro race and is not of such character as entitles defendant to the protection of freedom of speech guaranteed by the State and Federal constitutions."

48. *Beauharnais v. Illinois* 343 U.S. 250 (1952), at 257–258.

49. Ibid., 292.

50. *Beauharnais v. Illinois,* 343 U.S. 250, 272 (1952) (Black, J., dissenting).

51. *R. v. Osborne,* W. Kel. 230, 25 Eng. Rep. 584 (1732).

52. Ibid., at 585.

53. See *R. v. Osborn,* 2 Barnardiston 138 and 166, 94 Eng. Rep. 406 and 425 for an acceptance of this as group libel. See also the ambiguous account of the same case embedded in the opinion in another case, *In re Bedford Charity,* (1819) 2 Swans 502, 36 Eng. Rep. 696, 717.

54. Joseph Tanenhaus, "Group Libel," *Cornell Law Quarterly* 35 (1949–1950), 261, at 266.

55. *Palmer v. Concord,* 48 N.H. 211 (1868).

56. *Sumner v. Buel,* 12 Johnson 475 (1815), at 478.

57. *People v. Beauharnais,* 408 Ill. 512 (1951) at 517.

58. *Beauharnais v. Illinois,* 343 U.S. 250, 263 (1952) (Frankfurter, J., for the court).

59. In this area, the fact/opinion mantra casts precious little light. It is plain that both the public peace and, in a broader sense, public order as I

understand it can be undermined by expressions of virulent opinion as much as by false imputations of fact.

60. *R. v. Keegstra*, [1990] 3 S.C.R. 697.

61. MacKinnon, *Only Words*, 99.

62. I discuss this case at the beginning of Jeremy Waldron, "Boutique Faith," *London Review of Books*, July 20, 2006 (reviewing John Durham Peters, *Courting the Abyss: Free Speech and the Liberal Tradition*).

63. See Evan P. Schultz, "Group Rights, American Jews, and the Failure of Group Libel Laws, 1913–1952," *Brooklyn Law Review* 66 (2000–2001), at 96.

64. See also Waldron, "Dignity and Rank," *European Journal of Sociology* 48 (2007), 201; and Waldron, "Dignity, Rank and Rights," in *The Tanner Lectures on Human Values*, vol. 29, ed. Suzan Young (University of Utah Press, 2011), 207.

65. See Immanuel Kant, *Groundwork to the Metaphysics of Morals*, trans. Mary Gregor (Cambridge University Press, 1998), 42–43 (4: 435 of the Prussian Academy edition of Kant's works): "In the kingdom of ends everything has either value or dignity. Whatever has a value can be replaced by something else which is equivalent; whatever, on the other hand, is above all value, and therefore admits of no equivalent, has a dignity. Whatever has reference to the general inclinations and wants of mankind has a market value; . . . but that which constitutes the condition under which alone anything can be an end in itself, this has not merely a relative worth, i.e., value, but an intrinsic worth, that is, dignity. Now morality is the condition under which alone a rational being can be an end in himself, since by this alone is it possible that he should be a legislating member in the kingdom of ends. Thus morality, and humanity as capable of it, is that which alone has dignity." (This Kantian sense of "dignity" is somewhat different from the one I mentioned in note 36 above.)

66. As Michael Ignatieff argued, in *Human Rights as Politics and Idol-*

atry (Princeton University Press, 2001), 166, dignity is mainly an individualist idea. True: we do on occasion talk of the dignity of nations or of peoples (see Waldron, "The Dignity of Groups," *Acta Juridica* [Cape Town, 2008], 66). I do not want to rule this out, but this is not what is involved when we talk about group libel.

67. I think, therefore, that it is a serious mistake to suggest, as Robert Post does in "Racist Speech, Democracy, and the First Amendment," *William and Mary Law Review* 32 (1991), at 294, that the difference between the laws of European countries that prohibit group defamation and American law, which on the whole does not, is that the latter tends to view groups as mere "collections of individuals," whose claims are no greater than those of their constituent members. That individualism is characteristic of the approach taken here, though I recognize—as Post does not—that lots of people can be harmed individually by what people say about the group.

68. *President of the Republic of South Africa v. Hugo*, 1997 (4) SA (CC) 1, at §41 (my emphasis).

69. See, e.g., *Dworkin v. Hustler Magazine Inc.*, 867 F.2d 1188, 1200 (9th Cir. 1989); and *Collin v. Smith*, 578 F.2d 1197, 1205 (7th Cir. 1978). On the other hand, one should consider the interesting and not unfavorable comments about *Beauharnais* in *Smith v. Collin*, 439 US 916 (1978), at 919 (Blackmun, J., dissenting from denial of certiorari).

70. Laurence H. Tribe observed, in *American Constitutional Law*, 2nd ed. (Foundation Press, 1988), at 926–927, that "subsequent cases seem to have sapped *Beauharnais* of much of its force."

71. Lewis, *Freedom for the Thought That We Hate*, 159.

72. *New York Times Co. v. Sullivan*, 376 U.S. 254, at 270 (1964).

73. "[O]bnoxious leaflet" is Justice Jackson's term in his dissenting opinion in *Beauharnais v. Illinois*, 343 U.S. 250, at 287 (1952).

74. *New York Times Co. v. Sullivan*, 376 U.S. 254, at 301 (1964).

75. Ibid., at 263–264 and note (1952), cited and approved in *New York*

Times Co. v. Sullivan, 376 U.S. 254, at 268 (1964), by Brennan, J., for the court.

76. *Nuxoll v. Indian Prairie School District,* 523 F3d 688, 672 (7th Circuit, 2008).

77. But see the excellent discussion in Samuel Walker, *Hate Speech: The History of an American Controversy* (University of Nebraska Press, 1994), especially in ch. 5: "The Curious Rise and Fall of Group Libel in America, 1942–1952."

4. The Appearance of Hate

1. Actually the phrase is much older than Rawls's use of it. Denis Diderot used "well-ordered society" several times in "Observations sur le Nakaz," in *Diderot: Political Writings,* ed. John Hope Mason and Robert Wokler (Cambridge University Press, 1992), 87 (§5) and 128 (§81).

2. See John Rawls, *Political Liberalism* (Columbia University Press, 1993), 35 and 43–46. Parenthetical numbers in the text, preceded by *PL,* are references to this work.

3. John Rawls, "Kantian Constructivism in Moral Theory" (1975), in John Rawls, *Collected Papers,* ed. Samuel Freeman (Harvard University Press, 1999), at 355. See also *PL,* 66, suggesting that in a well-ordered society "citizens accept and know that others likewise accept those principles, and this knowledge in turn is publicly recognized."

4. In Rawls, "Kantian Constructivism in Moral Theory," at 355: "Our society is not well-ordered: the public conception of justice and its understanding of freedom and equality are still in dispute."

5. George Wright, "Dignity and Conflicts of Constitutional Values: The Case of Free Speech and Equal Protection," *San Diego Law Review* 43 (2006), 527, concluded that Rawls has really "not contributed substantially to the underlying logic of genuine respect or civility, in hate speech or any other context." Richard H. Fallon, "Individual Rights and the

Powers of Government," *Georgia Law Review* 27 (1993), at 351–352, argued that "the basic rights that Rawls derives—including rights to freedom of speech and religious autonomy—are so abstract as to settle few practical questions. Does freedom of speech encompass hate-speech directed at racial or religious minorities? . . . To answer questions such as these, a fuller set of considerations must be brought to bear." However, see also the discussion in T. M. Scanlon, "Adjusting Rights and Balancing Values," *Fordham Law Review* 72 (2004), 1485–86, of whether hate speech might be dealt with under the heading of the fair value of liberty. And see the suggestion in Richard Delgado and Jean Stefancic, "Four Observations about Hate Speech," *Wake Forest Law Review* 44 (2009), at 368, that a Rawlsian should approach hate speech through the difference principle: "one of the parties is more disadvantaged than the other, so . . . Rawls's difference principle suggests that . . . we break the tie in the victim's favor."

6. For Rawls's admiration of Kalven, see *PL,* 342–344. Kalven's own discussion of group libel in Harry Kalven, *The Negro and the First Amendment* (Ohio State University Press, 1965), 7–64, is nuanced, thoughtful, and complicated. Though he criticized the decision in *Beauharnais,* Kalven took a sophisticated view of its relation to the decision in *New York Times v. Sullivan.*

7. See *Ferdinand Nahimana v. The Prosecutor,* Case no. ICTR-99-52-A, Appeals Chamber (International Criminal Tribunal for Rwanda), partially dissenting judgment of Judge Meron at 374 (see esp. §§4–5 (pp. 375–376) and §§9–21 (pp. 378–381). See Catharine A. MacKinnon, "*Prosecutor v. Nahimana, Barayagwiza, and Ngeze* at International Criminal Tribunal for Rwanda, Appeals Chamber," *American Journal of International Law* 103 (2009), 97; and (for a different view) Susan Benesch, "Vile Crime or Inalienable Right: Defining Incitement to Genocide," *Virginia Journal of International Law* 48 (2008), 485.

8. Richard Delgado and Jean Stefancic, *Understanding Words That Wound* (Westview, 2004), 142.

9. Catharine MacKinnon, *Only Words* (Harvard University Press, 1993), 17.

10. Ibid., 25–26.

11. I have learned a great deal from Professor MacKinnon's discussion of pornography and her characterizations of the overlap (and the differences) between hate speech and pornography issues. I have also learned a great deal about the general character of this debate from the way in which MacKinnon's opponents have distorted and evaded the force of her arguments. I am grateful to MacKinnon for a number of helpful conversations on these issues.

12. Edmund Burke, *Reflections on the Revolution in France,* ed. J. C. D. Clark (Stanford University Press, 2001), 241 and 239.

13. Political aesthetics is taken very seriously in Ajume Wingo's excellent book, *Veil Politics in Liberal Democratic States* (Cambridge University Press, 2003), the first chapter of which has an admirable account of the presence and importance of monuments in modern society.

14. This is the paradox noted by Karl Marx in "On the Jewish Question," in *Nonsense upon Stilts: Bentham, Burke, and Marx on the Rights of Man,* ed. Jeremy Waldron (Methuen, 1987), 138–139.

15. Doreen Carvajel, "Sarkozy Backs Drive to Eliminate the Burqa," *New York Times,* June 23, 2009, quotes the president of France as saying: "The burqa . . . is a sign of the subjugation, of the submission, of women. . . . I want to say solemnly that it will not be welcome on our territory." Since Sarkozy spoke, a ban on the wearing of the burqa in public has come into effect in France.

16. I am grateful to Wendy Brown for this way of putting it.

17. West's Code of Georgia §16-11-38: "Wearing masks, hoods, etc." There are exceptions for gas masks, masquerade costumes, and safety devices.

18. See the discussion in Wayne R. Allen, "Klan, Cloth and Constitution: Anti-Mask Laws and the First Amendment," *Georgia Law Review* 25 (1991), 819.

19. For these terms, see John Rawls, *A Theory of Justice,* rev. ed. (Harvard University Press, 1999), 7–8.

20. See ibid., 109–112, on the circumstances of justice. On "limited strength of will," see H. L. A. Hart, *The Concept of Law,* rev. ed. (Clarendon Press, 1994), 197–198.

21. Rawls, *A Theory of Justice,* 211.

22. Ibid..

23. See Emile Durkheim, *The Division of Labor in Society,* trans. Lewis Coser (Free Press, 1997), 61. For an application to hate speech regulation of the Durkheimian idea of the expressive function of law, see Thomas David Jones, *Human Rights: Group Defamation, Freedom of Expression and the Law of Nations* (Martin Nijhoff, 1998), at 88.

24. My reference here to the fundamentals of justice is similar to, but not quite the same as, Rawls's idea of "constitutional essentials" (*PL,* 214 and 227). The idea is that some claims of justice are based on or presuppose others; some represent controversial developments of or extrapolations from others. The fundamentals of justice are the claims that lie at the foundations of these derivations and controversies. They include propositions establishing everyone's right to justice and elementary security, everyone's claim to have their welfare counted along with everyone else's welfare in the determination of social policy, and everyone's legal status as a rights-bearing member of society. They also include repudiations of particular claims of racial, sexual, and religious inequality that have historically provided grounds for denying these rights.

25. David Bromwich, *Politics by Other Means: Higher Education and Group Thinking* (Yale University Press, 1994), 157. See also George F. Will, *Statecraft as Soulcraft* (Touchstone Books, 1984), 87.

26. For a fine discussion of the details—the "microaggressions"—of racism, see Patricia Williams, *Seeing a Color-Blind Future: The Paradox of Race* (Farrar, Straus, and Giroux, 1998).

27. *R. v. Keegstra* [1990] 3 SCR 697.

28. See Stephen L. Darwall, "Two Kinds of Respect," *Ethics* 88 (1977), 36; and Darwall, *The Second-Person Standpoint: Morality, Respect, and Accountability* (Harvard University Press, 2006), esp. 122–123.

29. Darwall, "Two Kinds of Respect," 38.

30. MacKinnon, *Only Words*, 25.

31. Catharine A. MacKinnon, "Pornography as Defamation and Discrimination," *Boston University Law Review* 71 (1991), 793.

32. Ibid., 802–803. MacKinnon's reservations about the defamation model follow immediately in the article I am quoting—"When pornography's reality is examined against the terms of group defamation as a legal theory, some of the theory fits, but much of it does not" (ibid., 803)—and they can be seen also in MacKinnon, *Only Words*, at 11 and 38.

33. MacKinnon, "Pornography as Defamation and Discrimination," 802.

34. On the distinction between public goods whose ultimate payoff is collectively consumed and public goods that redound ultimately to the benefit of individuals, see also Joseph Raz, *The Morality of Freedom* (Clarendon Press, 1986), 199; and Jeremy Waldron, "Can Communal Goods Be Human Rights?" *Archives Européennes de Sociologie* 27 (1987), 294, reprinted in Waldron, *Liberal Rights: Collected Papers, 1981–1991* (Cambridge University Press, 1993). On public goods like security that have both aspects, see Jeremy Waldron, "Safety and Security," *Nebraska Law Review* 85 (2006), 454, reprinted in Waldron, *Torture, Terror and Trade-Offs: Philosophy for the White House* (Oxford University Press, 2010).

35. William Peirce Randel, *The Ku Klux Klan: A Century of Infamy* (Chilton Books, 1965), 224, quoted in Cedric Merlin Powell, "The Mythological Marketplace of Ideas: *R.A.V., Mitchell,* and Beyond," *Harvard Blackletter Law Journal* 12 (1995), at 32.

36. Quoted in Philippa Strum, *When the Nazis Came to Skokie: Freedom for Speech We Hate* (University Press of Kansas, 1999), 15.

37. See Derek Parfit, *Reasons and Persons* (Oxford University Press, 1984), ch. 3, entitled "Five Mistakes in Moral Mathematics."

38. For a discussion of the idea of self-application, see Henry M. Hart and Albert Sacks, *The Legal Process: Basic Problems in the Making and Application of Law,* ed. William N. Eskridge and Philip P. Frickey (Foundation Press, 1994), 120–121.

39. See, e.g., Ronald Dworkin, *Law's Empire* (Harvard University Press, 1986), pp. 295–301.

40. Rawls, *A Theory of Justice,* 109ff.

5. Protecting Dignity or Protection from Offense?

1. The intransitive sense involves violating a rule—as in the Book of Common Prayer's confession at Morning Prayer: "We have offended against thy holy laws."

2. See Jeremy Waldron, "Dignity, Rank and Rights," in *The Tanner Lectures on Human Values,* vol. 29, ed. Suzan Young (University of Utah Press, 2011), 207.

3. I have discussed this in Jeremy Waldron, "Inhuman and Degrading Treatment: The Words Themselves," *Canadian Journal of Law and Jurisprudence* 22 (2010), at 283–284; reprinted in Jeremy Waldron, *Torture, Terror, and Trade-Offs: Philosophy for the White House* (Oxford University Press, 2010), ch. 9, esp. 311–313.

4. *Regina (Burke) v. General Medical Council* (Official Solicitor intervening) [2005] QB 424, at §178.

5. *Lynch v. Knight* (1861) 11 Eng. Rep. 854 (H.L.) 863. See also Geoffrey Christopher Rapp, "Defense against Outrage and the Perils of Parasitic Torts," *Georgia Law Review* 45 (2010), 107.

6. *Wilkinson v. Downton* [1897] 2 QB 57, *Molien v. Kaiser Foundation Hospitals,* 27 Cal.3d 916, 616 P.2d 813 (1980).

7. See, e.g., *R.A.V. v. City of St. Paul* 505 U.S. 377 (1992) at 414

(White, J., concurring): "The mere fact that expressive activity causes hurt feelings, offense, or resentment does not render the expression unprotected." See also Nadine Strossen, "Regulating Racist Speech on Campus: A Modest Proposal?" 1990 *Duke Law Journal* 484, at 497–498: "Traditional civil libertarians recognize that [racist] speech causes psychic pain. We nonetheless agree with the decision of the Seventh Circuit in *Skokie* that this pain is a necessary price for a system of free expression."

8. This paragraph is adapted from something I wrote long ago, in a discussion of the views of John Stuart Mill—a discussion that began by thinking about the phenomenology associated with someone's being disturbed by viewing pornography. See Jeremy Waldron, "Mill and the Value of Moral Distress," *Political Studies* 35 (1987), at 410–411; reprinted in Jeremy Waldron, *Liberal Rights: Collected Papers, 1981–1991* (Cambridge University Press, 1993), at 115–116. I said there that it is wrong to assume we can disentangle, in someone's reaction to pornography, the elements of disapproval, the perception of threat, the perception of insult, the perception of symbol or representation, the vehemence of moral condemnation, the feeling of outrage, the elements of pity, contempt, outrage, pain, offense, sublimated guilt, uncomfortable pleasure, and so on. And so I tried to emphasize how sensitive we must be not to discount the importance of some of these feelings simply because we are uneasy about others.

9. See *Whitehouse v. Lemon* [1979] 2 WLR 281; *Whitehouse v. Gay News Ltd* [1979] AC 617; and *Gay News Ltd and Lemon v. United Kingdom* 5 EHRR 123 (1982), App. no. 8710/79.

10. See Ronald Dworkin, *Freedom's Law: The Moral Reading of the American Constitution* (Harvard University Press, 1996), 1–15. See also Jeremy Waldron, "Thoughtfulness and the Rule of Law," *British Academy Review* 18 (July 2011), available also online at ssrn.com/abstract=1759550.

11. See, e.g., Charles R. Lawrence, "If He Hollers Let Him Go: Regulating Racist Speech on Campus," *Duke Law Journal* 431 (1990), at 452–456. There Professor Lawrence writes eloquently about "the immediacy of the injurious impact of racial insults," the "visceral emotional response"—the "instinctive, defensive psychological reaction" of rage, flight, or paralysis, the "state of semi-shock, nauseous, dizzy," that more or less precludes any speech as a reaction.

12. *Kunz v. New York,* 340 U.S. 290, 299 (1951) (Jackson, J., dissenting).

13. See *Aguilar v. Avis Rent-a-Car System, Inc.,* 980 P.2d 846 (Cal. 1999), which upheld an injunction prohibiting use of racial epithets directed at Latino employees in their workplace. See also Lawrence, "If He Hollers Let Him Go." For a good though not uncritical discussion of campus speech codes, see Jon B. Gould, *Speak No Evil: The Triumph of Hate Speech Regulation* (University of Chicago Press, 2005).

14. I am most grateful to Joseph Singer for pressing this point in discussion after the Holmes Lectures at Harvard in 2009. See also Cynthia Estlund, "Freedom of Expression in the Workplace and the Problem of Discriminatory Harassment," *Texas Law Review* 75 (1997), 687.

15. Stephen Sedley, *Ashes and Sparks: Essays on Law and Justice* (Cambridge University Press, 2011), 400–401. I am grateful to Sedley for some discussion of these issues.

16. William Blackstone, *Commentaries on the Laws of England* (London: Cavendish Publishing, 2001), vol. 4, ch. 4, p. 46.

17. *Whitehouse v. Gay News Ltd and Lemon* [1979] AC 617, at 665.

18. *R. v. Chief Metropolitan Stipendiary Magistrate, ex parte Choudhury* [1991], 1 All ER, 306.

19. Religious and Racial Hatred Act 2006 (U.K.), sect. 1.

20. Criminal Justice and Immigration Act 2008 (U.K.), sect. 79(1): "The offences of blasphemy and blasphemous libel under the common law of England and Wales are abolished."

21. This is the definition given in the new section 29A which the 2006 statute inserted into the U.K.'s Public Order Act of 1986.

22. Public Order Act, sect. 29J, as amended by the 2006 statute.

23. This last case is particularly important for people in detention, whose lives and schedules of worship are utterly under the control of others. At Guantánamo Bay and elsewhere, the religious beliefs of Muslims have been perceived by their captors and interrogators as an opportunity for inflicting inhumane treatment, in order to break the spirit of those from whom they want to elicit information. Korans have been abused, for example, ripped up and flushed down a toilet in front of a detainee, eliciting from him a maddening combination of suffering, outrage, and heartbreak, which is thought to be exploitable as a "softening-up" process for interrogation. I believe that the deliberate infliction of this sort of distress is wrong and unlawful, and I have written about these abusive practices elsewhere. See Jeremy Waldron, "What Can Christian Teaching Add to the Debate about Torture?" *Theology Today* 63 (2006), at 341; reprinted in Waldron, *Torture, Terror and Trade-Offs*, 273–274. But the specific concerns about dignity, hate speech, and group libel that I am exploring in this book do not encompass these things.

24. See Jeremy Waldron, "The Dignity of Groups," *Acta Juridica* (Cape Town, 2008), 66.

25. Corinna Adam, "Protecting Our Lord," *New Statesman*, February 13, 2006 (originally published July 15, 1977): "'I simply had to protect Our Lord,' Mrs. Mary Whitehouse told me, in the Old Bailey coffee-bar, on the first day of the blasphemy trial." She was referring to a poem by James Kirkup that described necrophiliac acts performed upon the body of Jesus after his crucifixion.

26. However, there seems to have been a recent shift, as indicated in a recent Reuters news story. See Robert Evan, "Islamic Bloc Drops U.N. Drive on Defaming Religion," March 25, 2011, available online at in.reuters.com/article/2011/03/24/idINIndia-55861720110324 (accessed May 30,

2011): "Islamic countries set aside their 12-year campaign to have religions protected from 'defamation,' allowing the U.N. Human Rights Council to approve a plan to promote religious tolerance on Thursday. Western countries and their Latin American allies, strong opponents of the defamation concept, joined Muslim and African states in backing without vote the new approach that switches focus from protecting beliefs to protecting believers."

27. Jonathan Turley, "The Free World Bars Free Speech," *Washington Post*, April 12, 2009.

28. This is in section 29J, "Protection of Freedom of Expression," which the 2006 statute inserts into Part 3A of the Public Order Act.

29. See Lorenz Langer, "The Rise (and Fall?) of Defamation of Religions," *Yale Journal of International Law* 35 (2010), 257.

30. Originally published in the Danish newspaper *Jyllands-Posten* as Flemming Rose, "Muhammeds Ansigt" [Muhammed's Face], September 30, 2005.

31. Meital Pinto, "What Are Offences to Feelings Really About? A New Regulative Principle for the Multicultural Era," *Oxford Journal of Legal Studies* 30 (2010), 695, at 721.

32. I am grateful to Henning Koch for this point. See also Stéphanie Lagoutte, "The Cartoon Controversy in Context: Analyzing the Decision Not to Prosecute under Danish Law," *Brooklyn Journal of International Law* 33 (2008), 379, at 382.

33. But compare Ronald Dworkin, "The Right to Ridicule," *New York Review of Books*, March 23, 2006. Though Dworkin bitterly opposes laws against fomenting religious hatred, he began this article by saying: "The British and most of the American press have been right, on balance, not to republish the Danish cartoons that millions of furious Muslims protested against in violent and terrible destruction around the world. Reprinting would very likely have meant—and could still mean—more people killed and more property destroyed. It would have caused many British and American Muslims great pain because they would have been

told by other Muslims that the publication was intended to show contempt for their religion, and though that perception would in most cases
have been inaccurate and unjustified, the pain would nevertheless have
been genuine."

34. I argued this a long time ago in Jeremy Waldron, "A Right to Do
Wrong," *Ethics* 92 (1981), 21; reprinted in Waldron, *Liberal Rights,* ch. 3.

35. See Jeremy Waldron, "Too Important for Tact," *Times Literary
Supplement* (London), March 10–16, 1989, at 248 and 260; reprinted in
Waldron, *Liberal Rights,* at 134 (chapter entitled "Rushdie and Reli-
gion").

36. Book of Job 1:6–12.

37. Public Order Act, section 29J, as amended by the 2006 statute.

38. See Jeremy Waldron, "Cultural Identity and Civic Responsibility,"
in *Citizenship in Diverse Societies,* ed. Will Kymlicka and Wayne Norman (Oxford University Press, 2000), for a broader argument against
identity politics, along these lines.

39. I said, in that earlier work (ibid., 160): "It is widely—I think correctly—believed that this liberal task of securing proper respect for all
the interests that demand it becomes immeasurably more difficult when
identity is associated with culture whilst retaining the flavour of rights.
It is hard enough to set up a legal framework that furnishes respect for
persons as individuals, and which ensures that the interests and freedoms basic to individual identity are not sacrificed for the sake of the
common good. But if respect for an individual also requires respect for
the culture in which his identity has been formed, and if that respect is
demanded in the uncompromising and non-negotiable way in which respect for rights is demanded, then the task may become very difficult
indeed, particularly in circumstances where different individuals in the
same society have formed their identities in different cultures."

40. C. Edwin Baker, "Harm, Liberty, and Free Speech," *Southern California Law Review* 70 (1997), 979, at 1019–20.

41. See *Employment Division of Oregon v. Smith,* 494 U.S. 872 (1990),

in which the Supreme Court considered whether generally applicable narcotics laws required strict scrutiny in light of their impact on the petitioner's sacramental use of peyote. See also Religious Freedom Restoration Act 1993 (codified at 42 U.S.C. §2000bb), in which Congress purported to insist on strict scrutiny for cases like this, in defiance of the Supreme Court decision in *Smith*.

42. Rebecca Mason, "Reorienting Deliberation: Identity Politics in Multicultural Societies," *Studies in Social Justice* 4 (2010), 7.

43. I am particularly grateful to Timothy Garton Ash for pressing me on this point.

44. For a brusque critique of dignity talk, see Steven Pinker, "The Stupidity of Dignity," *New Republic*, May 28, 2008.

45. Arthur Schopenhauer, *The Basis of Morality*, trans. Arthur Brodrick Bullock (Swan Sonnenschein, 1903), 129: "For behind that imposing formula they concealed their lack, not to say, of a real ethical basis, but of any basis at all which was possessed of an intelligible meaning; supposing cleverly enough that their readers would be so pleased to see themselves invested with such a 'dignity' that they would be quite satisfied."

46. Christopher McCrudden, "Human Dignity in Human Rights Interpretation," *European Journal of International Law* 19 (2008), 655, at 678.

47. See Immanuel Kant, *Groundwork of the Metaphysics of Morals*, ed. Mary Gregor (Cambridge University Press, 1998), 42–43 (4: 434–435 of the Prussian Academy edition of Kant's works); Pope John Paul II's encyclical *Evangelium Vitae* (March 25, 1995), para. 3; Ronald Dworkin, *Justice for Hedgehogs* (Harvard University Press, 2011), 191ff.; Jeremy Waldron, "Dignity and Rank," *Archives Européennes de Sociologie* 48 (2007), 201.

48. Nor am I suggesting that it be used as a judicial principle: compare the debate in Canada about the use of dignity as a guiding principle

in discrimination law. Recently the Supreme Court of Canada had occasion to say that dignity is "an abstract and subjective notion ... confusing and difficult to apply" (*R. v. Kapp* [2008] SCC 41 at §22). But the court emphasized that this does not mean the concept is useless in our understanding of the values that law protects.

49. James Weinstein and Ivan Hare seem to assume—wrongly, in my view—that this is what the dignitarian case for hate speech legislation must presuppose. See "General Introduction: Free Speech, Democracy, and the Suppression of Extreme Speech Past and Present," in *Extreme Speech and Democracy,* ed. Ivan Hare and James Weinstein (Oxford University Press, 2009), 1, at 6–7.

50. Of course, the human-dignity principle is used as a constitutional principle in other contexts, such as in American Eighth Amendment jurisprudence: see *Trop v. Dulles,* 356 U.S. 86 (1958), at 100 (Warren, C.J., for the Court); and *Gregg v. Georgia* 428 US 153 (1976), at 173 and 182–183 (plurality opinion). But I am not relying on that here.

51. There is a good critique of McCrudden's analysis in Paolo G. Carozza, "Human Dignity and Judicial Interpretation of Human Rights: A Reply," *European Journal of International Law* 19 (2008), 931.

52. Ronald Dworkin talks about free speech "and the dignity it confirms" in his foreword to Hare and Weinstein, eds., *Extreme Speech and Democracy,* viii.

53. David Feldman, "Human Dignity as a Legal Value: Part 1," *Public Law* [1999], 682, speaks (at 685) of "[t]he perplexing capacity of dignity to pull in several directions."

54. In other contexts, the notion of dignity is present on both sides of a human-rights argument: consider the French "dwarf-throwing" case, where the Conseil d'Etat said that closing down the exhibition was a legitimate way of protecting human dignity, while the dwarf in question claimed that his dignity was compromised by this paternalistic intrusion into his ability to contract for the use of his body for entertainment pur-

poses. See the decision in *Commune Morsange-sur-Orge* CE, Ass., 27 October 1995, 372, and the decision of the U.N. Human Rights Committee in the same case, under the title *Wackenheim v. France,* U.N. Human Rights Committee, 75th session, July 15, 2002 (2002). Again, there is no contradiction here.

6. C. Edwin Baker and the Autonomy Argument

1. For Baker's claims about free-speech absolutism, see C. Edwin Baker, *Human Liberty and Freedom of Speech* (Oxford University Press, 1989), 161ff. See also C. Edwin Baker, "Harm, Liberty, and Free Speech," *Southern California Law Review* 70 (1997), 979. At 981: "[T]he thesis of this article is that the harmfulness of a person's speech itself never justifies a legal limitation on the person's freedom of speech."

2. Holmes's exact words in *Schenck v. U.S.,* 249 U.S. 47 (1919), at 52, were these: "The most stringent protection of free speech would not protect a man in falsely shouting fire in a theatre."

3. But there was an incident in 1913, recorded in Woodie Guthrie's ballad "1913 Massacre," in which a provocateur shouted "Fire!" at a party given for the children of striking miners in Calumet, Michigan. In the ensuing stampede, seventy-three people were killed, most of them children. See Larry D. Lankton, *Cradle to Grave: Life, and Work and Death at the Lake Superior Copper Mines* (Oxford University Press, 1991). This has been cited as the background to Justice Holmes's famous image: see Baker, "Harm, Liberty, and Free Speech," at 982–983.

4. See Joseph Raz, *The Morality of Freedom* (Oxford University Press, 1986), 380: "[H]as autonomy any value qua autonomy when it is abused? Is the autonomous wrongdoer a morally better person than the non-autonomous wrongdoer? Our intuitions rebel against such a view. It is surely the other way round. The wrongdoing casts a darker shadow on its perpetrator if it is autonomously done by him." See also the discussion in Jeremy Waldron, "Autonomy and Perfectionism in Raz's *The*

Morality of Freedom," *Southern California Law Review* 62 (1989), 1097. But as far as I know, Raz himself does not apply this doctrine to the case of hate speech. This may be on account of a view that he also holds: that even if autonomy has no value when exercised in the choice of an option that is morally wrong, still we cannot trust our lawmakers to distinguish correctly between right and wrong options.

5. This insistence on the gravity of the harm that is in prospect is doubly justified, because in the best-drafted hate speech regulations, legislators go out of their way to concentrate on the most serious cases and install various filters—such as the requirement in the United Kingdom that no prosecution may be brought under the racial-hatred provisions without the consent of the attorney general. See Public Order Act 1986 (U.K.), section 27(1).

6. See, e.g., Ronald Dworkin, Foreword, in *Extreme Speech and Democracy,* ed. Ivan Hare and James Weinstein (Oxford University Press, 2009), vi.

7. A similar conclusion is reached by Martha Minow, "Regulating Hatred: Whose Speech, Whose Crimes, Whose Power?" *UCLA Law Review* 47 (2000), 1261–62: "[T]oo often, the advocates of the First Amendment ignore or try to minimize the ways in which slurs and bias-based comments both produce psychological damage for individuals and perpetuate the dehumanization of members of particular groups (which in turn can invite further degradation and violence). . . . Acknowledging such harms might seem threatening to those who believe that protection for freedom of expression and thought is or should be absolute. Yet, it is only honest to acknowledge the harms first, and then decide what to do."

8. Robert Post, in his article "Racist Speech, Democracy, and the First Amendment," *William and Mary Law Review* 32 (1991), at 278–279, talks about the need for "serious engagement with the question of why we really care about protecting freedom of expression." He writes (and I agree with him): "What is most disappointing about the expanding lit-

erature proposing restrictions on racist speech is the palpable absence of that engagement. The most original and significant articles in the genre concentrate on uncovering and displaying the manifold harms of racist communications; the harms of regulating expression are on the whole perfunctorily dismissed. . . . I agree, of course, that the question of regulating racist speech ought not to be settled simply by reference to present doctrine. But it is equally important that the question ought not to be settled without serious engagement with the values embodied in that doctrine." Post's own work is a model in this regard, not only for his engagement with free-speech values but also for his open and sustained engagement with the arguments in favor of the regulation of hate speech.

9. See, e.g., Alexander Tsesis, "Dignity and Speech: The Regulation of Hate Speech in a Democracy," *Wake Forest Law Review* 44 (2009), at 499–501: "Hate speakers seek to intimidate targeted groups from participating in the deliberative process. Diminished political participation because of safety concerns, in turn, stymies policy and legislative debates. . . . When harassing expression is disguised as political expression it adds nothing to democratic debate." See also Mari J. Matsuda, "Public Response to Racist Speech: Considering the Victim's Story," *Michigan Law Review* 87 (1989), 2320.

10. C. Edwin Baker, "Autonomy and Hate Speech," in Hare and Weinstein, eds., *Extreme Speech and Democracy,* at 143.

11. Laurence H. Tribe, *American Constitutional Law* (Foundation Press, 1988), 790, quoting the U.S. Supreme Court in *Police Department of Chicago v. Mosley,* 408 U.S. 92, 95–96 (1972).

12. For a helpful discussion of the antinomies surrounding this distinction, see R. George Wright, "Content-Based and Content-Neutral Regulation of Speech: The Limitations of a Common Distinction," *University of Miami Law Review* 60 (2006), 333.

13. Public Order Act 1986, section 18(1): "A person who uses *threatening, abusive or insulting words or behaviour,* or displays any *written mate-*

rial which is threatening, abusive or insulting, is guilty of an offence if—(a) he intends thereby to stir up racial hatred, or (b) having regard to all the circumstances, racial hatred is likely to be stirred up thereby" (my emphasis). However, a later savings clause, section 18(5), does seem to emphasize adverbial elements that are independent of content: "A person who is not shown to have intended to stir up racial hatred is not guilty of an offence under this section if he did not intend his words or behaviour, or the written material, to be, and was not aware that it might be, threatening, abusive or insulting."

14. Geoffrey Stone, "Content-Neutral Restriction," *University of Chicago Law Review* 54 (1987), at 56–57. See also Geoffrey R. Stone, "Content Regulation and the First Amendment," *William and Mary Law Review* 25 (1983), at 208–212.

15. I dwelt on this in more detail with regard to the impact of cross-burning, in the latter part of Chapter 4.

16. Stone, "Content-Neutral Restriction," at 55, citing Alexander Meiklejohn, *Political Freedom: The Constitutional Powers of the People* (Greenwood Press, 1979), 27.

17. *R. v. Keegstra* [1990] 3 SCR 697.

18. See the discussion in Vincent Blasi, "Holmes and the Marketplace of Ideas," *Supreme Court Review* (2004), 1.

19. Ibid., 6–13. See also Darren Bush, "The 'Marketplace of Ideas': Is Judge Posner Chasing Don Quixote's Windmills?" *Arizona State Law Journal* 32 (2000), 1107; and Paul H. Brietzke, "How and Why the Marketplace of Ideas," *Valparaiso University Law Review* 31 (1997), 951.

20. Ivan Hare and James Weinstein, "General Introduction," in Hare and Weinstein, eds., *Extreme Speech and Democracy*, 6.

21. Dworkin, *Taking Rights Seriously*, 198 (my emphasis).

22. Ibid., 191ff.

23. Cf. Dworkin's celebrated "Lexington Avenue" example (ibid., 269).

24. Compare Charles Taylor's "fiendish defense of Albania" (saying

that although Albania has restrictions on freedom of worship, it balances that by having fewer traffic lights) in his essay "What's Wrong with Negative Liberty?" *in The Idea of Freedom: Essays in Honour of Isaiah Berlin* (Oxford University Press, 1979), 183.

25. Baker, "Harm, Liberty, and Free Speech," 992.

26. Immanuel Kant, *Groundwork to the Metaphysics of Morals,* ed. Mary Gregor (Cambridge University Press, 1997), 41–42 (4:433–435 of the Prussian Academy edition of Kant's works).

27. C. Edwin Baker, "Autonomy and Informational Privacy, or Gossip: The Central Meaning of the First Amendment," *Social Philosophy and Policy* 21 (2004), at 224.

28. See Baker, "Autonomy and Hate Speech," 142–146; Baker, "Autonomy and Informational Privacy, or Gossip," 205ff.; Baker, "Harm, Liberty, and Free Speech," 979ff.; and Baker, *Human Liberty and Freedom of Speech,* ch. 4.

29. Baker, "Autonomy and Informational Privacy, or Gossip," at 225–226.

30. See the discussion in Jeremy Waldron, "One Law for All: The Logic of Cultural Accommodation," *Washington and Lee Law Review* 59 (2002), 3, at 3–35.

31. Baker, "Harm, Liberty, and Free Speech," 1019–20.

32. Baker, "Autonomy and Hate Speech," 143.

33. For a review of the conventional theories, and for some valuable proposals, see T. M. Scanlon, "A Theory of Freedom of Expression," in his collection *The Difficulty of Tolerance: Essays in Political Philosophy* (Cambridge University Press, 2003), 6.

34. Baker, "Harm, Liberty, and Free Speech," 990–991.

35. On the idea of performatives, see J. L. Austin, *How To Do Things with Words* (Oxford University Press, 1975).

36. The example is from John Stuart Mill, *On Liberty* (Penguin Books, 1985), ch. 3.

37. Baker, "Harm, Liberty, and Free Speech," 991–992.

38. Ibid., 992–993.

7. Ronald Dworkin and the Legitimacy Argument

1. See, e.g., Alexander Meiklejohn, *Political Freedom: The Constitutional Powers of the People* (Greenwood Press, 1979). Meiklejohn's position is that "the principle of the freedom of speech springs from the necessities of the program of self-government" (26–27), but he elaborates it at considerable length without really producing a sharp and compelling argument. See also Robert C. Post, *Constitutional Domains: Democracy, Community, Management* (Harvard University Press, 1995).

2. For example, James Weinstein, "Extreme Speech, Public Order, and Democracy," in Ivan Hare and James Weinstein, eds., *Extreme Speech and Democracy* (Oxford University Press, 2009), at 23, 28, and 38.

3. Ronald Dworkin, Foreword, in Hare and Weinstein, eds., *Extreme Speech and Democracy,* v–ix. See also Ronald Dworkin, "A New Map of Censorship," *Index on Censorship* 35 (2006), 130.

4. Dworkin, Foreword, viii.

5. Ibid., vii.

6. Ibid.

7. Ibid., viii.

8. Ibid.

9. Ibid., vi. Dworkin says this also about claims concerning the effects of pornography: compare his attack on Catharine MacKinnon's claims about pornography in Chapters 8 and 9 of Ronald Dworkin, *Freedom's Law: The Moral Reading of the American Constitution* (Oxford University Press, 1996). Though Dworkin concedes that pornography is "often grotesquely offensive" to women (218), he asserts that "no reputable study has concluded that pornography is a significant cause of sexual crime" (230). For Professor MacKinnon's rebuttal of Dworkin's assertion,

see her letter in the *New York Review of Books,* March 3, 1994, responding to an *NYRB* article by Dworkin which he used as the basis for a chapter in *Freedom's Law.*

10. I will discuss issues about incitement in Chapter 8 below.

11. Dworkin, Foreword, viii.

12. Dworkin, *Freedom's Law,* 219.

13. Consider the remarks in Isaiah Berlin, "Two Concepts of Liberty," in his collection *Liberty,* ed. Henry Hardy (Oxford University Press, 2002), 171–173, about the importance of facing up to the moral reality of both terms in any situation of trade-off or sacrifice. It is true that in some contexts, Dworkin has argued that liberals are forbidden from considering reasons of a certain kind. For example, he suggests that a person's "external" preference that another be treated with less than equal respect should to be counted alongside other preferences in a utilitarian calculus; see Ronald Dworkin, *Taking Rights Seriously* (Duckworth, 1977), 235–238. But the reasons he proposes to dismiss from consideration here cannot possibly be brought within the ambit of that argument. They are simply reasons concerning the causation of certain diffuse harms; they do not embody prejudices or any other disqualifying element.

14. See Dworkin, Foreword, vii: "[W]e must protect it even if it does have bad consequences and we must be prepared to explain why."

15. In his book *Law's Empire* (Harvard University Press, 1986), 190–192, Dworkin recognizes that these two elements may come apart. But mostly he deals with them together.

16. Public Order Act 1986 (U.K.), Parts 3 and 3A.

17. See, e.g., Race Relations Act, 1976, section 70.

18. Dworkin, Foreword, viii.

19. Cf. John Stuart Mill, *On Liberty* (Penguin Books, 1985), ch. 2, p. 81: "Strange it is, that men should admit the validity of the arguments for free discussion, but object to their being 'pushed to an extreme'; not see-

ing that unless the reasons are good for an extreme case, they are not good for any case."

20. See text accompanying note 7 above.

21. Robert C. Post, "Racist Speech, Democracy, and the First Amendment," *William and Mary Law Review* 32 (1991), at 290 (my emphasis).

22. Ronald Dworkin, *Is Democracy Possible Here? Principles for a New Political Debate* (Princeton University Press, 2006), 97.

23. Public Order Act 1986 (U.K.), section 18(1)(a).

24. Ibid., section 18(5).

25. Racial Discrimination Act 1975 (Commonwealth of Australia), section 18d.

26. Mill, *On Liberty,* ch. 2, p. 106.

27. Ibid.

28. Ibid., ch. 2, pp. 99 and 106.

29. Ibid., ch. 2, p. 108.

30. See Ivan Hannaford, *Race: The History of an Idea in the West* (Woodrow Wilson Center Press, 1966), for the history of disputation on these issues. And consider this example: in 1907, the Clarendon Press at Oxford published the following in a two-volume treatise on moral philosophy by the Reverend Hastings Rashdall, concerning trade-offs between high culture and the amelioration of social and economic conditions: "It is becoming tolerably obvious at the present day that all improvement in the social condition of the higher races of mankind postulates the exclusion of competition with the lower races. That means that, sooner or later, the lower well-being—it may be ultimately the very existence—of countless Chinamen or negroes must be sacrificed that a higher life may be possible for a much smaller number of white men." Hastings Rashdall, *The Theory of Good and Evil: A Treatise on Moral Philosophy,* 2nd ed. (Oxford University Press, 1924), vol. 1, 237–238.

31. Of course, there are still some discussions of race—for example, of the kind initiated in the "bell curve" controversy: see Richard Herrnstein

and Charles Murray, *The Bell Curve: Intelligence and Class Structure in American Life* (Free Press, 1994).

32. But see Post, "Racist Speech, Democracy, and the First Amendment," 291, for a sense of how careful we need to be here.

33. See Waldron, "Dignity and Defamation," *Harvard Law Review* 123 (2010), 1596, at 1646–52.

34. It is not merely the fact that serious debate has died away on these topics. We regard them as settled also in the sense that we have erected whole swaths of social policy on their settlement. The falsity of the racist's claim, for example, is one of the fundamentals of our scheme of justice, not only in the sense that we take it for granted but in the sense that we feel entitled to build great edifices of law and policy on its foundation—education policy, strategies for equal opportunity, permanent mechanisms for securing equal concern and respect. And we most emphatically do not think we have to regard these edifices as temporary, liable to be dismantled next year or the year after, depending on how the debate about race comes out. We treat the falsity of the claim about race as one of the fundamentals of our approach to justice, and we distinguish it now from contestable elements like economic equality, affirmative action, progressive taxes, social provision in the public realm, and so on—all of which *are* the subject of vital and ongoing debate whose suppression would give rise to a genuine problem of legitimacy for current social policy.

35. The account that follows summarizes the argument in Post, "Racist Speech, Democracy, and the First Amendment."

36. See Jeremy Waldron, *Law and Disagreement* (Oxford University Press, 1999), 302–306, for a discussion of what it means for everything to be "up for grabs."

37. Robert Post, "Hate Speech," in Hare and Weinstein, eds., *Extreme Speech and Democracy,* at 128, quoting from *Wingrove v. U.K.* (1997) 24 EHRR 1, 7.

38. Section 2 of the act provided for the exemption of ninety peers from this provision, and arrangements were made for the ninety to be elected from among the body of more than a thousand hereditary peers, making the House of Lords in part a representative assembly (rather than a plenary assembly) of peers for the first time in its history. Life peers, on the other hand, continue their membership of the House of Lords on a nonrepresentative basis: all life peers are members of the House.

39. This is based on comments by Professor Stone to the author, in conversation.

40. *Dennis v. United States,* 341 U.S. 494 (1951). On the Sedition Act, see the discussion in Chapter 2 above.

41. See, for example, Waldron, *Law and Disagreement,* pp. 211–312; and Jeremy Waldron, "The Core of the Case against Judicial Review," *Yale Law Journal* 115 (2006), 1346.

8. Toleration and Calumny

1. See Jeremy Waldron, "Locke, Toleration and the Rationality of Persecution," in *Justifying Toleration,* ed. Susan Mendus (Cambridge University Press, 1988), reprinted in Waldron, *Liberal Rights: Collected Papers, 1981–1991* (Cambridge University Press, 1993); "Toleration and Reasonableness," in *Reasonable Tolerance: The Culture of Toleration in Diverse Societies,* ed. Catriona McKinnon and Dario Castiglione (Manchester University Press, 2003); *God, Locke, and Equality: Christian Foundations of Locke's Political Thought* (Cambridge University Press, 2002), 217ff.; and "Hobbes and Public Worship," in *Nomos XLVIII: Toleration and Its Limits,* ed. Melissa Williams and Jeremy Waldron (New York University Press, 2008).

2. *R. v. Osborne,* W. Kel. 230, 25 Eng.Rep. 584 (1732); or *R. v. Osborn,* 2 Barnardiston 138 and 166 (94 Eng.Rep. 406 and 425).

3. This description is taken from an observation on Osborne's case in another case concerning Jews, *In re Bedford Charity*, 2 Swans. 471, at 532; 36 Eng.Rep. 696 (1819), at 717.

4. Ibid. Fazakerly appears to have been a most prolific attorney. He is mentioned in the English Reports hundreds of times.

5. *R. v. Osborne*, W. Kel. 230, 25 Eng.Rep. 584 (1732).

6. *R. v. Osborn*, 2 Barnardiston 138, 94 Eng.Rep. 406.

7. *R. v. Osborn*, 2 Barnardiston 166, 94 Eng.Rep. 425.

8. *R. v. Osborne*, W. Kel. 230, 25 Eng.Rep. 584 (1732).

9. *In re Bedford Charity*, 2 Swans. 471, at 532; 36 Eng.Rep. 696 (1819), at 717.

10. Ibid., at 502 note 4; at 717. It's a law report within a Law Report.

11. Ibid., at 502; at 705, citing Calvin's Case, 7 Co. Rep. 17a, 77 Eng. Rep. 397 (1609).

12. Counsel for the petitioners argued as follows (*In re Bedford Charities*, 512; 707): "It is painful to comment on the doctrine cited from Lord *Coke's* report of *Calvin's* case; a doctrine disgraceful to the memory of a great man. . . . That passage has never been cited without reprobation. In *The East India Company v. Sandys*, Sir *George Treby* condemned it in the strongest terms. 'I must take leave to say that this notion of Christians not to have commerce with infidels is a conceit absurd, monkish, fantastical, and fanatical.'"

They cited in a footnote the opinion of Coke's contemporary Lord Littleton, who insisted (1 Salkeld 47; 91 Eng.Rep. 46) that "Turks and Infidels are not *perpetui inimici*, nor is there a particular enmity between them and us; but this is a common error founded on a groundless opinion . . . ; for though there be a difference between our religion and theirs, that does not oblige us to be enemies to their persons; they are the creatures of God, and of the same kind as we are, and it would be a sin in us to hurt their persons."

They also cited Chief Justice Willes in *Omichund v. Barker*, Willes, 538, at 542; 125 Eng.Rep. 1310 at 1312 (1727), to the effect that "[t]his notion, though advanced by so great a man [Coke], is, I think, contrary not only to the Scripture, but to common sense and common humanity; and I think that even the devils themselves, whose subjects he says the heathens are, cannot have worse principles; and besides the irreligion of it, it is a most impolitic notion and would at once destroy all that trade and commerce from which this nation reaps such great benefits."

13. My American friends tell me this phrase was invented by Thomas Jefferson. But Richard Hooker used it in *Ecclesiastical Polity* almost two centuries before Jefferson did, and Hooker used it in a way that indicated it was in common circulation in Elizabethan times. (Hooker, of course, opposed the idea.)

14. John Locke, *A Letter Concerning Toleration,* ed. Patrick Romanell (Bobbs Merrill, 1955), 24.

15. Public Order Act 1986, section 29J.

16. Locke, *Letter Concerning Toleration,* 29.

17. Ibid., 28.

18. Ibid., 23 (my emphasis).

19. John Locke, *A Second Letter Concerning Toleration* (Awnsham and Churchill, 1690), 7–8.

20. John Locke, "The Fundamental Constitutions of Carolina," in *Locke: Political Essays,* ed. Mark Goldie (Cambridge University Press, 1997), 179. I am most grateful to Teresa Bejan for this reference. (Bejan tells me that rules of this sort were not uncommon in Tudor England and contemporary America.)

21. For a discussion, see Waldron, *God, Locke, and Equality,* 202–204.

22. Locke, *Letter Concerning Toleration,* 24.

23. John Locke, *Two Treatises of Government,* ed. Peter Laslett (Cambridge University Press, 1988), I, §42, p. 170.

24. John Marshall, *John Locke, Toleration and Early Enlightenment Culture* (Cambridge University Press, 2006), 656–657: "Although political scientists nowadays tend to pass by Locke's arguments in the *Letter* for toleration on the basis of charity . . . , there is no question that for

Locke, as for his contemporaries arguing for toleration, the duty of charity was a crucial argument for toleration, as charity was the most important duty of Christianity."

25. Locke, "Pacific Christians," in *Locke: Political Essays*, 305.

26. Ibid.

27. Pierre Bayle, *Commentaire philosophique sur ces paroles de Jésus-Christ, "Contrain-les d'entrer"; ou, Traité de la tolérance universelle* (1686); translated in 1708 as *Philosophical Commentary on These Words of the Gospel, Luke 14.23, "Compel Them To Come In, That My House May Be Full,"* ed. John Kilcullen and Chandran Kukathas (Liberty Press, 2005), 363.

28. Ibid., 317.

29. Ibid., 312. Bayle criticizes the common practice of "giving things very hard names o' purpose to create a horror for 'em" (ibid., 205). And the theme is continued in his sarcastic comment against those who say that sometimes law is needed to act against the pride of heretics. Bayle says: "Why not force those, who make an ill use of their Youth and Beauty, to take Pouders or Potions to destroy their Complexion and Vigor, or get defamatory Libels against 'em publickly dispers'd, that they might never dare shew their faces abroad?" (ibid., 359).

30. Ibid., 104.

31. Ibid., 209.

32. Ibid., 199–200.

33. Voltaire, *Lettres philosophiques sur les Anglais* (1734); translated as *Letters on England*, trans. Leonard Tancock (Penguin Books, 1980), 41 ("Letter VI: On the Presbyterians").

34. Voltaire, "Mahométans," in *Dictionnaire philosophique* (1764); translated as "Mohammedans," in *Voltaire's Philosophical Dictionary* (NuVision Publications, 2008), 145.

35. Voltaire, "Persecution," in *The Philosophical Dictionary*, quoted in David George Mullan, ed., *Religious Pluralism in the West* (Blackwell, 1998), 187–188.

36. Denis Diderot, *Political Writings*, trans. and ed. John Hope Mason

and Robert Wokler (Cambridge University Press, 1992), 29. The last sentence of this quotation is replaced by an ellipsis in this edition, but can be found online at quod.lib.umich.edu/cgi/t/text/text-idx?c=did;cc= did;rgn=main;view=text;idno=did2222.0000.564.

37. Denis Diderot, *Political Writings,* 29.

38. Adam Smith, *The Wealth of Nations,* ed. Edwin Cannan (University of Chicago Press, 1976), book I, ch. 2, p. 18.

39. Immanuel Kant, *Grundlegung zur Metaphysik der Sitten* (1785); translated as *Groundwork of the Metaphysics of Morals,* ed. Mary Gregor (Cambridge University Press, 1998), 42–43 (4: 434–435 of the Prussian Academy edition of Kant's works).

40. Peter Gay, *The Enlightenment: The Science of Freedom* (W. W. Norton, 1969), 398–406.

41. See Waldron, "Locke, Toleration and the Rationality of Persecution."

42. Locke, Second *Letter Concerning Toleration,* 23.

43. Locke, *Letter Concerning Toleration,* 23.

44. Ibid., 39.

45. I differ here from John Marshall, who reads this passage as showing that Locke was willing to echo common denunciations of religious promiscuity; see Marshall, *John Locke, Toleration and Early Enlightenment Culture,* 706ff.

46. On the complexities of Locke on the toleration of Roman Catholics, see the discussion in Waldron, *God, Locke, and Equality,* 218–223.

47. John Stuart Mill, *On Liberty* (Penguin Books, 1982), 144 (my emphasis). See also the extended discussion in Jeremy Waldron, "Mill as a Critic of Culture and Society," in an edition of John Stuart Mill, *On Liberty,* ed. David Bromwich and George Kateb (Yale University Press, 2002), 224.

48. Voltaire, "Mahométans," 145.

49. S. G. Tallentyre, *The Friends of Voltaire* (G. P. Putnam's Sons, 1907), 199.

50. See John Durham Peters, *Courting the Abyss: Free Speech and the Liberal Tradition* (University of Chicago Press, 2005), 156–157.

51. The context is: "If a Roman Catholic believe that to be really the body of Christ which another man calls bread, he does no injury thereby to his neighbour. If a Jew do not believe the New Testament to be the Word of God, he does not thereby alter anything in men's civil rights. If a heathen doubt of both Testaments, he is not therefore to be punished as a pernicious citizen. . . . I readily grant that these opinions are false and absurd. But the business of laws is not to provide for the truth of opinions, but for the safety and security of the commonwealth and of every particular man's goods and person." Locke, *Letter Concerning Toleration*, 45.

52. Ibid., 19.

53. I actually don't accept this as a definitional move. Many thinkers in the Enlightenment tradition based what they called "toleration" in part on principles of relativity or uncertainty or indifference toward religious belief; and I don't think much is gained in modern philosophical debate by saying they used the word "toleration" wrongly. What we may say is that the case for toleration is usually thought to require that practices and beliefs should not be persecuted even if they are (or turn out to be) wrong; but we don't necessary postulate their wrongness as a starting point. So toleration need not necessarily commit us to finding an outlet for the condemnation that it presupposes.

I mention this because it helps a bit with what Bernard Williams and others have called "the paradox of toleration." See Bernard Williams, "Toleration: An Impossible Virtue?" in *Toleration: An Elusive Virtue*, ed. David Heyd (Princeton University Press, 1996), 18. According to Williams, toleration seems to commit us, by way of presupposition, to the judgment that a given practice or belief is wrong or mistaken; and it seems to commit us, as a matter of principle, to refrain from doing what we would ordinarily do in regard to stuff that is wrong or mistaken—namely, try to stamp it out.

54. Locke, *Letter Concerning Toleration*, 46: "I would not have this understood as if I meant . . . to condemn all charitable admonitions and affectionate endeavours to reduce men from errors, which are indeed the greatest duty of a Christian. Any one may employ as many exhortations and arguments as he pleases, towards the promoting of another man's salvation. But . . . [n]othing is to be done imperiously."

55. Mill, *On Liberty*, 144. See also the discussion in Waldron, "Mill as a Critic of Culture and Society," at p. 224.

56. Locke, *Letter Concerning Toleration*, 46: "[S]eeing [as] one man does not violate the right of another by his erroneous opinions and undue manner of worship, nor is his perdition any prejudice to another man's affairs; therefore, the care of each man's salvation belongs only to himself."

57. Lord Shaftesbury, 3rd Earl of Shaftesbury (Anthony Ashley Cooper), *Characteristics of Men, Manners, Opinions, Times* (1711), ed. Lawrence E. Klein (Cambridge University Press, 1999), 31.

58. From a sermon preached by Bartholomew Stosch, court chaplain, before the Brandenburg Landtag in 1653, and printed by the Elector's special order in 1659; quoted in Oliver H. Richardson, "Religious Toleration under the Great Elector and Its Material Results," *English Historical Review* 25 (1910) 93, at 94–95.

59. John Locke, *A Third Letter for Toleration to the Author of the Third Letter Concerning Toleration* (Awnsham and Churchill, 1792), 104.

60. Thomas Hobbes, *Leviathan*, ed. Richard Tuck (Cambridge University Press, 1996), ch. 14.

61. Niccolò Machiavelli, *Discourses on Livy*, trans. Harvey Mansfield and Nathan Tarcov (University of Chicago Press, 1996), 27 (I, 8). See also the excellent discussion in David Cressy, *Dangerous Talk: Scandalous, Seditious, and Treasonable Speech in Pre-Modern England* (Oxford University Press, 2010). Cressy remarks that sixteenth- and seventeenth-century Englishmen "knew from the Bible, from literature, from legal proceedings, and from everyday discourse that speech could provoke violence,

discord, unhappiness, or sedition. An oath or a slur, an insult or a curse, a joke or a lie, could all intensify divisions within communities and erode the fabric of society" (6).

62. For example, they are not unhappy with John Stuart Mill's condemnation, in the essay *On Liberty* a century or so later, of the public expression of an opinion that "corn dealers are starvers of the poor . . . when [that opinion is] delivered orally before an excited mob assembled before the house of a corn dealer." Mill, *On Liberty*, 119.

63. Locke, *Letter Concerning Toleration*, 56.

64. Montesquieu, *The Spirit of the Laws*, trans. and ed. Anne M. Cohler, Basia Carolyn Miller, and Harold Samuel Stone (Cambridge University Press, 1989), 193 (book XII, ch. 5).

Index